1. Creamed fish with onions

FISH, MEAT, POULTRY AND GAME

HAMLYN
LONDON · NEW YORK · SYDNEY · TORONTO

Published by
The Hamlyn Publishing Group Limited
LONDON • NEW YORK • SYDNEY • TORONTO
Hamlyn House, Feltham, Middlesex, England

© Copyright Paul Hamlyn Ltd. 1962
First published 1962
Revised edition 1970
Reprinted 1972

ISBN 0 600 02458 X

Printed in Czechoslovakia by Svoboda, Prague

CONTENTS

LIST OF COLOUR PLATES

1. Creamed fish with onions
2. Halibut with provencale sauce on croutons
3. Fish Doria
4. Pickwick fish pie, Plaice fillets with asparagus, Scallops and bacon
5. Mackerel in foil
6. Dressed crab
7. Scallop mayonnaise
8. Beef scone pie, Roast beef
9. Beef casserole provencale, Lancashire hot pot
10. Spaghetti with meat sauce
11. Italian meat balls with mixed vegetables and mashed potatoes
12. Steak and kidney pie
13. Glazed forehock
14. Stuffed shoulder of veal
15. Steak with orange salad
16. Grilled liver and bacon
17. Braised topside, Stuffed breast of lamb
18. Kidney kebabs
19. Lamb and apple curry, as recipe for Chicken curry
20. Sweet and sour pork, Roast pork with apple and raisin sauce
21. Irish stew, Southern pork casserole
22. Roast duck
23. Grilled chicken joints with caper sauce
24. Rabbit and bacon pie

INTRODUCTION

In this book you will find the correct way of cooking fish, meat, poultry and game by those traditional methods which still remain the favourite in most homes. However, since we all get a little tired of continually cooking the same thing in the same way, you will also find a great variety of new ideas for dealing with familiar foods.

I particularly recommend many of the recipes in the fish section. Not only for use when the family needs a light diet in case of illness, but for your everyday enjoyment. Fish is a very valuable and nourishing food. And today, when so much stress is laid on careful transport and storage, we are in the fortunate position of not only being able to get better quality, fresher fish, but also a remarkably wide variety all the year round.

I would also like you to try some of the delicious stews and casseroles you will find in the meat section of the book. Many butchers say housewives do not take advantage of the cheaper cuts of meat. This is a great mistake, as they contain just as much food value as the more expensive steaks and chops, and can be put to a number of imaginative uses.

Game and poultry also lend themselves to an infinite variety of dishes. I have tried to give you as varied selection as possible ranging from the simple to the elaborate.

Once again, as in past books, I would like to convey my appreciation to the Home Economists who have helped in producing the special pictures you will find in these pages. Pictures are very important to this series. Not only because they add interest and colour, but, as so many readers have written to say, they also help to create enthusiasm and a willingness to experiment by showing just how delicious a dish looks when it is cooked. It is comparatively easy to take exciting pictures of cakes and puddings. But I am sure you will agree that the pictures here prove that our main dishes – which after all are the most essential part – can look just as tempting as any sweet dish.

WEIGHTS AND MEASURES

English weights and measures have been used throughout this book. 3 teaspoonsful equal 1 tablespoon. The average English teacup is ¼ pint or 1 gill. The average English breakfast cup is ½ pint or 2 gills.

When cups are mentioned in recipes they refer to a B.S.I. measuring cup which holds ½ pint or 10 fluid ounces. The B.S.I. standard tablespoon measures 1 fluid ounce.

In case it is wished to translate any of the weights and measures into their American, Canadian or French counterparts, the adjacent tables give a comparison.

LIQUID MEASURE
The most important difference to be noted is that the American pint is 16 fluid ounces, as opposed to the British Imperial pint and Canadian pint which are 20 fluid ounces. The American ½-pint measuring cup is therefore actually equivalent to two-fifths of a British pint.

FRENCH WEIGHTS AND MEASURES
It is difficult to convert to French measurements with absolute accuracy, but 1 oz. is equal to approximately 30 grammes, 2 lb. 3 oz. to 1 kilogramme.

For liquid measure approximately 1¾ pints may be regarded as equal to 1 litre. 1 demilitre is half a litre, and 1 decilitre is one-tenth litre.

SOLID MEASURE

ENGLISH	INGREDIENTS	AMERICAN
1 pound	Butter or other fat	2 cups
1 pound	Flour	4 cups
1 pound	Granulated or Castor Sugar	2 cups
1 pound	Icing or Confectioners' Sugar	3 cups
1 pound	Brown (moist) Sugar	2½ cups
1 pound	Golden Syrup or Treacle	1 cup
1 pound	Rice	2 cups
1 pound	Dried Fruit	2 cups
1 pound	Chopped Meat (finely packed)	2 cups
1 pound	Lentils or Split Peas	2 cups
1 pound	Coffee (unground)	2½ cups
1 pound	Soft Breadcrumbs	4 cups
½ ounce	Flour	1 level tablespoon*
1 ounce	Flour	1 heaped tablespoon
1 ounce	Sugar	1 level tablespoon
½ ounce	Butter	1 tablespoon smoothed off
1 ounce	Golden Syrup or Treacle	1 level tablespoon
1 ounce	Jam or Jelly	1 level tablespoon

* must be standard measuring tablespoon

OVEN TEMPERATURES

In most recipes in this book reference has been given to the oven temperature or the gas setting. This is an approximate guide only. Different makes of cooker vary and it is a fact that even the same make of cooker can give slightly different individual results at the same temperature or setting.

If in doubt as to whether the temperature given is EXACTLY right for your particular cooker, then do at all times refer to your own manufacturer's temperature chart. It is impossible in a general book to be exact for every cooker, but you will find that the following are a good average in every case.

Oven	Electricity °Fahrenheit	Gas Regulo	°Centigrade
COOL	225–250	0–½	107–121
VERY SLOW	250–275	½–1	121–135
SLOW	275–300	1–2	135–149
VERY MODERATE	300–350	2–3	149–177
MODERATE	375	4	190
MODERATELY HOT	400	5	204
HOT	425–450	6–7	218–233
VERY HOT	475–500	8–9	246–260

BASIC METHODS OF COOKING

Baking	Cooking in dry heat in the oven.
Boiling	Cooking by immersing the food in a pan of liquid, which must be kept boiling gently—all the time.
Braising	Almost a combination of stewing and roasting. Meat is placed on a bed of vegetables with a little liquid surrounding, in a covered vessel, and cooked slowly in the oven.
Casseroling	Cooking slowly in the oven in a covered casserole dish—usually meat, rabbit, etc.
Frying	Cooking in a little hot fat in an open pan. Deep frying is cooking by immersion in a deep pan of smoking hot fat.
Grilling	Cooking quickly under a red-hot grill; used for small tender pieces of meat, fish, etc.
Poaching	Cooking gently in water which is just below boiling point: usually eggs or fish.
Pressure Cooking	Cooking at higher temperatures than usual, so that food is cooked much more quickly.
Roasting	Cooking with a little fat in a hot oven. Fat is poured from the baking tin over the meat or poultry from time to time, using a long-handled spoon: this is known as basting.
Simmering	The rate of cooking used for stews—just below boiling point, so that the liquid bubbles gently at the side of the pan.
Steaming	Cooking either in a steamer over a pan of boiling water, or in a basin standing in (but not covered by) boiling water.
Stewing	Cooking slowly until the food is tender. It is done in just enough liquid to cover the food, as the liquid is served with it and should be rich. Stews may be cooked in covered saucepans or casseroles, either on a hotplate or in the oven—but always at a low temperature.

WHITE FISH

1 *To fillet fish*

In a number of the recipes reference is made to filleted fish. Many fishmongers will fillet it for you, but if not it is quite easy to do it yourself. You must, however, have a really sharp knife. To fillet fish make a definite slit down the centre and round the edge of the whole fish, insert the knife at the tip by the tail and with your left hand begin to lift the flesh while the knife, held in your right hand, cuts the flesh away from the bones. Continue slowly like this. A little salt on the tip of the knife often helps.

2 *To skin fish*

Use a very sharp knife, as for filleting, then make a small slit in the flesh just about the beginning of the tail or at the end of a fillet. Working slowly and carefully, loosen the skin well at this point, then gradually lift the flesh away from the skin with the tip of the knife. Dipping the knife in salt, as for filleting often proves helpful.

3 *To cook fish perfectly*

Fish, one of the most delicious and easily digested foods, can easily be spoiled with bad cooking. The general fault is to OVER-cook fish – it is ready when the flakes come away from the bone very slightly. Great care should be taken in choosing really fresh fish. If you are in an area where it is difficult to purchase really fresh fish, you are well advised to try frozen fish – which is frozen within a very short time of being caught. You can tell if fish is fresh, for the flesh should be firm, the eyes bright, and there should be no unpleasant or strong smell.

4 *To poach fish*

One hears of 'boiled' fish, but in fact fish should never be boiled, it should be simmered. Rapid boiling destroys both flavour and texture; the fish is inclined to break, and will certainly become very dry. Simmering or poaching means cooking very gently in either salted water, or in a fish stock made from the bones and skin of the fish and flavoured with bay leaf, onion and carrot. Allow 7 minutes per lb. for thin fillets of fish and 10 minutes per lb. for thick cutlets. If poaching in 1 piece then allow 12 minutes first lb. and 10 minutes after that for second lb. For very large fish allow 7-8 minutes per lb. for any weight after the first 2 lb.

5 *Court-Bouillon*

1 pint water
1 tablespoon lemon juice
few peppercorns
1 sliced onion
1 teaspoon salt
bouquet garni (see Recipe 638)

This is the liquid often used for poaching fish. One can vary it according to personal taste.

Allow sufficient ingredients to cover the fish and poach as in above recipe.

6 *Fried fish*

This is one of the most popular ways of serving any fish. It is important to remember the following:
1 Dry the fish well and coat very thinly with seasoned flour.
2 Dip in fritter batter (see Recipe 7) or in beaten egg and crumbs. Shake off surplus crumbs or allow excess batter to drain away.
3 For shallow frying make sure the fat (which can be oil, cooking fat or butter) is hot. Put in the fish, cook steadily until brown, turn and cook on the other side. For shallow frying allow 2-3 minutes on either side for filleted fish, 4-5 minutes for thicker fish cutlets or whole fish. For deep frying allow 3-4 minutes total cooking time for fillets, 7-8 minutes for whole fish or cutlets. If using deep fat make sure this is not too hot otherwise the outside browns before the fish is cooked.
4 Always drain fried fish. Use kitchen paper. The latest absorbent kitchen rolls are excellent, but never use greaseproof paper.
5 Do not over-cook the fish.
The ideal accompaniment is beautifully fried chips.

To fry fish whole
Most fish can be fried whole but it is correct to fry small codling, fresh haddock, sole, plaice, trout, herring or mackerel whole rather than fillet them.

7 *Fritter batter*

4 oz. flour
seasoning
1 egg
¼ pint and 4 tablespoons or
½ pint milk and water

Sieve flour and seasoning, add egg, gradually beat in liquid. For fillets use large quantity of liquid, for more solid cod, etc., you can use ¼ pint and 4 tablespoons.

8 *To coat in egg and crumbs*

Add little water or milk to egg to make it easier to brush over fish. Put crumbs into paper bag or on sheet of paper and turn fish in this, pressing crumbs firmly on to fish. Use either very fine soft white crumbs or dried breadcrumbs.

9 *Grilled fish*

Most fish is suitable for grilling. Fillets of fish, unless very thick, can be grilled without turning. Whole fish should be turned so that it is cooked on both sides. Make sure that the grill is hot before you begin cooking and keep the fish well brushed with melted butter so that it doesn't dry. Never over-cook fish. For fillets allow approximately 4 minutes, turning the heat down after the first 2-3 minutes, if desired. For thicker fish grill quickly for 2-3 minutes on either side, then reduce heat for a further 3-4 minutes. An ideal accompaniment for any grilled fish is grilled mushrooms which can be cooked at the same time.

10 *Baked fish*

Most fish can be baked, but care should be taken with fillets of fish to keep them moist. Butter the dish well, put in the seasoned fish, cover with buttered paper, and add a little stock, milk or white wine to keep fish moist. Use this stock in sauces.
Bake fillets of plaice, sole, etc., for approximately 12-20 minutes.
Bake cutlets of white fish for approximately 20 minutes.
Bake whole fish for approximately 12 minutes per lb. (if stuffed weigh with stuffing).
The heat of the oven should be moderate to moderately hot (375°-400°F. – Gas Mark 4-5).

11 *To cook fish without fat*

Clean fish thoroughly, then put on a piece of greaseproof paper, sprinkling over a little salt, pepper, lemon juice. Wrap up the fish thoroughly; this makes certain that all flavour is retained. Put between 2 plates and stand over a saucepan of boiling water. Cook for approximately 10 minutes until just tender. In my opinion this gives a better flavour than poaching (see Recipe 4).

12 *How to recognise and cook white fish*

Fish and when in season	
BASS May-September	Sea bass the best of the various bass. Striped fish that can be cooked like salmon.
BRILL May-August	Large flat fish, only small supplies available. Use like turbot (see Recipes 82-84).
BREAM July-December	Generally a fresh-water fish. Buy whole or in fillets. Not very plentiful but a good flavour. Bake with a savoury stuffing or grill. Allow 6-8 oz. on bone, 4-6 oz. filleted, per person.
COD Throughout year: best October-March	Excellent all-purpose fish because of its definite flavour; particularly good in 'made-up' dishes. Poach, fry, bake or grill. It has large flakes, so when frying it is inclined to break unless floured well before being coated with egg and crumbs or batter.
FLOUNDER November-March	Not quite such a delicate flavour as sole or plaice, but very much like them. Can be used in just the same way. Allow 8 oz. per person or 1 small fish, or 4-6 oz. when filleted.
HADDOCK October-February	Can be used in every way like cod. Buy fillets, cutlets or whole fish. May be slightly dry when cooked unless kept well moistened. 8 oz. per person when whole but 4-6 oz. when in fillets or steaks.
HAKE June-January	Again not unlike cod, but more delicate flavour. Best fried or baked. Buy steaks or fillets. 4-6 oz. per person. Good with various sauces.
HALIBUT July-April	More expensive fish, though generally cheaper than turbot. Excellent poached, grilled or baked. Small halibut under 3 lb. should be baked whole. A 'filling' fish, so allow 4-6 oz. per person when buying steaks or a good 6 oz. when buying whole.
DOG FISH or HUSS September-May	Will be skinned and filleted. Best baked or fried. Not very 'fleshy' so allow 6-8 oz. per person. Best with good flavoured sauce.
JOHN DORY or DORY September-early January	Good flavour, but ugly appearance. Buy fillets and cook in any way suitable for sole or turbot. Allow 6 oz. per person.
PLAICE Late May-December	One of the most popular of fish easily distinguished from other flat fish by yellow to reddish brown spots on the dark skin. Bake, fry, grill or serve in the same way as sole. Steam or poach for invalids, 1 small fish per person or approximately 6 oz.

SKATE November-May	An ugly but undoubtedly delicious fish. Generally sold in rather triangual-shaped pieces. Fry, bake or poach or use cold in salads. It is recommended that the fish be steamed a few minutes before being fried. Because of the large heavy bones allow about 10 oz. per person.
SOLE Some kind available all year	Considered by many people the finest fish of all, and certainly the one that has produced more delicious fish dishes and sauces than any other. Dover sole does not mean it comes from Dover, but is so called to distinguish it as the finest sole. Others, lemon, Torbay, witch, dabs are all good though. Bake, fry, poach, steam, grill and serve with lemon, melted butter or other sauces. Allow 1 fish or 8 oz. per person.
TURBOT April-early September	Can be distinguished from halibut by the spots on its skin. Bake, grill, fry or poach and serve with sauce. Excellent cold in fish salads too. It is a substantial and expensive fish. Allow 4-6 oz. as fillet or good 6 oz. when in steaks or whole.
WHITING October-April	An ideal fish for children and invalids since it is a very fine delicate-flavoured and small flaked fish. Much less expensive than sole or plaice, and can be filleted and served in the same way. Poach, bake or grill or fry. Allow 1 fish or 8 oz. when filleted per person.

13 *White fish turbans*

Steamed white fish fillets – whiting, plaice, sole, codling – look and taste most appetising curled into these turbans. Simply season the skinned and filleted fish and sprinkle with lemon juice before steaming in a covered colander (if you haven't got a real steamer) over just boiling water for 10 minutes. Drain well, curl into turbans (these can be held in place if necessary with a toothpick headed by a piece of mushroom) and serve with duchesse potatoes, peas, quarters of lemon and a good white sauce (see Recipe 216) flavoured with a few mushrooms or, still more simply, with a little fresh grated nutmeg or mace. A fresh tomato salad adds colour, freshness and vitamins to this meal.

14 *Fish with savoury rice stuffing*

4 servings

4 fillets sea bream, haddock
    or cod

Stuffing:
1 medium sized onion
2 sticks celery
2 oz. margarine
4 oz. cooked rice
¼ level teaspoon sage
¼ level teaspoon thyme

1½ oz. chopped stuffed or
    green olives (optional)
seasonings to taste

To garnish:
3 rashers streaky bacon, cut
in long thin strips
tomato halves
parsley

Skin the fish and chop the onion and celery. Prepare the stuffing; melt the margarine in a pan, add the onion and celery and fry gently for about 3 minutes. Add the rice and remaining ingredients and mix thoroughly over the heat for 2-3 minutes. Wipe the fillets with a damp cloth, season with salt and lay two of them flat in the bottom of a greased shallow ovenproof dish. Spread the stuffing over and around the fillets and cover sandwich-wise with the remaining two fillets arranged skinned side downwards. Top with criss-crossed strips of bacon, place the tomato halves around the sides and cover with greased greaseproof paper or foil. Bake in a moderately hot oven (400°F – Gas Mark 5) for about 30 minutes. Remove the paper and serve garnished with parsley.

Fish with Savoury Rice Stuffing

15 Fish Fricassée

4 servings

2 rounded tablespoons
  dehydrated mixed
  vegetables
½ pint cold water
¼ pint milk
salt

¾ oz. margarine
¾ oz. flour
1 lb. cooked flaked fish

To garnish:
1 oz. packet potato crisps

Put the mixed vegetables into a saucepan with the water and milk, add a little salt, and bring to the boil. Cover, and simmer 15 minutes. Meanwhile, melt the margarine in another saucepan, stir in the flour, and allow to cook gently for 3 minutes. Gradually add the vegetables and cooking liquor and bring to the boil, stirring or whisking continuously. Simmer 5 minutes, then stir in the fish, adjust the seasoning and reheat. Serve on a hot dish garnished with potato crisps.

Fish Frieassée

16 Whiting with French mustard sauce

4 servings

4 whiting
salt and pepper
2 small shallots
1 level tablespoon French
  mustard
4 tablespoons dry white wine

juice ½ lemon
1 oz. butter
1 tablespoon finely chopped
  parsley

To garnish:
sprigs of parsley

Arrange the fish in a buttered ovenproof dish and season with salt and pepper. Peel the shallots, chop very finely and scatter over the fish. Blend together the mustard and wine and pour over the fish. Cover and bake in the oven until fish is thoroughly cooked. Pour cooking liquor off into a saucepan, stir in the lemon juice and heat 2-3 minutes, stirring throughout to reduce liquid. Stir in butter and chopped parsley and pour over the prepared fish. Decorate with sprigs of parsley.

17 Fish Pie

4-5 servings

Rough puff pastry:
8 oz. plain flour
½ teaspoon salt
5 oz. margarine
6 tablespoons cold water

Filling:
1½ lb. cooked white fish
¼ pint white sauce (see
  Recipe 216)
lemon juice
pepper and salt

To glaze:
beaten egg

Sieve flour and salt, add fat in walnut-sized pieces. Mix with cold water to an elastic dough, leave in a cool place for 30 minutes. Roll and fold 4 times as flaky pastry (see Recipe 338). Roll out half pastry and line a 9-inch pie plate. Pile in prepared filling. Dampen edges, cover with remaining pastry. Knock up and flute edges. Make hole in centre, decorate with leaves and rose made from trimmings. Brush with egg and bake in centre of hot oven (425°-450°F. – Gas Mark 7) for 35-40 minutes, lower heat after 25 minutes if necessary.

Fish Pie

18 Fish loaf

4 servings

8 oz. cooked white fish
2 oz. white breadcrumbs
1 can condensed cream of
  mushroom soup or
  mushroom sauce (see
  Recipe 216)

1 lightly beaten egg
½ small onion (finely
  chopped)
1 teaspoon salt
pinch cayenne pepper

Bone and flake fish. Add crumbs and 5 tablespoons of soup. Mix in egg, onion, salt and pepper. Place in a lightly greased loaf tin (4 x 8 inches). Bake in a very moderate oven (350°F – Gas Mark 3) for 1 hour. Put remaining soup in a pan and, stirring, heat gently. Turn loaf into a hot dish, pour over sauce and serve.

Fish Loaf

19 Fish cakes

4 servings

12 oz. flaked cooked fish*
8 oz. mashed potato
either ¼ pint thick white
   sauce (see Recipe 216) or
   egg to bind
seasoning
egg

crisp breadcrumbs *or* flour
fat for frying

To garnish:
parsley
slices of lemon

*Cod, fresh haddock, turbot,
   hake are best, because of
   more definite flavour

Mix fish, potato, sauce or beaten egg together. Add seasoning.
Form into flat cakes and brush these with egg and breadcrumbs
or flour. Fry in hot fat until crisp and brown on both sides and
very hot right through to the middle. Drain carefully on kitchen
paper so that they are not greasy. Garnish with parsley and
slices of lemon.

Fish Cakes

20 Quick tartare sauce

4 tablespoons thick
   mayonnaise
½ teaspoon chopped parsley

½ teaspoon chopped capers
½ teaspoon chopped gherkins

Mix together the thick mayonnaise, chopped parsley, capers and gherkins
and serve with crisp newly fried fish cakes or fried fish.

21 Fish cutlets with piquant sauce

4 servings

4 cutlets (approximately
   1½ lb.) haddock or cod
1 oz. margarine
¼ pint milk
pinch salt and pepper
4 oz. cooked rice

Sauce:
2 oz. luxury margarine
1 large onion, peeled and
   finely chopped
4 oz. mushrooms,
   peeled and chopped

1 small pepper, chopped
1 oz. flour
8 oz. can or 8 oz. fresh
   tomatoes
salt
pepper
fish stock, drained from the
   fish

To garnish:
parsley
lemon

Wash and trim fish. Place in baking tin, brushed with melted margarine. Add
milk and seasoning. Cover with greased paper. Bake in a moderate oven
(375°F. – Gas Mark 4) for 20 minutes. Drain off fish stock for sauce. Keep fish
hot.
Sauce:
Melt the margarine slowly in a saucepan. Add the chopped onion, pepper and
mushrooms; fry gently for 10 minutes until just tender but not browned. Add the
flour and, stirring, cook about 1 minute until the mixture bubbles. Add the
tinned or fresh tomatoes, seasoning and fish stock. Stir over a gentle heat until
boiling and continue to boil for 3 minutes. Pour over the hot fish and serve
immediately with 4 oz. boiled rice, sprinkled with chopped parsley and garnished
with lemon.

Fish Cutlets with Piquant Sauce

22 Lemon fried fish

Rub the insides of the fish (see Recipe 6 for suitable fish for frying whole) with
fresh lemon and sprinkle with salt. Then dip and roll in seasoned flour and fry in
melted butter or margarine to which the juice of half a lemon has been added.
Use medium heat. Turn once.
Serve garnished with fresh zesty lemon quarters.

23 Cod à la Portugaise

4 servings

4 cod steaks
¼ teaspoon salt
3 tablespoons apple purée*
1 tablespoon tomato purée
2½ tablespoons quick-cooking
   rolled oats
1 teaspoon sugar

To garnish:
lemon

**3-4 apples cooked and
   mashed in a very firm
   purée*

Wash fish and sprinkle with salt. Mix apple and tomato purée in saucepan. Add rolled oats and sugar and cook for 1 minute. Transfer fish to a greased casserole and cover with apple mixture. Bake in a moderate oven (375°F. – Gas Mark 4) for 30-40 minutes. Garnish with lemon and serve on a bed of cooked rice.

Lemon Fried Fish

Cod à la Portugaise

24 Brill Dugléré

4 servings

12 oz. tomatoes
1 onion, chopped
¼ pint claret, port wine or
   red wine

seasoning
4 fillets brill
2 oz. butter
1 oz. flour

Skin and chop tomatoes. Mix onion, tomatoes and claret. Season well and pour over fish. Put butter on top, leaving about 1 oz. Cover and bake for 25 minutes in a moderately hot oven (400°F. – Gas Mark 5). Meanwhile heat rest of butter, work in flour and cook for a few minutes. Put fish on to a hot dish. strain liquid on to roux, and cook until a smooth thickened sauce. Serve over fish.

25 Cod with bacon

4 servings

1 lb. cod
approximately 6 rashers
   bacon

To garnish:
parsley

Cut cod in thin strips, roll a bacon rasher round each. Bake in a moderate oven (375°F. – Gas Mark 4) for about 20 minutes or grill. This makes a quickly prepared breakfast, lunch or supper dish. Garnish with parsley.

26 Cod cutlets with cheese sauce

4 servings

4 cod cutlets
pepper
salt

Cheese sauce:
1 oz. butter or margarine

1 oz. flour
½ pint milk
3 oz. grated Cheddar cheese
pinch cayenne pepper and
   salt
1 teaspoon made mustard

Wash and dry the cutlets, sprinkle with pepper and salt and lay in a lightly buttered fireproof dish or baking tin. Place some buttered greaseproof paper over the fish and bake in a moderately hot oven (400°F. – Gas Mark 5) for about 20 minutes until the flesh is beginning to shrink from the bone. Prepare the cheese sauce: Melt the butter in a small pan, stir in the flour and cook for 1 minute. Gradually add the milk, stirring continuously, bring to the boil and cook for 1 minute, stirring. Add the grated Cheddar cheese and seasonings and heat without re-boiling until the cheese melts. Serve the fish hot, coated with the cheese sauce or hand the sauce separately.

27 Gourmet cod

4 servings

4 cod cutlets

Stuffing:
4 oz. fresh white breadcrumbs
1 rounded tablespoon
   chopped parsley
1 level teaspoon dry mustard
1 egg, beaten

2 tablespoons milk
seasoning to taste

Tangy Marinade:
(see Recipe 32)

Topping:
3 oz. grated cheese

Wash and trim cutlets. Mix together crumbs and parsley. Beat mustard into egg, add milk and stir into crumbs, mixing thoroughly. Season to taste. Divide stuffing equally between the 4 cutlets and secure each by tying round with thin string. Turn into a heatproof dish and cover with marinade. Leave to stand at least 1 hour, turning cutlets frequently. Bake in the centre of the oven (400°F. – Gas Mark 5 for 30 minutes, basting every 10 minutes. Take out of the oven and top cutlets with grated cheese. Brown under a medium grill, transfer to a warm serving dish and carefully remove string. Pour liquid from oven dish into a sauce jug and hand separately. Serve hot.

Gourmet Cod

28 *Cream fish au gratin*

4 servings

4 cod cutlets
salt and pepper
½ pint milk
8 oz. cheese spread or cream
  cheese

½ teaspoon Worcestershire
  sauce
1 tablespoon browned
  breadcrumbs
½ oz. margarine

Trim, wash and dry cutlets and place in a greased ovenproof dish. Season well and add milk. Cover tightly with greased greaseproof paper or aluminium foil. Bake in a moderately hot oven (400°F. – Gas Mark 5) for 20-25 minutes. Drain off liquid into saucepan, cut cheese spread into cubes, add to liquid and, stirring, bring gently to boil. Continue to heat and stir until cheese is dissolved. Add Worcestershire sauce, pour over fish, sprinkle with browned breadcrumbs and dot with margarine. Brown under a moderate grill.

29 *Cod Provençale*

4 servings

1 medium sized onion
1 clove garlic
12 oz. tomatoes
1-1¼ lb. skinned cod fillet
1 oz. seasoned flour
oil for frying

1 level teaspoon chopped
  fresh herbs as available,
  e.g. parsley, thyme, sage
salt and pepper

To garnish:
black olives (optional)

Slice the onion and crush the garlic. Peel the tomatoes, remove pips and slice. Cut the fish into 2-inch squares then roll it in the seasoned flour. In a frying pan heat a little oil then fry the fish quickly until golden-brown on both sides, approximately 8 minutes. Drain, arrange in a shallow serving dish and keep hot. Strain off surplus oil leaving 1 good tablespoon in the pan. Fry the onion until tender, then add the garlic, tomato and herbs. Toss quickly over a brisk heat for 2-3 minutes. Season to taste and add olives if used. Reheat and pour over the fish, or serve alongside.

30 *Mimosa fish mould*

4 servings

1 oz. margarine or butter
1 oz. flour
2 oz. breadcrumbs
1 egg
8 oz. white fish (flaked)
5-6 dashes liquid seasoning
¼ pint evaporated milk

½ pint hollandaise sauce (see
  Recipe 217)
1 hard-boiled egg yolk

To garnish:
lemon or tomato slices or
asparagus tips

Rub the margarine into the flour, mix with breadcrumbs, raw egg, fish, seasoning and milk. Pour into a greased basin or mould, cover with greased paper and steam until firm (45 minutes – 1 hour). Coat with the sauce and sprinkle the sieved hard-boiled egg over the top, garnish with lemon or tomato slices or asparagus tips. Serve hot.

31 *Fish and rice croquettes*

4 servings

3 oz. rice, cooked (weight
  before cooking)
8 oz. flaked, cooked cod
2 teaspoons chopped parsley
½ teaspoon anchovy essence
salt and pepper
1 egg yolk
4 stuffed olives

1 egg white
12 tablespoons water
breadcrumbs for coating
whipped-up cooking fat for
  frying

To garnish:
2 stuffed olives
parsley sprigs

Mix rice, cod, parsley, essence, seasoning and egg yolk together then form into 4 fish-shaped croquettes placing a stuffed olive inside each. Mix together the egg white and water. Dip each croquette into the mixture and coat with browned breadcrumbs. Heat the cooking fat to 375°F., place in the croquettes and fry for 3-4 minutes. Drain on crumpled tissue paper. Serve on a hot dish with parsley for the tails and cut olives for the eyes.

Fish and Rice Croquettes

32 *Tangy marinade*

For fish, especially fresh cod, hake, haddock, plaice, turbot: 4 tablespoons cider, white wine, apple juice or orange juice (or 2 tablespoons wine vinegar), 2 level teaspoons dry mustard, $\frac{1}{2}$ level teaspoon salt, shake of pepper, 2 tablespoons olive oil.

Blend mustard with a spoonful of the cider. Add pepper, salt and the remaining cider. Gradually whisk this into the oil. Sufficient for 4 cutlets. Spoon over the fish and stand for at least 15 minutes, preferably 1 hour or longer. Spoon over the fish as it grills or bakes.

33 *Cod's roe*

All fish roes are particularly good for children. The roe should first be steamed for about 10 minutes, then the outer skin removed. It can then be cut into slices, which are delicious fried with bacon or potato cakes or served with a little white sauce poured over, or even used as a sandwich filling. For older children you can dip the slices of roe in a thick batter and fry, making them into fritters.

34 *Baked stuffed haddock*

Small haddock, like small cod, is excellent if stuffed and served whole. Choose either a veal stuffing, adding plenty of lemon juice to flavour, or a sage and onion stuffing (see Recipes 377, 375). Bone the fish or ask the fishmonger to bone it for you, insert the stuffing and skewer or tie in place. Allow approximately 12 minutes per lb. in a moderately hot oven (400°F. – Gas Mark 5). Put the fish in a well buttered dish and cover with buttered paper. Garnish with lemon, tomatoes and olives. Serve with creamed potato or boiled rice.

Baked Stuffed Haddock

35 Creamed fish with onions

4 servings

1½ lb. haddock or cod fillet
salt and pepper
2 oz. butter
6 anchovy fillets, chopped
3 small onions, chopped

3 tomatoes, quartered
1½ tablespoons chopped
   parsley
¼ pint cream

Cut the fish in pieces for serving and season well. Melt butter in a small saucepan, add anchovies and cook for 2 minutes. Add onions and brown lightly. Stir in tomatoes and cook gently. Add parsley and arrange in a fireproof dish. Place the haddock portions on top, dot with butter and grill until brown and cooked – about 7-10 minutes. Baste with cream during the last few minutes of cooking. Serve with green beans.

36 Newburg haddock stew

4-5 servings

1½ lb. smoked haddock fillet
2 oz. butter
½ teaspoon sweet paprika
   pepper
pepper
¼ pint sherry

¼ pint cream
2 egg yolks
½ pint milk
8 oz. rice
salt

Newburg Haddock Stew

Put the fish into a frying pan or skillet, cover with water and just bring to the boil. Drain well, divide into 2-inch cubes. Heat the butter in top of a double boiler, drop in the fish and turn it over and over for 3-4 minutes. Season with the paprika and pepper (salt should not be necessary in the fish). Pour in the sherry and simmer gently for 10 minutes, add the cream. Stir together to blend well; just before serving add the egg yolks thoroughly beaten with the milk. Cook and stir over a gentle heat without letting the sauce come to the boil, until it is of a creamy consistency. Take care not to break up the fish. Serve with the plain boiled rice cooked rather dry in slightly salted water, stirring it well with a fork to separate the grains.
NOTE. Fresh haddock may be used but the dish will not have the same piquant flavour of that made with the smoked variety.

37 Haddock with egg and dill sauce

4 servings

1½ lb. haddock fillet
½ pint milk
1 teaspoon dill
salt and pepper

1 oz. butter
1 oz. flour
1 hard-boiled egg

Divide the haddock into four portions. Place in a saucepan and cover with the milk. Add dill and seasonings, simmer gently for 8-10 minutes. Drain and keep hot. Melt the butter in a saucepan, stir in the flour and make the white sauce in the usual way using the milk from the fish. Taste and season as necessary. Chop the egg and stir into the sauce. Serve with the fish.

38 Fish pudding

4-5 servings

1½-2 lb. hake or cod
2 oz. margarine or butter
2 eggs
1 oz. flour

3 tablespoons milk or cream
   from the top of the milk
seasoning

Bone the uncooked fish, and put it through a mincer twice so that it is very fine and smooth. Melt the margarine, then add this to the fish together with the other ingredients. The eggs should be well beaten and added 1 at a time. Put the mixture into a well greased basin and cover with margarined paper and a cloth. Either steam for 45 minutes, or stand the pudding in a dish of cold water in a moderate oven (375°F. – Gas Mark 4) and cook for 30 minutes.
To make an even lighter pudding, separate the egg yolks from the whites, add the yolks first, then FOLD in the stiffly beaten egg whites. Serve this pudding with shrimp or mushroom sauce (see Recipes 216).

39 Fish soufflé

4 servings

8 oz. white fish*
1 oz. butter or margarine
1 oz. flour
¼ pint milk or fish stock

seasoning
3 egg yolks
2 tablespoons cream
4 egg whites

* While any fish can be used,
  fresh haddock or hake are
  ideal. Turbot or halibut
  are also excellent in a
  soufflé.

A better and stronger flavour is given in this recipe if raw fish is used. This should be put through the mincer twice to give a very fine texture. If the fish is cooked it should be flaked well and no skin used. Heat the butter in a pan, stir in the flour and cook for 1 minute, then gradually work in the milk. Bring to the boil and cook until thickened and smooth, add the fish, seasoning and the egg yolks. Mix well, then stir in the cream and the stiffly beaten egg whites. Put into a soufflé dish, filling just above ¾ of the dish. If wished, put a band of paper round the outside, buttering this well where it comes above the dish. Bake for approximately 35 minutes in the centre of a moderate oven (375°F. – Gas Mark 4). Serve at once with a shrimp, mushroom or cheese sauce (see Recipe 216).

Variations:
Add a small amount of chopped gherkin or cucumber, parsley or capers.
Use salmon or shell fish and a few drops of anchovy essence.
Use tomato juice instead of milk.
Use less fish and a little grated cheese.

40 Hake pimento

4 servings

½ oz. butter
2 onions
2 lb. hake
salt

black pepper
1 large green pepper
2 cartons plain yoghourt
   (½ pint)

Grease a baking dish with the butter. Blanch the onions for about 10 minutes, then cut into rings and lay on the bottom of the dish. Place the fish on top and season well with salt and pepper. Remove the seeds from the green pepper; cut into thin rings and lay decoratively on the fish. Pour the yoghourt over and bake for 20-30 minutes in moderate oven (timing depends on thickness of fish). This is also extremely good made with halibut.

41 Halibut with Provençale sauce on croutons

3 servings

3 halibut steaks
salt and pepper
2 oz. butter or margarine
2 tablespoons cream
2 oz. grated cheese
3 large or 6 small slices of
   French bread fried in
   butter

For the sauce:
½ oz. butter
1 onion, sliced
½ oz. flour
½ pint water or stock
3 tablespoons tomato purée
a few sliced black or green
   olives

Season the fish, brush with the butter and cream and sprinkle with cheese, grill until the fish is well cooked. Place the fish on the croutons. Meanwhile melt the butter and sauté the onion until soft and transparent. Add the flour and cook for a few minutes. Gradually stir in the water or stock and tomato purée. Finally add the olives and boil for a few minutes; season and serve poured over the hot fish steaks.

42 Summer fish mousse

4 servings

½ oz. gelatine soaked in 3
   tablespoons cold water
¼ sweet green pepper
1½ lb. cooked halibut
celery salt
freshly milled black pepper

Cream dressing:
½ teaspoon salt
2 teaspoons sugar
1 teaspoon dry mustard

pinch cayenne pepper
2 tablespoons wine vinegar
1 egg (an extra yolk makes a
   richer, thicker dressing)
¼ pint double cream

To garnish:
tomatoes
parsley
lemon slices

Make the cream dressing by combining all the dry ingredients in the top of a double saucepan. Pour in vinegar and blend to a smooth paste. Slightly beat egg (and extra yolk if used) and add. Cook slowly, stirring all the time, until mixture begins to thicken. When cool, add the whipped cream. Dissolve gelatine over hot water and add to cream dressing. Chop the green pepper (having carefully removed the pips and veins which are too hot to eat) as fine as you possibly can, and combine with flaked halibut and cream dressing. Season with celery salt and freshly milled black pepper to taste. Pour into a well-wetted mould and chill. Garnish with tomatoes, parsley and lemon slices.

Summer Fish Mousse

43 Fish Doria

4 servings

4 fillets of plaice or sole
4 oz. prawns
1 oz. butter
1 tablespoon milk
4 oz. rice, boiled and rinsed
paprika pepper
½ cucumber
knob of butter

Shrimp cream sauce:
2 oz. butter
2 oz. flour
½ pint milk
salt and pepper
2 tablespoons cream
a few chopped prawns

To garnish:
thin strips of cucumber

Lay fillets out flat and season. Place a few prawns on the skin side of each fillet. Fold into 3. Place in an ovenproof dish with butter and milk and bake in a moderate oven (350°-375°F. – Gas Mark 4-5) for about 10 minutes. Place on a bed of rice. Sprinkle each fillet with paprika pepper and garnish with thin strips of cucumber. Serve with a shrimp cream sauce (made by preparing a white sauce in the usual way, then adding 2 tablespoons of cream and a few chopped prawns) and poached cucumber. To poach cucumber: peel half a cucumber and cut across into three pieces; then cut lengthwise into batons about the thickness of a little finger. Place in boiling salted water and simmer for 3-4 minutes. Drain, add a small piece of butter and place in a separate serving dish.

44 Plaice or sole in raisin and wine sauce

4 servings

2 medium-sized sole or plaice
  (filleted and skinned)
salt and pepper
¼ pint white wine
4 oz. seedless raisins
¼ pint water
few peppercorns
1 medium-sized onion (sliced)
1 small bay leaf

Sauce:
1 oz. butter
1 oz. flour
¼ pint milk
salt and pepper

To garnish:
sprigs parsley
lemon slices

Rinse and dry fillets, sprinkle with salt and pepper and roll lightly from tail to head. Place fillets in a buttered, shallow ovenproof dish. Put 3 tablespoons of wine in another shallow tin or dish and add raisins and cover closely. Pour remaining wine and water over fish, add peppercorns, onion and bay leaf and cover closely with buttered paper or foil. Cook fish and seedless raisins in a very moderate oven (350° F. – Gas Mark 3) for 20 minutes. Drain fish and place on dish, keep hot. To make sauce, melt butter in small pan, add flour and stirring, cook for a few minutes. Strain liquid from fish and seedless raisins into milk and stir into pan a little at a time, cooking gently. Season, add raisins and pour over fish. Garnish with lemon slices and parsley.

Fillets in raisin and wine sauce

45 Plaice fillets with asparagus

4 servings

4 plaice fillets
1 packet frozen asparagus
  spears
  or canned asparagus tips
juice of ½ lemon
seasoning

For the sauce:
1 oz. butter
2 oz. mushrooms
1 oz. flour
½ pint milk
seasoning

Skin the plaice fillets and wrap each around several spears of cooked, frozen or canned asparagus. Arrange in a shallow baking dish, sprinkle with lemon juice and season. Cover with a lid or foil and bake in a moderate oven (375° F. – Gas Mark 4) for 15 minutes or until the fish is opaque. Place in a serving dish and keep warm. To make the sauce: melt the butter and fry the chopped mushrooms for 2-3 minutes. Stir in the flour and cook for a further 2 minutes. Add the milk and bring to the boil, stirring and cook for 3 minutes. Season and pour over the fish and serve.

46 Skate with cream sauce

4 servings

4 portions of skate
parsley
onion
1 oz. butter
1 oz. flour
½ pint milk
2 tablespoons cream

1 hard-boiled egg
2 teaspoons chopped chives
  or spring onions
½ teaspoon grated lemon rind
little lemon juice
seasoning

Put skate into cold salted water, bring to the boil then skim. Add sprig of parsley and onion and simmer for just 10 minutes. Meanwhile make sauce of butter, flour and milk, add cream, chopped hard-boiled egg and other ingredients. Strain fish, and cover with sauce.

47 Skate with tomato sauce

Cook as above, make same sauce but omit cream and egg. When sauce is cooked take off heat for a few minutes, and whisk in 2 tablespoons tomato ketchup.

48 Using plaice

Plaice may be used instead of sole in Recipes 51-81. While the flavour is not as fine, the price is generally more reasonable.

49 Using flounder

This is the name given to flat fish, other than plaice and sole. The true flounder has a row of sharp little 'prickles' on upper side. Use in any recipe for plaice and sole, but it is best with a good flavoured sauce, since the flavour is not very good in comparison with these two.

2. Halibut with provencale sauce on croutons
3. Fish Doria

4. Pickwick fish pie, Plaice fillets with asparagus, Scallops and bacon

50 Pickwick fish pie

4 servings

1 oz. butter	For the sauce:
3 small onions	milk
¼ pint white wine (Graves or	1 oz. butter
Chablis)	1 oz. flour
1½ lb. mixed fish – plaice,	fish liquid
haddock, mussels, 3-4	¼ pint cream
scallops if wished	
seasoning	6 oz. bought or home-made
	puff pastry

Heat the butter and fry the chopped onions. Add the wine and diced fish and season. Cook for about 5 minutes only. Lift fish from liquid and put into a pie dish. Measure liquid and add milk to give ½ pint. Make a sauce with the butter, flour, fish liquid, cream and seasoning. Cook until thickened and pour over fish. Cover the pie with the pastry and cook for 20 minutes in a pre-heated very hot oven (475 F. Gas Mark 8) and then lower the heat to 400°F. Gas Mark 5 and cook for a further 10-15 minutes.

51 Baked sole

Wash, dry and season the fish. It can be coated lightly with flour, or with egg and breadcrumbs as for frying. Put into a well-buttered dish and cover the top of the fish with pats of butter. Bake for 20-30 minutes, according to thickness of the fish, in a moderate to moderately hot oven (375°-400°F. – Gas Mark 4-5). Serve at once, covered with the melted butter from the dish, and garnished with lemon and parsley.

52 Sole Bercy

4 servings

4 large or 8 small fillets of	salt and pepper
sole	½ pint white wine
extra butter	¼ pint water or fish stock
2 shallots or small onions	1 oz. butter
2 teaspoons chopped parsley	1 oz. flour

Fold the fillets of fish, put into a buttered dish, with the chopped shallots, parsley, seasoning, ¼ pint white wine, and fish stock. Cover with buttered paper and bake in a moderate oven (375°F. – Gas Mark 4) for approximately 20 minutes. Meanwhile heat the butter, stir in the flour and cook gently for several minutes. Add remainder of the wine and cook until smooth. Lift the fillets of sole on to a hot dish, add the liquid from the dish, with chopped shallots, etc. and cook the sauce until smooth and thick. Do not strain. Pour over the fish.

53 Sole bonne femme

Recipe as Sole Bercy – but use sliced mushrooms instead of shallots and use ¼ pint cream or milk instead of water or fish stock. Put the sole on to a hot dish in a border of creamed or duchesse potatoes (see below) and garnish with cooked, sliced or whole mushrooms.

Sole Bonne Femme

54 Duchesse potatoes

1 or 2 eggs	To garnish:
2 oz. butter	parsley
1¼ lb. well-mashed potatoes	

Mix the beaten egg and butter with the potatoes, pipe on to greased baking tins, or as border on dish, and bake for about 20-25 minutes in a moderately hot oven (400°F. – Gas Mark 5).

55 Sole Bretonne

4 servings

4 large or 8 small fillets sole	¼ pint tomato purée or
¼ pint hollandaise sauce (see	sauce (see Recipe 360)
Recipe 217)	
	To garnish:
	1 or 2 onions
	butter

Poach the fillets of sole carefully in salted water. Drain well and arrange on a hot dish. Whisk the hot sauces together (away from the stove) taking care they do not curdle. Coat the fish with this and garnish with rings of onion fried in a little butter.

56 Sole Bréval

Recipe as Sole Bercy, but use both shallots and 2 or 3 skinned and sliced tomatoes. Use a little less wine or stock, since the tomatoes provide liquid. Garnish with creamed or duchesse potatoes (see Recipe 54).

57 Sole caprice

Fry fillets of sole – coating them with egg and breadcrumbs, and serve with fried halved bananas and watercress. Delicious with espagnole sauce (see Recipe 355).

58 Sole cardinal

4 servings

4 large or 8 small fillets of
  sole
salt and pepper
little extra butter
½ pint cider

coral (roe) from female
  lobster
2 oz. butter
1 oz. flour

To garnish:
lemon

Fry or bake the well-seasoned fillets of sole in butter. If baking add a little of the cider. Meanwhile blend the coral with 1 oz. of the butter until smooth. Heat the other ounce of butter in a pan, stir in the flour and cook for a few minutes, add the cider, bring to the boil, and cook until smooth. Stir in the lobster butter. Arrange the fillets of sole on a hot dish, adding any liquid to the sauce. Pour over the sauce, and garnish with lemon.

59 Sole Casanova

Recipe as Sole Cardinal, but instead of lobster butter use about 12 prepared mussels, adding this to the cider sauce, just before serving.

60 Sole Cécilia

Season fillets of sole and fry in butter. Arrange on a hot dish and cover each fillet with several well drained asparagus heads. Cover with grated cheese and a little melted butter and brown under the grill.

61 Sole à la Colbert

Skin whole sole (see Recipe 2). With a sharp knife slit down the centre back – being careful not to spoil the fish. If possible remove the backbone. Coat the fish in seasoned flour or egg and breadcrumbs and fry in deep fat. Serve with maître d'hôtel butter (see Recipe 68) and lemon.

62 Sole Florentine

Serve baked, poached or fried fillets of sole in a border of creamed spinach. Coat with cheese sauce and put under the grill to brown.

63 Fried sole

Follow the directions for frying fish (see Recipe 6), and be particularly careful NOT to over-cook sole.

64 Sole au gratin

Poach or grill the fillets of sole, cover with the cheese sauce (see Recipe 216) add grated cheese and breadcrumbs and a little butter. Brown under the grill.

65 Grilled sole

When grilling sole it is usual to cook the whole fish rather than filleting. Make sure the grill is very hot before starting to cook, brush the fish with melted butter, grill until tender on one side, turn over, brush again with melted butter and cook on the second side. Seasoning and lemon juice can be added as required.

66 Sole à l'indienne

Poach the seasoned fillets of sole, using milk if wished. Coat with a fairly mild curry sauce and serve in a border of boiled rice.

67 Sole maître d'hôtel

Bake the fillets of sole with butter and a little milk in the oven. Make a white sauce (see Recipe 216) adding a squeeze of lemon juice and top the fish with maître d'hôtel butter (see below) if desired or add chopped parsley to the sauce.

68 Maître d'hôtel butter

Work 1 good teaspoon finely chopped parsley into 2 oz. fresh butter, then add a little lemon juice and a good pinch chopped fresh tarragon and lemon thyme and chervil. Season well. Spread out until about ¼-inch thick, allow to become hard and cut into tiny shapes.

69 Sole meunière

This is one of the best ways of cooking sole – the sole can either be cooked whole or in fillets. Follow the directions for trout meunière (see Recipe 192).

70 Piquant sole fillets in mushroom sauce

4 servings

8 medium-sized sole fillets
2 level teaspoons mustard
1 can cream of mushroom
  soup
2 tablespoons milk

To garnish:
few whole cooked
  mushrooms

Skin, trim and wash fillets. Spread with mild mustard to heighten flavour. Roll up. Put into greased heatproof dish. Pour over soup mixed with milk. Cover dish with greased paper. Bake 20 minutes in centre of moderately hot oven (400°F. – Gas Mark 5). Remove paper. Garnish with mushrooms. Serve with potato swirls (see following recipe).

Piquant Sole Fillets in Mushroom Sauce with Potato Swirls

71 Potato swirls

4 tablespoons milk
1 oz. butter
1 lb. mashed potatoes

seasoning
2 rounded teaspoons
  mustard

Heat milk with butter. Add to potatoes. Season well. Beat with fork till smooth and creamy. Add mustard. Arrange in small heaps on greased baking tray or pipe in swirls, using meringue tube and forcing bag. Bake towards top of oven (same temperature as fish) for 25 minutes.

72 Sole Mornay

Poach or bake fillets of sole. Coat with a thick cheese sauce (see Recipe 216) cover with grated cheese, and brown slightly – either under the grill or in the oven.

73 Sole Normande

Cook the fillets of sole as in white wine sauce (see Recipe 80); garnish with mussels or mushrooms and mussels.

Sole Normande

74 Sole Niçoise

Cook the fillets of sole in white wine sauce (see Recipe 80) but add a little anchovy essence to the sauce. Garnish with olives, anchovy butter (see Recipe 222) and serve in a border of cooked tomatoes.

75 Sole Orly

This is the name given to fried fillets of sole when coated in batter and served with a good tomato sauce.

76 Sole Rachel

4 servings

4 large or 8 small fillets sole
  skinned (reserve skin and
  bones)
1½-2 oz. onion peeled
bay leaf
3 peppercorns
1 teaspoon salt
6 oz. mushrooms
1 oz. butter
3 tablespoons cream

seasoning
¼ pint dry white wine
¾ oz. flour
1 egg yolk

To garnish:
slices of mushroom
fleurons of puff pastry
  (optional)

Place fish skin and bones with onion, bay leaf, peppercorns and 1 teaspoon salt in a saucepan and just cover with water. Boil for 20-30 minutes. Wipe or wash the mushrooms. Slice some for the garnish and chop the rest finely. Cook gently in ¼ oz. of the butter, 1 tablespoon of the cream, seasoning, in a covered pan for 4-5 minutes: strain. Place equal portions of the mushroom on ½ of each fillet, skinned side downward, fold over and lay in a heatproof dish. Pour over wine and ¼ pint of the strained fish stock. Season. Cover with greaseproof paper and bake (375°F. – Gas Mark 4) for 20-25 minutes, or until fish is cooked.

Melt rest of butter in a small saucepan, blend in flour, add strained liquor from the fish and bring to the boil, stirring with a wire whisk. Boil for 1 or 2 minutes, remove from heat, beat in rest of cream and the egg yolk, adjust seasoning, heat through and then pour over the fish. Garnish with slices of mushroom and fleurons of pastry if desired.

Sole Rachel

77 Sole ribbons

4 servings

2 medium soles
1 tablespoon seasoned flour
beaten egg

browned breadcrumbs
cooking fat for frying
little cayenne pepper

Skin the sole, fillet, wash and dry well. Cut the fillets across into ½-inch ribbons. Roll in seasoned flour, dip into the beaten egg and coat well with breadcrumbs. Fry in cooking fat heated to 350°F. for 4-5 minutes until crisp and golden-brown. Drain well and serve sprinkled lightly with a little cayenne pepper.

78 Sole en goujons

This is just another name for sole ribbons; one often hears the dish called just 'Goujons'. It is served either as a main course, accompanied by several different sauces: tartare, hollandaise, etc. (see Recipes 365, 217) or small portions can be served as an hors d'oeuvre.

79 Sole Walewska

4 servings

4 large or 8 small fillets of
  sole
salt and pepper
¼ pint white wine
little butter

hollandaise sauce (see
  Recipe 217)
small lobster
lobster butter if desired (see
  Recipe 223)

Season the fillets of sole and bake in a moderately hot oven (400°F. – Gas Mark 5) for approximately 15 minutes or until tender, adding the white wine and a little butter. Meanwhile make the hollandaise sauce. Lift the fillets of fish on to a hot dish and strain the liquid gradually into the hollandaise sauce, re-heating gently to thicken. Add the lobster pieces and pour over the fish. The lobster butter can either be stirred into the sauce, or put on top of the dish just before serving.

80 Sole in white wine sauce

To make this sauce, which can be the basis of many flavourings, the sauce is prepared with 1 oz. butter, 1 oz. flour and just over ¼ pint white wine. Meanwhile, cook the sole in the oven with another ¼ pint white wine, seasoning and a little butter. When the sole is cooked, lift on to a hot dish, then strain the liquid into the sauce and re-heat, stirring until smooth.

81 *Sole Véronique*

4 servings

2 medium-sized soles
seasoning
3 tablespoons white wine
  (optional)
1 shallot
1 or 2 button mushrooms

Stock:
fish bones
2-3 peppercorns

few parsley stalks
1 small onion
½ pint water

Sauce:
1 can evaporated milk
1 oz. butter
1 oz. flour

To garnish:
4 oz. green grapes

Have the soles skinned and filleted. Put the heads and bones into a saucepan with the peppercorns, parsley stalks, onion and water, simmer for 30 minutes. Strain off the liquor. Season the fillets and roll them skin side in and place upright on a buttered deep plate or dish. Add the stock, wine, shallot and mushrooms, cover and poach in a moderate oven (375°F. – Gas Mark 4) or over a pan of water until cooked. Keep fish hot and strain off the liquor. Make up to just over ½ pint again with evaporated milk. Make a sauce with the butter, flour and liquor. Skin and stone the grapes. They may be heated in a little wine or brought to the boil before skinning. Coat the fish with the sauce and garnish with the grapes.

82 *Turbot Florentine*

1 serving

2 good tablespoons cooked
  spinach
2 tablespoons cream or milk
seasoning

1 oz. margarine or butter
1 small piece of turbot
2 teaspoons grated cheese
1 teaspoon soft breadcrumbs

Sieve the spinach or chop until very smooth. Mix with the cream or milk and a little extra seasoning, if desired, and half the margarine. Put the spinach at the bottom of a deep scallop shell or individual dish with the piece of turbot on top. Sprinkle over the cheese and breadcrumbs, a pinch of salt and pepper and the knob of margarine. Bake near the top of a moderately hot oven (400°F. – Gas Mark 5) for a good 10 minutes. Serve with creamed or duchesse potatoes (see Recipe 54).

83 *Turbot Mornay*

4 servings

4 fillets turbot
seasoning
½ pint milk
¼ lemon

1 oz. margarine
1 oz. flour
2 oz. grated cheese

Put the fillets of fish into a dish, add seasoning, ¼ pint milk and the sliced lemon. Bake in the middle of a moderate oven (375°F – Gas Mark 4) for 15-20 minutes. While the fish is cooking prepare the sauce. Melt the margarine in the saucepan, stir in the flour and cook the roux for 3 minutes. Remove the pan from the heat and gradually stir in the cold milk. Bring slowly to the boil, stirring all the time. Put the turbot on to a hot dish and strain the liquid into the sauce, stirring well to keep it smooth. Simmer the sauce for a further 1 minute then add the grated cheese and cook until dissolved. Season well. Pour over the sauce and serve with creamed spinach.

84 *Turbot or halibut soufflé*

4 servings

good 8 oz. cooked and
  flaked fish
5 oz. well mashed potatoes

¼ pint thick white sauce (see
  Recipe 216)
2 eggs
seasoning

Any other white fish may be substituted, but turbot or halibut give a better and more definite flavour.

Mix the fish, potato and sauce together, add the well beaten egg yolks and season well. Lastly FOLD in the stiffly beaten egg whites. Put into a greased soufflé dish and bake in the centre of a moderately hot oven (400°F – Gas Mark 5) for 25-30 minutes, i.e. until golden brown and firm on top. Serve at once accompanied by creamed potatoes and spinach.

85 *Whiting (Merlan)*

Whiting has a rather delicate flavour and is easily digestible, but it is not a fish which keeps well. Be sure to check that the eyes are bright and clear and the fish silver in colour. Skin the fish before frying and fasten the tail between the eyeholes. To remove the backbone slit the fish down the back at each side of the bone, break the bone at either end and carefully lift it out. Whiting can be served in any of the ways one serves sole or plaice. Fried fillets are good served with fried parsley or thick tomato sauce, or with béarnaise sauce (see Recipes 360, 217). Small whiting are delicious baked in the oven in a good mushroom sauce or cooked with chopped shallots in white wine or cider.

86 *Whiting Portugaise*

4 servings

4 whiting (each cut into 2
  fillets)
1 onion
2 or 3 tomatoes

salt and pepper
1 oz. grated cheese
1 oz. butter

This recipe is extremely quick and easy to prepare.

Fold fillets in half and place in a greased fireproof dish. Slice onion very thinly and place on the top with sliced tomatoes. Sprinkle over salt and pepper and grated cheese. Put small pieces of butter on top. Bake for 20-30 minutes in moderate oven (375°F – Gas Mark 4). Take care not to over-cook the fish, for whiting is very easily dried.

OILY FISH

87 How to recognise and cook oily fish

Fish and when in season	
HERRINGS Obtainable from various sources throughout year, from Britain in season June-February	Buy whole, but most fishmongers will bone and fillet if wished. Make sure herrings are very firm and bright-eyed. Can be grilled, fried, baked (with stuffing if wished) or pickled and soused to have with salads. Most economical. 1-2 herrings per person.
MACKEREL March-July	Looks like a larger, more silvery herring. Take great care to see they are fresh, since stale mackerel can be particularly dangerous. Cook as herrings, particularly good served with a thick gooseberry purée as sauce. 1 per person.
MULLET April-October	Both grey and red. Bake or grill with plenty of butter. Red mullet is particularly delicious baked in covered bags of buttered paper. Always retain liver of fish, as this has particularly good flavour. 1 grey or 2 red (smaller) mullet per person.
SALMON March-August	Serve hot or cold. Take great care in cooking not to dry the fish and lose both oily texture and flavour, and colour. A substantial fish. Allow approximately 6 oz. per person.
SALMON TROUT April-August	Cook as salmon, but generally best to buy a small salmon trout and cook it whole. Allow 8 oz. fish when buying whole per person.
SPRATS October-March	These tiny fish can be baked or fried. Remove heads, dust with seasoned flour before cooking. Very easily digested and quite delicious. Allow 6-8 oz. per person.
WHITEBAIT May-August	The tiniest fish used. Do not take off heads, dust well in seasoned flour and cook in deep fat until crisp and tender. Drain well and serve either as a main course or an hors d'oeuvre with cayenne pepper, lemon and brown bread and butter. Allow 4-8 oz. per person.

88 Baked herrings and tomato

4 servings

4 herrings
8-12 oz. tomatoes
1 small onion
2 level teaspoons dry mustard

2 teaspoons vinegar
½-1 level teaspoon salt
¼ level teaspoon pepper
1 tablespoon stock or water

Bone herrings, remove the heads, skin and slice tomatoes and onion. Mix the mustard and vinegar together. Open the herrings out flat and if large, cut each into two or three pieces. Spread with the mustard mixture. Arrange a thick layer of tomatoes at the bottom of the dish: top with herrings and season well. Add the stock and put the onion rings over the herrings. Cover the dish. Bake in the centre of a moderate oven for 45 minutes (350-375°F – Gas Mark 4). Serve hot.

Baked Herrings and Tomato

89 Stuffed baked herrings

4 servings

4 herrings
1 small onion
2 oz. breadcrumbs

1 teaspoon chopped parsley
salt and pepper
½ teaspoon butter

Remove heads, clean and wash the fish. Split open and remove the backbone. To make the stuffing, chop the onion very finely and add the breadcrumbs, parsley and seasoning. If the fish have roes mix two with the stuffing and this will bind it. If there are no roes use a little beaten egg. Sprinkle the inside of each herring with salt and pepper and spread a portion of the stuffing down the centre. Roll up and tie with cotton or pierce with a small wooden skewer. Cook in a buttered fireproof dish, covered with greaseproof paper in moderately hot oven (400°F – Gas Mark 5) for 15 minutes. Remove paper and allow to brown.

90 To bone herrings

1 Cut off head, slit along stomach of herring.
2 Remove the intestines and roe. Clean the herring. (Cook the roe with the fish).
3 Open the herring, and put cut side downwards on to a board.
4 Run your thumb very firmly along the centre, feeling the back bone; do this several times.
5 Turn fish over, you will find the back bone completely loosened and easy to remove.

91 Herrings fried in salt

There is so much oil in the flesh of a herring that it is quite possible to fry it without other fat. Use only a strong, thick frying pan, a thin one will burn. Sprinkle the pan with salt, heat gently at first, shaking the pan occasionally. Continue heating until the pan is very hot then lay in the herrings, previously scaled, cleaned, washed and dried. Fry on each side 4-5 minutes until golden brown and crisp. Serve at once.

92 Crispy oat herrings

4 servings

4 herrings
1 egg, beaten
4 oz. oatmeal
4 oz. pure cooking fat

To garnish:
lemon
parsley

Sauce:
¼ pint tomato ketchup
4 pickled gherkins, chopped
1 tablespoon capers

Clean the herrings and remove the eyes. Wash and dry them thoroughly. Dip in beaten egg and coat thoroughly with oatmeal. Heat the fat in a frying pan until hot. Cook the herrings on both sides over a gentle heat for 4-5 minutes. Serve hot garnished with lemon and parsley. Heat the tomato ketchup in a small saucepan, stir in the gherkins and capers, serve with the herrings.

Crispy Oat Herrings

93 Grilled herrings and mustard sauce

4 servings

4 large or 8 small herrings
little butter

Sauce:
2 oz. butter
1 oz. flour
1 tablespoon mustard

¼ pint and 4 tablespoons water
1 teaspoon vinegar
salt

To garnish:
parsley
lemon

Trim and clean herrings. Brush with butter, grill on both sides. To make sauce: Heat 1 oz. butter in the pan, stir in the flour and cook for one minute, then blend the mustard with the water until very smooth, add to the butter and flour and bring to the boil slowly, stirring until smooth; add the vinegar, butter and pinch of salt. Garnish with parsley and lemon.

94 Herring slices

4 servings

6 oz. short crust or flaky pastry

Filling:
12 oz. cooked flaked herring
1½ level tablespoons chopped pickle

2 level teaspoons salt
1½ tablespoons vinegar
pinch of pepper
1 dessertspoon grated or finely chopped onions

Divide pastry in half and roll out thinly into 2 square pieces. Place 1 square on a baking sheet. Mix ingredients for filling and spread over square and cover with other square. Seal edges. Mark a lattice work on top. Bake in centre of a hot oven, 425°-450°F – Gas Mark 6-7, for 25-30 minutes. Serve hot or cold.

Herring slices

95 Spiced herrings

4 servings

8 oz. onion, finely sliced
1 oz. dripping
2 tablespoons chopped
   parsley
4 herrings boned

1-2 teaspoons salt
1 teaspoon pepper
1 tablespoon vinegar
6 tablespoons stock or water
½ teaspoon cinnamon

Fry the onion in the dripping until lightly browned. Remove from the heat and cover with the parsley. Arrange the herrings on the onions, sprinkle with the seasoning and add the vinegar and stock or water. Cover the pan with a lid and cook over a gentle heat for 20 minutes or until the herrings are tender. When cooked turn on to a hot dish, sprinkle with cinnamon; serve with potato and a green vegetable.

96 Soused herrings

4-6 servings

6 or 8 herrings
1 tablespoon mixed pickling
   spice
3 pickled onions

1 level teaspoon salt
¼ pint vinegar
¼ pint water

Cut off the heads and tails and scale and clean the fish. Arrange in a baking dish (not a tin) alternately thick end to thin end. Scatter pickling spice over the fish and add the onions sliced. A bay leaf may be added, if liked. Sprinkle in the salt, pour in the vinegar and water mixed together. Bake in a very slow oven (275°F. – Gas Mark 1) for 1½ hours. Serve cold.

Soused Herrings

97 Cornish herrings

4 servings

2 large cooking apples
6 medium herrings
1 teaspoon mixed spice
good pinch white pepper
1 level teaspoon salt
3 bay leaves
¼ pint cider
¼ pint malt vinegar

For the sauce:
½ pint cider
pinch salt
1 tablespoon malt vinegar
2 teaspoons cornflour
few slices apple

Peel and quarter the cooking apples and slice the quarters thinly. Grease a shallow ovenproof dish and arrange a layer of apple slices on it. Cover with a layer of 3 herrings, split open and boned. Cover with more apple slices and half spice, pepper and salt, also the bay leaves. Top with the other 3 herrings, also split and boned. Sprinkle over remaining spice, pepper and salt, and decorate round edge of dish with the rest of the apple slices, reserving a few for the sauce. Pour in the cider and vinegar and bake in a moderate oven (375°F – Gas Mark 4) for about 30 minutes or until fish is creamy-white and tender when tested with a fork. To make the sauce, heat the cider, together with the salt and vinegar. Blend the cornflour with a little water, stir in and continue cooking and stirring until the sauce thickens. Allow to reduce a little then serve in a hot sauceboat with the herrings, with a few pieces of chopped apple floating on top.

98 Herrings diablette

2 servings

1 tablespoon breadcrumbs
1 tablespoon grated onion
pinch cayenne
1 teaspoon salt
1 tablespoon mustard

2 herrings
1 oz. fat
2 tablespoons flour

To garnish:
fried breadcrumbs

Mix together the breadcrumbs, grated onion, cayenne, salt and half mustard (previously made up with water). Split and bone the herrings, spread each fillet with the stuffing and roll it up so that the end of the fillet is tucked underneath. Heat the fat in a frying pan and secure each roll with a wooden cocktail stick or short skewer. Turn the rolls in the flour, mixed with the remainder of the dry mustard. When the fat is beginning to smoke put in the rolls and lower the heat slightly. Fry for 5 minutes on each side. Remove the sticks or skewers and transfer the herring rolls to a serving dish. Garnish with fried breadcrumbs.

99 Stuffed mackerel and paprika sauce

3 servings

3 medium-sized mackerel
2 oz. chopped mushrooms
1 large skinned and chopped tomato
2 oz. cooked rice
2 teaspoons suet or ½ oz. margarine

few drops lemon juice
seasoning

For sauce:
1 oz. margarine or butter
1 oz. flour
½ pint milk
2 level teaspoons paprika pepper

Split the mackerel and take out the backbone. Make the stuffing by mixing the finely chopped mushrooms, tomato, rice, suet or margarine, lemon juice and seasoning together. Put into the mackerel and secure with small cocktail sticks. Bake in a well greased dish covered with greased greaseproof paper for 15 minutes in the middle of a moderate oven (375°F – Gas Mark 4). If the fish are fairly large they will take 20 minutes. While the fish is cooking prepare the sauce. Heat the margarine or butter in a saucepan, stir in the flour and cook for 3 minutes. Take the pan away from the heat and gradually add the cold milk. Bring gently to the boil, stirring all the time until the sauce thickens. Add a little salt and the paprika pepper, whisking to make sure it is thoroughly mixed. Serve with the fish.

100 Mackerel in foil

4 servings

4 mackerel
salt and pepper
2 firm tomatoes

1 lemon
parsley
1 oz. butter

Clean the fish and remove the heads. Season well with salt and pepper. Lay each fish on a piece of buttered foil. Cut the tomatoes and lemon into slices and arrange alternate slices on each fish. Place a good sprig of parsley on top and dot with butter. Fold the foil up and seal into neat parcels. Place on a baking sheet and bake in a moderate oven (350°F – Gas Mark 4) for 25-30 minutes. The fish can be served in the foil or transferred in a serving dish together with the juices formed during the cooking.

101 Mackerel macedoine salad

2 servings

2 medium mackerel
8 oz. cooked potatoes
1 small packet frozen beans or fresh beans cooked and chopped

1 tablespoon chopped chives
¼ pint mayonnaise

To garnish:
lettuce
tomato wedges

Gently poach the mackerel until tender, remove and allow to become cold. Divide the fish into bite-size pieces, carefully removing all skin and bones. Mix fish, chopped potatoes, beans and chives with the mayonnaise. Arrange in the centre of a bed of lettuce leaves and garnish with the tomato wedges.

102 To boil or poach whole salmon

Salmon is probably more easily spoiled by bad cooking than any other fish. It is essential that it should not be over-cooked, for if it is, you lose colour, flavour and moistness.

When buying salmon make sure that the fish looks stiff and firm, with bright red gills, and the flesh a true salmon pink. The scales will be bright and shiny.

If you have a sufficiently large fish kettle or saucepan you can poach the fish whole. Scale and clean it carefully, then put into cold salted water, adding several slices of lemon, a small bunch parsley and 1 or 2 tablespoons olive oil, which help to keep the fish moist. Bring the water fairly quickly to boiling point, then turn the heat very low immediately, so that the liquid does no more than simmer very gently.

Allow 10 minutes per lb. cooking time for the first 6 lb., i.e. a 5 lb. fish would take 50 minutes.

Allow 5 minutes per lb. cooking time for the next 6 lb., i.e. a 10 lb. fish would take 1 hour 20 minutes.

Allow 2 minutes per lb. for each lb. over 12 lb., i.e. a 15 lb. fish would take 1 hour 36 minutes (6 lb. at 10 minutes per lb. 6 lb. at 5 minutes per lb. and 3 lb. at 2 minutes per lb.).

Take the pan off the heat, then allow the whole salmon to remain in the water for a short time to cool slightly before lifting out.

103 To poach slices of salmon

With cut salmon it is undoubtedly best to wrap it in well-buttered or oiled paper. Season the salmon, add a little lemon juice if wished, and tie carefully in a neat 'parcel' of buttered paper. Put into cold salted water with a little lemon and oil in the water. Bring slowly to boiling point, then simmer gently and allow 10 minutes per lb. or better still, bring just to boiling point, put a tightly fitting lid on the saucepan, and allow the fish to stay in the water, until it is quite cold. This is an ideal way of cooking the fish to be served cold in a salad.

104 Baked salmon

Whole salmon or slice of salmon can be baked in the oven. Wrap the well seasoned fish in buttered greaseproof paper or better still in buttered or oiled foil. Tie firmly so all the moisture is kept in during cooking. Stand in a tin in the oven and bake in a moderate oven (375°F – Gas Mark 4). Allow 20 minutes per lb. for any weight up to 2½ lb. (i.e. this will take 50 minutes). After this allow 10 minutes per lb. up to 6 lb. and 7 minutes per lb. for any weight above this. Serve both boiled and baked salmon with hollandaise sauce (see Recipe 217).

105 Grilled salmon

Season the slices of salmon well, and brush liberally with melted butter. Cook steadily under the grill until just golden coloured on the top surface, turn and brush again with more melted butter and grill on the second side, until just tender. Serve with hollandaise, tartare or shrimp sauce or top with maître d'hôtel butter (see Recipes 217, 365, 216, 68).

106 Fried salmon

Dry the slices of salmon and coat with a thin layer of seasoned flour. Fry steadily in hot butter. Serve with lemon and tartare sauce (see Recipe 365) or with mousseline sauce (see Recipe 217).

107 Salmon salad

In this dish the cooked salmon is served on a bed of mixed salad, which can be tossed in French dressing (see Recipe 362), and the mayonnaise is served separately. The salmon is either flaked or served in one piece. (*Illustrated in colour on the jacket*).

108 Salmon mayonnaise

In this dish the salmon is tossed in mayonnaise or coated with mayonnaise. In the picture is a piece of salmon and the thick mayonnaise has been put into a piping bag or syringe with a writing pipe and a design drawn on this. Ordinary mayonnaise or green mayonnaise are delicious with salmon (see Recipes 361, 363).

Salmon Mayonnaise

109 Salmon mould

4 servings

¼ pint aspic jelly
1 level teaspoon powder
   gelatine
¼ pint mayonnaise
2 tablespoons cream from the
   top of the milk

8 to 12 oz. flaked cooked
   salmon
2 hard-boiled eggs
2 sliced gherkins
seasoning

When making the aspic jelly, dissolve the extra teaspoon powder gelatine in the liquid. Allow to cool, then mix with the mayonnaise, cream, flaked salmon and 1 of the chopped hard-boiled eggs and 1 of the gherkins. Season well. Put into a rinsed mould and allow to set. Turn out and decorate with the other egg and gherkin.

110 Salmon mousse

4 servings

8-12 oz. salmon, canned or
    fresh
2 tablespoons vinegar
½ oz. butter
1 dessertspoon flour
2 teaspoons sugar
1 teaspoon dry mustard
2 eggs
fish stock
10 tablespoons milk
½ oz. powdered gelatine

2 tablespoons cold water
salt and pepper
few tablespoons cream

To garnish:
green pea salad
1 hard-boiled egg
radishes
stuffed olives

Drain off liquid from can of salmon (or stock in which fish was cooked) into a measuring jug. Add enough vinegar (preferably 1 tablespoon tarragon and the remainder malt) to bring liquid to ¼ pint. Add butter and heat until fat has just melted. Allow to cool. Flake the fish. Mix flour, sugar and mustard in top of double boiler. Add eggs, one at a time, and beat well to mix. When smooth gradually stir in fish liquids, followed by the milk. Cook, stirring constantly until mixture is thick, remove from heat. Soften gelatine in cold water, then stir until dissolved in hot mixture. Turn into large bowl and add fish. Set in cool place, stirring occasionally. When cold and thick season and fold in lightly whipped cream. Turn into 1½-2 pint mould that has been rinsed with cold water. Place in a cold place (refrigerator if possible) until set. When ready to serve, turn out on to serving dish, surround with green pea salad (cooked peas tossed in French dressing) and garnish with wedges of hard-boiled egg, radish roses and stuffed olives.

111 Salmon trout

The texture and flavour is very similar to salmon. It is, however, best if poached in salted water. Allow 10 minutes per lb. and 10 minutes over, with the water bubbling very gently.

112 Salmon in aspic

6-8 servings

1 small salmon
    (approximately 3-4 lb. or
    salmon trout
2 oz. margarine or butter

Sauce:
1 oz. margarine or butter
1 oz. flour
½ pint milk

Decoration:
½ oz. aspic jelly
½ pint water
¼ cucumber
2 oz. stuffed olives
1 bunch radishes
pickled walnuts
1 oz. capers
seasoning
2 tablespoons salad cream
    (see Recipe 364)
chopped parsley

Leaving on head and tail, bake the salmon for 30-40 minutes in moderate oven, covered with melted margarine, greaseproof paper or foil. Skin when cool. Make white sauce with margarine, flour and milk, cover with wet greaseproof paper to prevent a skin forming, allow to cool. Dissolve aspic in hot water, leave until cool. Add half aspic to two-thirds sauce, when mixture starts to thicken, coat body of fish with this. Decorate fish with half the cucumber sliced, slices of stuffed olives, sliced radishes, pieces of pickled walnut and capers as in photograph. Finally coat fish with remaining aspic jelly. Leave to set. Place a whole olive for the salmon's eye and one in the mouth. Decorate dish with remaining cucumber, sliced, and serve with salad and remaining sauce to which has been added seasoning, salad cream, chopped olives and parsley.

Salmon in Aspic

113 Grilse

The name given to very young salmon. Cook as salmon being particularly careful the fish does not become dry.

114 Baked sprats

Wash and trim sprats, coat very lightly with seasoned flour. Arrange in a casserole dish and cover with melted margarine. Put on the lid and bake for 25-30 minutes in a moderately hot oven (400°F – Gas Mark 5).

115 Fried sprats

Wash, dry and coat the sprats in well seasoned flour. Use little fat since they have a high fat content and fry steadily in the pan. The butter or fat can be flavoured with chopped parsley and lemon juice and poured over sprats when cooked.

116 *Whitebait*

4 servings

1 lb. whitebait
flour
fat for frying
salt

cayenne pepper
slices of lemon
brown bread and butter

As whitebait is not drawn, take great care to see it is fresh and keep it in a very cold place, a refrigerator if possible, until ready to eat. Wash and dry carefully, then dredge in flour. Fry until crisp and brown in boiling fat, drain and dust with salt and cayenne pepper. Serve with sliced lemon and brown bread and butter.

117 *Double frying of whitebait*

The above recipe gives a good result, but if you wish the whitebait to be very crisp they should be fried in hot fat for about 1-2 minutes until very pale coloured. Lift out the frying basket containing the fish, and allow the fat to heat up again, then lower the whitebait into the fat for the second time.
If whitebait are not available then use small sprats instead, but it is possible to obtain frozen whitebait, these should be allowed to defrost then be dried, floured and cooked as above.

118 *Devilled whitebait*

When whitebait is cooked, toss in the salt and pepper, then serve sprinkled liberally with Worcestershire sauce and wafer-thin slices of fried onion.

119 *Whitebait bites*

Whitebait make an excellent party savoury. Coat in well seasoned flour and cook in hot deep fat until crisp and golden brown. Drain well and put 3 or 4 on to cocktail sticks. Push one end of stick in a grapefruit.

120 *Sturgeon*

This is regarded as a 'Royal fish', since it is the property of the Crown, and is therefore rarely available. The fish has a very firm texture and a taste rather more like veal than anything else. When fresh the flesh should be white, and the veins clear blue. The fish can be baked, either just in butter or butter and white wine. Allow approximately 20 minutes per lb. in a moderate oven (375°F. – Gas Mark 4). It is excellent with a stuffing – either veal stuffing (see Recipe 377) or some people like sage and onion stuffing (see Recipe 377). Sturgeon can also be sliced and fried, grilled or poached in a court-bouillon (see Recipe 5).

121 *Smoked fish and how to serve it*

COD	This is filleted then cured. Cook as smoked haddock. Allow 8 oz. per person.
HADDOCK	Either filleted and smoked or cured whole. Poach in water or milk and serve with butter or a sauce. Top with poached egg if wished. Take care not to over-cook. Excellent as kedgeree (see Recipe 132). Allow 8-10 oz. per person.
HERRING	Kippers can be fried, grilled, baked or boiled. Bloaters are best grilled or fried. Buckling are served as smoked trout.
SALMON	Serve as hors d'oeuvre.
SPRATS	Unusual but very good. Grill or fry. Allow 8 oz. per person.
TROUT	An excellent hors d'oeuvre. Serve with horseradish sauce, lemon and brown bread and butter. Allow 1 fish per person.
WHITING	Cook as haddock, generally called 'golden fillets'. Allow 2 fillets per person.
EEL	An unusual but excellent hors d'oeuvre. Serve as smoked trout, removing tough skin. Allow 3-4 oz. per person.

122 *Kippers maître d'hôtel*

2 servings

2 kippers
paprika
lemon juice

maître d'hôtel butter (see Recipe 68)
chopped parsley

Remove heads from kipper and dust inside of each with paprika then sprinkle with lemon juice. Put 2 kippers together and wrap in greaseproof paper. Place in baking tins in moderate oven for about 20 minutes. Turn out on to hot serving dish and pour juices from wrapping paper over top. Blend ingredients for maître d'hôtel butter, and mould into small squares, placing one on each fish before serving. Garnish with sprigs of parsley and serve with plain or French mustard.

123 *Jugged kippers*

Roll up the kippers, put them in a jug and pour in enough fast boiling water to cover them. Cover the jug and let it stand for 5 minutes in a hot place, beside the hot plates on the kitchen stove for instance. Remove the fish, drain and serve with a pat of butter on top.

Kippers

124 *Grilled bloaters*

as many bloaters as required   a little margarine or dripping for frying the roes

Break off the heads of the fish, split open the back and remove the roes and backbone. Toss the roes in a little hot margarine or dripping in a small pan until golden brown. Make the grill hot, grease the grid in the grill pan and place the fish in it, the insides to the heat. When brown turn over and grill the backs. Serve very hot with the fried roes.

125 *Kipper pâté*

Cook the kippers by frying, grilling or by method given in jugged kippers (see Recipe 123). Flake all the fish away from skin and any bones. Pound well with plenty of butter, grated nutmeg and pepper. Excellent for toast or sandwiches.

126 *Kippers as mock smoked salmon*

Raw kippers are a very good substitute for smoked salmon in salads, hors d'oeuvre and for sandwich fillings. Choose really thick, moist kippers and divide into neat fillets. Cover with a little oil and vinegar, also chopped onion if wished and leave. Lift out of this mixture after several hours.

127 *Herring roe*

There are several ways in which herring roes may be cooked, but they are one of the most digestible forms of food and can be served to very young children.

128 *Fried herring roes*

Allow 2-4 oz. roe per person. Wash under running cold water then dry and toss in well-seasoned flour. Fry in hot fat until pale golden brown. Garnish with finely chopped parsley.

129 *Steamed herring roes*

2-4 oz. roe per person   seasoning
little milk   knob of margarine

Put roes into a colander and let the cold water run over them, then pat them dry. Put on a plate, covered with the milk, seasoning and margarine. Cover with a second plate and steam over a saucepan of hot water for about 15 minutes. Serve on toast or with mashed potato. These can be dusted with paprika or cayenne pepper.

130 *Herring roe pie*

4 servings

1 lb. herring roes   seasoning
1 hard-boiled egg   2 oz. finely grated cheese
½ pint white sauce (see Recipe 216)   2 tablespoons breadcrumbs

Wash the roes under running cold water. Put into a pie dish with the chopped egg and white sauce, seasoning the mixture well. Sprinkle the cheese and crumbs on top, and bake for 25 minutes in the centre of a moderately hot oven (400°F – Gas Mark 5).

131 *Hard herring roes*

When you are not cooking the roes with the fish you can make them into an appetising separate dish. Here's one good way of using hard roes. Wash the roes, dry them and coat with seasoned flour. Cook in a little fat until lightly brown. Add chopped parsley, a little lemon juice and a dash of Worcestershire sauce. Pound together with the fat they were cooked in and add enough extra margarine to form a paste. Add seasoning if needed and serve on hot buttered toast.

132 *Kedgeree*

There are many variations on a kedgeree: basically you need smoked haddock and cooked rice.

Allow 1½-2 oz. rice per person and about 2 oz. smoked haddock. Toss both together in hot butter, then add a little cream if wished and heat gently.

If you like several beaten eggs can be used to bind the mixture together.

The kedgeree can be topped with fried onion rings, rolls of bacon, hard-boiled eggs.

133 *Boston kedgeree*

4 servings

about 8 oz. smoked haddock
6 oz. rice
1 onion
2 oz. butter
2 hard-boiled eggs

pepper, salt and cayenne
chopped parsley

To garnish:
toast triangles, lemon

Pour boiling water over the haddock, leave it to stand for 5 minutes, remove any bones and skin and flake coarsely. Bring a pint of water to the boil in a large saucepan with seasonings to taste, pour in the rice, cover closely and cook over a very low heat until all the water is absorbed – about 25 minutes. While it is cooking fry the finely chopped onion in a little of the butter till soft and transparent, chop the whites of the hard-boiled eggs and sieve the yolks. Stir in the flaked fish, the onion, the egg whites and the rest of the butter into the cooked rice and season rather highly. Heat through gently and pile up on a flat warm dish. Make a big yellow cross over the top with the sieved egg yolks and then scatter the whole dish with parsley. Garnish with toast and lemon.

Boston Kedgeree

134 *Russian fish pie*

4 servings

6 oz. short or flaky pastry
  (see Recipes 207, 338)
approximately 12 oz. cooked
  flaked smoked haddock
1 hard-boiled egg
2 tablespoons cream

1 tablespoon fine
  breadcrumbs
1 teaspoon parsley
little finely grated lemon rind
seasoning
egg or milk to glaze

Roll out the pastry in a large square. Mix fish, chopped egg, and other ingredients together and put in centre of the pastry. Bring up the corners of the pastry into centre, brushing them with a little egg or milk to make sure they do not come apart. Decorate with rose of pastry. Brush with egg or milk to glaze. Bake for approximately 40 minutes, starting at a hot oven (450°F. – Gas Mark 7) for 20 minutes, then reduce the heat to moderate (375°F. – Gas Mark 4). Serve hot or cold.

135 *Easy fish casserole*

4 servings

8 oz. fresh haddock
8 oz. smoked haddock (or
  1 lb. white fish as
  available)
1 large carrot
1 small onion
1-2 sticks celery
1 chicken bouillon cube

1 pint boiling water
milk
1 oz. butter
1 oz. cornflour
seasoning
few cooked green peas
lemon juice
parsley

Cut the fish into pieces and cook with the diced carrot, onion and celery in 1 pint stock, make by dissolving the chicken cube in the boiling water. When cooked, strain the liquor carefully from the fish and make it up to 1 pint with milk if necessary. Melt the butter in a pan, add the cornflour and cook for 1-2 minutes. Remove from the heat and stir in the liquor. Return to the heat, stir till boiling and boil for 3 minutes, stirring constantly. Add the fish, flaked and free from skin and bone, and the vegetables. Add seasoning if required, the peas and a squeeze of lemon juice. Re-heat, then turn into a casserole and serve garnished with parsley.

136 *Haddock balls*

4 servings

1 large smoked haddock
6 oz. cold mashed potatoes
pepper
2 heaped teaspoons chopped
  parsley

1 egg
browned crumbs
cooking fat for frying

Cook the haddock, remove skin and bone, or use left-over cooked haddock. Chop finely, add the potatoes, pepper, chopped parsley, and form into 6 balls. Dip in beaten egg and coat with browned crumbs. Fry in hot cooking fat (heated to 356°F) for 3 minutes or until brown and crisp. Drain, serve hot or cold with tomatoes and watercress.

Haddock Balls

137 *Finnan haddock rarebit*

4 servings

1 smoked haddock
1 oz. butter
1 oz. flour
¼ pint milk
seasoning
1 teaspoon made mustard

1 tablespoon Worcestershire
    sauce (light ale can be
    used)
3-4 oz. grated cheese
3 oz. soft breadcrumbs
knob butter

Cook the haddock and remove the bones and break into **LARGE** flakes. Put into the casserole. Heat the butter in the pan, stir in the flour and cook for several minutes slowly then add the milk, bring to the boil and cook until thick and smooth. Add seasonings, the sauce or light ale and the cheese, keeping a little back for the topping. Spread over the fish (the mixture is fairly thick) then cover with the crumbs and cheese and knob of butter. Bake for about 25 minutes in a moderate oven (375°F. – Gas Mark 4).

SHELL FISH AND FRESH WATER FISH

138 *Shell fish*

Be particularly careful that the fish is really fresh, since stale shell fish can be very harmful.

Fish
and when in season

CLAM
September-April

Smaller than oyster, but can be served in the same way (see Recipes 168-172).

COCKLES
September-April

Tiny shell fish served cold. To cook, wash very well, put into salted water, then into either roasting tin in moderate oven or saucepan containing very little water. Heat until shells open. Take out and serve with seasoning and a little vinegar. Excellent added to sauces.

CRAB
May-August

Dress and serve hot or cold (see Recipes 139-145). Be sure to remove the stomach bag and grey brown fingers. To cook put into boiling salted water, simmer for 20-25 minutes, rinse in cold water. Best selection is male crab, distinguished by larger claws.

CRAWFISH (Langouste) May-August	Although no large claws, use as lobster.
CRAYFISH (Ecrevisse) October-March	Small fresh water shell fish, similar to lobster. If caught fresh, cook for 10 minutes only. Otherwise cook as lobster.
LOBSTER February-October	Serve hot or cold (see Recipes 152-164). To cook, wash well, tie claws and put into boiling water. Simmer for 20-25 minutes according to size, BUT NO MORE, then put into cold water. Hen lobster has wide tail and red coral which is delicious. If buying ready-cooked lobster, make sure it has been freshly cooked. The lobster should feel heavy for its size and the tail should spring back when tested. Be sure to take out intestinal vein and the lady 'fingers'.
MUSSELS September-April	Serve raw as oysters or in sauce (see Recipes 165-167).
OYSTERS September-April	Generally served raw as hors d'oeuvre, can be used in sauces or as main dish, delicious as filling in omelettes (see Recipes 168-172). Imported oysters now cover closed season.
PRAWNS Small: February-October Large: March-December	Very excellent frozen small prawns or large prawns known as scampi; you can serve them throughout the year (see Recipes 180-185). Delicious hot or cold, in main dishes or with hot sauce.
SHRIMPS February-October	See prawns.
SCALLOPS (Coquilles St. Jacques) or SCOLLOPS or ESCALLOPS October-March	Use in sauces, main dishes. The roe (coral) should be firm and bright in colour. Remove the black part and gristly fibre. Save shells to use in scalloped dishes (see Recipes 146-151).
WHELKS September-April	Buy when alive, clean in plenty of water. Boil steadily in salted water for approximately 1 hour. Take out of shells with pin and serve with seasoning and vinegar.
WINKLES September-April	Like small whelks.

Never over-cook shell fish since it toughens it badly.

139 *To dress crab*

One medium sized crab is enough for two people, one large one for four people. Feel the crab when you buy it, and if it feels surprisingly light for its size, ask the fishmonger to break it open – for 'lightness' often indicates that it is 'watery' and you are not getting good solid crab meat. Open the main part of the shell by pulling up the rounded part. Take out the skin-like 'bag' and the greyish-brown fingers, both of which should be discarded. Remove all white meat and mix with the meat from the claws. Remove the brown meat and keep this separately.

140 *Devilled crab*
2 servings as a main dish
4 servings as an hors d'oeuvres

1 large crab or 2 smaller crabs	1 teaspoon Worcestershire sauce
seasoning	1 oz. fine breadcrumbs
1 teaspoon curry powder	1 oz. butter

Take the crab meat from the shell and flake, and mix with seasoning, curry powder, sauce and half crumbs. Fry the rest of the crumbs in the butter. Put the crab meat back into the shell, cover with the crumbs and heat under the grill.

141 *Crab au gratin*

Mix the crab meat with a little grated cheese. Cover the top of the crab meat (either in the shell or serving dish) with grated cheese and fried crumbs and brown under the grill.

5. Mackerel in foil

6. Dressed crab

142 Crab pilaff

4 servings

4 oz. butter or margarine
8 oz. cooked long grain rice
4 tomatoes, peeled and
   chopped
4 oz. sultanas
2 large cooked crabs or
   1¼ lb. crab meat

salt
ground black pepper
grated cheese (Parmesan or
   dry Cheddar), optional

To garnish:
strips of anchovy

Melt the butter or margarine in a pan and add the rice. Stir until the fat is absorbed and then add the tomatoes, sultanas, crab meat and seasonings. Stir until heated through. Divide the mixture between the two shells, or if crab meat is used pile on a heated dish; if desired, a generous sprinkling of cheese may be served on each portion. Top with anchovy fillets. With the pilaff serve a tossed green salad.

Crab Pilaff

143 King crab herb garden salad

4 servings

2 small cans Japanese
   crabmeat or 2 fresh crabs
lettuce
watercress
1 tablespoon fresh herb
   leaves (lemon thyme,
   verbena, sweet geranium,
   basil, tarragon as
   available)

To garnish:
parsley
radish rose

Gently remove cartilage from crab meat keeping big chunks whole. Mound crab flakes and small pieces on bed of torn lettuce, watercress and herbs. Top with the crab meat chunks and garnish centre with parsley and a radish rose. Serve with herb dressing; see recipe 144.

144 Herb dressing

¼ pint mayonnaise or salad
   dressing (Recipes 361 and
   364)
1 tablespoon cider vinegar
¼ teaspoon chopped lemon
   thyme leaves (or dill or
   basil)

¼ teaspoon chopped
   parsley
½ teaspoon chopped chives
¼ teaspoon salt
⅛ teaspoon pepper

Combine all ingredients.

145 King crab Newburg

4 servings

2 small cans Japanese crab
   meat or 2 fresh crabs
2 oz. butter or margarine
2 tablespoons sherry
2-4 egg yolks

¼ pint and 4 tablespoons
   cream or evaporated milk
   approximately.
½ teaspoon salt
paprika

Remove cartilage from crab meat, keeping chunks whole. Place crab, butter and sherry in top of double saucepan and cook for several minutes. Beat egg yolks and cream until smooth, add salt. Stir cream mixture into crab mixture. Cook, stirring, until mixture thickens. Sprinkle with paprika. Serve over rice.

King Crab Newburg

146 *Coquilles St. Jacques*

4 servings

4 medium-sized scallops	seasoning
½ pint milk	1 tablespoon white wine or
little mashed potato	sherry
2 oz. butter	few crisp breadcrumbs
1 oz. flour	1 oz. grated cheese

Simmer the scallops (often called 'escallops') in the milk for approximately 10 minutes, until quite soft. It is important that this is done slowly, for too quick cooking makes them tough. When cooked, put the scallops on to their shells. Pipe round a border of mashed potatoes. Melt the butter in the pan, stir in the flour and cook gently for 3 minutes. Gradually add the milk made up again to the ½ pint. Cook the sauce until thick, adding seasoning and the wine. Carefully mask the tops of the scallops with this. Sprinkle with the crumbs and cheese and either put into a hot oven or under the grill until heated through and crisp and brown on top.

147 *Coquilles St. Jacques bonne femme*

4 servings

4 scallops	salt and pepper to taste
½ pint milk	creamed potato
4 tablespoons white wine	
1 oz. margarine	*To garnish:*
2 oz. mushrooms, sliced	sprigs of parsley
¾ oz. flour	

Slice the scallops and simmer in the milk and wine until tender, about 10 minutes; drain them carefully, place in the deep shells and keep hot. Melt the margarine and fry the mushrooms until soft, about 3-4 minutes, then add the flour and cook for a further 1-2 minutes. Stir in the fish liquor and bring to the boil, stirring all the time. Boil gently for 5 minutes then season to taste. Pipe a firm border of creamed potato round the edge of each scallop shell and pour the sauce over the fish. Re-heat under the grill until lightly browned and garnish with a sprig of parsley.

148 *Scallop mayonnaise*

4 servings as a main meal
8 servings as a starter

	4 oz. cooked rice
8 scallops	4 tablespoons French
small piece shallot, thinly	dressing
sliced	
¼ pint dry white wine	*To garnish:*
salt	paprika
freshly ground black pepper	lemon
¼ pint thick mayonnaise	sprigs of parsley

Wash the scallops and cut into 1-inch pieces. Simmer the shallot in the wine for 5 minutes. Add the scallops and seasoning and simmer for a further 7 minutes. Drain off any surplus wine and leave to cool. Add the mayonnaise and correct the seasoning. Mix together the rice and French dressing and add a little paprika to make it faintly pink. Arrange the rice in crescent shapes on individual plates with the mayonnaised scallops in front of the rice. Garnish the scallops with paprika, lemon butterflies and parsley.

149 *Fried scallops*

Lift the scallops from the shells, dry and coat in well seasoned flour, or a thin batter. Put into deep or shallow fat and fry steadily for approximately 5 minutes.

150 *Scallops and bacon*

Lift the scallops from the shells, season and add a little lemon juice. Wrap round with rashers of bacon, secure with skewers and fry or grill for 5 minutes.

151 *Scallops in sauces*

One can use scallops instead of lobster or sole with any of the 'classic' sauces. Either serve on the shells or in entrée dishes.

152 *Lobster in salad*

Choose the lobster with care – see details in table (Recipe 138), and use as soon as possible after it is cooked.

Split the lobster, remove the intestinal vein, and the lady 'fingers'. These are found where the small claws join the body, and shouldn't be eaten. Crack the large claws very carefully and remove the lobster meat. One way of serving lobster for lobster mayonnaise or salad is to leave the meat on the shells, and serve a ½ shell on each plate or for each person, garnished with salad, meat from the large claws and the small claws. Many people like to add a few capers to the mayonnaise piped or spread over the top of the lobster meat.

The second way of serving the salad is to remove all the meat from the body, dice this, mix with mayonnaise and arrange on a bed of salad. Cold lobster looks attractive garnished with whisked aspic jelly.

153 *Lobster Americaine*

4 servings

1 large or 2 medium lobsters	¼ pint white wine
1 onion or 2 shallots	¼ pint brandy
2 oz. butter	seasoning
3 tomatoes	

Many chefs like to cut up a live lobster for this dish, but few housewives will enjoy doing this. However, use one as soon after boiling as possible. Dice the onion finely and fry in the butter, add the skinned tomatoes, wine and brandy and simmer for about 10 minutes. Remove all lobster meat from shell and claws, dice and add to the tomato mixture, season, heat for about 5 minutes. Serve with crisp toast or rice.

154 *Lobster à la crème*

4 servings

2-3 mushrooms	1 cooked lobster or can of
1 onion	lobster
1 oz. butter	seasoning
½ oz. flour	
½ chicken bouillon cube in	*To garnish:*
¼ pint water	watercress
¼ pint evaporated milk or	
thin cream	

Peel and slice mushrooms and onion and fry them, but do not brown, in the butter, add the flour and stir in the liquids gradually. Simmer until thickened and vegetables are tender, season to taste. Remove lobster flesh from shell and claws or drain canned lobster. Add it to the sauce and heat through. Pile in the shell or in individual fireproof dishes. Garnish with watercress.

Au gratin

Recipe as above, but top the lobster and sauce with 1 oz. sieved processed Gruyère or grated Cheddar cheese, a few breadcrumbs, and grill until brown.

155 *Lobster cutlets*

1 oz. margarine	1 egg
1 oz. flour	1 teaspoon finely grated
¼ pint milk	onion
seasoning	egg and browned
1 medium-sized lobster	breadcrumbs for coating
4 oz. fine breadcrumbs	fat for frying

This is an economical method of serving lobster, for 1 medium-sized one will be ample for 4 people.

Melt the margarine in a saucepan, stir in the flour and cook for 3 minutes. Remove the pan from the heat and stir in the cold milk, bring to the boil, stirring all the time until a thick sauce is formed, and add seasoning. Let this cool, then mix in the lobster, breadcrumbs and the well-beaten egg and onion. Form into cutlet shapes, brush with egg and coat in breadcrumbs. Heat fat in a frying pan and cook until brown and crisp on either side, then lower heat to cook gently for a further few minutes to make sure the cutlets are heated through to the middle. Serve with fried or creamed potatoes, peas or creamed spinach.

156 *Curried lobster*

Make a curry sauce – using the shell of the lobster to provide the stock (see Recipe 353). Add the diced lobster meat and cook for 5-8 minutes. Serve on a bed of rice.

157 *Lobster cardinal*

For this recipe it is essential to have hen lobsters (see Recipe 138). The lobster is heated gently in a creamy white sauce (see Recipe 216), to which can be added a little sherry or white wine, then the lobster butter (see Recipe 223) stirred in at the end to colour the mixture a delicate pink.

158 *Grilled lobster*

Split the lobster and prepare and spread with well seasoned butter of, if a hen lobster, with lobster butter (see Recipe 223). Season the meat from the large claws too, and spread with the butter. Put for a few minutes only under a really hot grill and serve at once.

159 Lobster Mexicaine
4 servings

For 2 lobsters fry 1 small onion, ½ chopped green and ½ chopped red pepper in 2-3 oz. butter. Add 4 skinned chopped tomatoes and 4 good sized chopped mushrooms, season well then stir in the chopped lobster meat.

160 Lobster pancakes

Heat lobster meat in a creamy sauce and use as a filling for pancakes or omelettes, garnish with the small lobster claws. The pancakes can be coated with grated cheese and put for 1 minute under a hot grill.

161 Lobster Newburg
4 servings

1 large or 2 medium lobsters	¼ pint milk
2 oz. butter	¼ pint brandy *or* sherry
¼ pint cream	seasoning
yolks of 2 eggs	

Dice the lobster meat and toss in the butter, add the cream, egg yolks blended with the milk and seasoning. Heat very gently, taking care not to boil sherry or brandy (a double saucepan is ideal for this). Serve at once, garnished with the small lobster claws.

A less rich Lobster Newburg is made by using ½ pint good white sauce (see Recipe 216), adding the diced lobster, sherry and a little cream or an egg yolk and heating gently.

162 Lobster Thermidor (1)
4 servings

1 oz. butter for sauce	1 small onion or shallot
1 oz. flour	2 oz. butter
¼ pint and 4 tablespoons milk	2 tablespoons white wine or
2 tablespoons cream	sherry
seasoning	2 oz. grated cheese
1 large or 2 medium lobsters	

Make the sauce with the butter, flour, milk and cream, and season well. Add the diced lobster meat and heat gently. Meanwhile fry the very finely chopped shallot or onion in the butter, add to the mixture together with the sherry. Pile back in the lobster shells, cover the tops with grated cheese and brown under a hot grill.

163 Lobster Thermidor (2)

In this recipe 2 or 3 skinned tomatoes and several chopped mushrooms are fried and added to the sauce instead of the onion.

164 Lobster vol-au-vent

Lobster makes a delicious filling for a large vol-au-vent case or for small pastry patties. Dice the lobster meat and mix with a thick white sauce (see Recipe 216) to which can be added a little mayonnaise or cream. If using a hen lobster use the red coral for garnish on top.

When using lobster in hot dishes take care not to over-cook for this toughens it.

165 Mussels marinière
4 servings

2 pints mussels	seasoning
1 tablespoon tarragon vinegar	1 bunch parsley
1 small onion	*To garnish*
2 or 3 pieces celery when available	chopped parsley

Scrub the mussels well, discarding any that are open and will not close when sharply tapped. Put into a large saucepan together with water to cover, vinegar, onion, celery, a good pinch of salt and pepper and the bunch of parsley. Heat slowly until the mussels open. Remove the beards from the mussels. Sometimes you will find a small growth, looking like a weed, in the mussels – this must be taken out. Leave the mussels on half the shell. Re-boil the liquid and strain over them. Garnish with chopped parsley. A little wine can be added if wished.

Mussels Marinière

166 *Poached mussels*

Cook the mussels until they open (see Recipe 165), then serve on buttered toast with lemon slices or parsley sauce, or put into scallop shells and coat with tomato purée.

167 *Fried mussels*

Cook the mussels until they open (see recipe 165), save a little of the liquid, and use instead of milk in a coating batter. Dip mussels in this, then fry for a few minutes in deep fat. Serve with lemon.

168 *Oysters*

Get the fishmonger to open these for you. Serve in one shell, with paprika or cayenne pepper, slices of lemon and brown bread and butter. Some people like a little vinegar with them.

169 *Helford angels*

Butter generously thin slices of brown bread and trim into neat 2-inch squares. Place a raw oyster on each, sprinkle with a shake of pepper and grated nutmeg and roll up cornerwise. Place on a greased ovenproof dish and bake in a moderately hot oven (400°F. – Gas Mark 5) about 10 minutes until the bread is crisp. Spear with cocktail sticks and serve immediately.

170 *Fried oysters*

Lift the oysters from the shells, being careful to retain all the juice. Put this, and the oysters into a pan, heat gently for a few minutes until the edges curl, then lift out and coat each oyster with fritter batter (see Recipe 7), and fry steadily.

171 *Oysters mornay*

Par-cook the oysters as in the previous recipe, then put into scallop shells or a dish. Cover with cheese sauce and heat gently in the oven.

172 *Oysters as an omelette filling*

Fry oysters, then cut into small pieces and heat with a little cream. Put into the omelette just before serving.

173 *Prawn Salad*

4 servings

1-1½ lb. fresh prawns or
  8-12 oz. shelled
lettuce

To garnish:
sprigs of cauliflower
watercress
sliced stuffed olives

Marinade:
4 tablespoons corn oil
2 tablespoons lemon juice
¼ level teaspoon salt
¼ level teaspoon pepper
½ clove garlic chopped
few drops Tabasco sauce

Dressing:
3 tablespoons corn oil
1 tablespoon wine vinegar
¼ level teaspoon salt
1 level teaspoon sugar

Combine all ingredients for the marinade together – pour over the prawns – cover and leave in the refrigerator for 1-2 hours stirring occasionally. Arrange a bed of lettuce in a salad bowl and place the prawns on top. The salad is given extra 'bite' with sprigs of raw cauliflower and is decorated with watercress and sliced stuffed olives. Just before serving pour over the dressing. To make this put all ingredients in a screw top jar and shake well.

174 *Curried prawns*

4 servings

8 oz. frozen or freshly shelled
  prawns
curry sauce (see Recipe 353)

Make the curry sauce and simmer well for an hour or so. Add the prawns and cook gently until hot. Do NOT over-cook or you will toughen shellfish.
Serve with Patna rice and interesting side dishes. To get grains of boiled rice really separate wash the uncooked rice in two changes of water, then drain. Cook in a large saucepan, covering with plenty of water. Bring to the boil quickly and simmer for 20 minutes or more until each grain is soft but not mushy. Drain through a colander, rinse in running cold water, then stand colander over a pan of simmering water or put rice in a shallow dish in a very low oven until it has warmed through. Suitable accompaniments for curry are bananas, currants (washed in boiling water to make them moist and juicy), chutney, shredded coconut, mandarin oranges, apple slices and poppadums, which can be bought in packets in shops specialising in Indian foods. Fry them in fat or grill until crisp.

175 Prawn barquettes

4 servings

6-8 short crust pastry (see Recipe 207)	1 bay leaf
about 3 oz. prawns (fresh or frozen)*	1 oz. butter
	1 oz. flour
½ pint single cream	1-2 oz. grated cheese
1 small shallot or a slice of onion	salt and pepper
	cayenne or curry powder
blade of mace	1 egg yolk, beaten

Roll out pastry thinly, put boat-shaped tins close together in a row (groups of 4 large or 6 small tins) lift pastry on rolling pin and put it over a group of tins at once. Press it well into each tin and then roll over tops of tins with a well-floured rolling pin, first in one direction then the other, to remove surplus pastry. Flute edges of the 'boats' and prick bottoms lightly. Bake 'blind' in hot oven (425°-450°F. – Gas Mark 6-7) for 10-15 minutes. Chop half the prawns coarsely, reserving the rest for decoration. Put cream in a pan with onion or shallot, mace, bay leaf and a few peppercorns if available, and leave covered to infuse over a low heat for about 10 minutes. (Do not let it boil). Melt butter in another pan and stir in flour. Gradually strain in warm cream, off heat; bring to boil and simmer for a few minutes. Stir in cheese and season with salt and pepper and either cayenne or a pinch of curry powder. Remove from heat, stir in egg yolk and chopped prawns and cook for 1-2 minutes longer without boiling. Turn into pastry cases and brown tops lightly under a hot grill. Then decorate with remaining prawns.

Prawn Barquettes

176 Potato and prawn mornay

4 servings

1-1½ lb. creamed potatoes	3 oz. grated cheese
margarine	2 hard-boiled eggs
½ pint white sauce (see Recipe 216)	½ pint picked prawns
	2 oz. breadcrumbs

Line the casserole at the bottom and sides with the creamed potatoes, brush with a little melted margarine and put into a hot oven (425°-450°F. – Gas Mark 6-7) for about 10 minutes to crisp. Meanwhile make the sauce, add most of the cheese, the chopped eggs and prawns. Pour into the potato-case and top with the crumbs, cheese and margarine. Return to the oven for about 10-15 minutes.

177 Cheese and shrimp or prawn ramekins

4 servings

4 eggs	2-3 oz. shelled shrimps or prawns
½ pint white sauce (See Recipe 216)	2 teaspoons chopped parsley
4 oz. grated Cheddar cheese	pinch cayenne pepper and salt

Boil the eggs for 7 minutes then plunge them into cold water for 1 minute. Remove the shells and roughly chop up the eggs in a small pan with the sauce. Add 2 oz. of the grated cheese, the shrimps or prawns and chopped parsley and heat through without boiling. Season and pour into buttered ramekin dishes. Sprinkle over the remainder of the grated cheese and brown under a hot grill. Garnish and serve at once with crisp toast.

Cheese and Shrimp Ramekins

178 Shell fish platter

Simply fill scallop shells with fish 'titbits' such as shrimps on paper-thin slices of cucumber, topped with creamy lemon mayonnaise; crisp fried whitebait garnished with 'butterflies' of sliced lemon; creamed, smoked haddock with slices of hard-boiled eggs and chopped chives; and dressed crab with sprigs of parsley. Arrange the shells on a large plate and garnish with unpeeled shrimps, parsley and slices of lemon.

Shell Fish Platter

179 *Paella*

4 servings

4 pieces of cooked or raw
   young chicken
1 onion
1 clove garlic
2 tablespoons olive oil
2 pints water
2 medium-sized tomatoes
4 oz. rice
2 chicken bouillon cubes

a little saffron if possible
1 small cooked lobster or tin
   lobster
4 Dublin Bay prawns or 8-10
   smaller prawns
6-8 mussels
8 oz. frozen peas
½ tin pimento or red pepper

Cut up chicken, onion and garlic and fry in the oil until golden. Add half the water and simmer for 15 minutes. Add the tomatoes skinned and cut up, add the rice and the remaining water and bouillon cubes. Simmer 5 minutes, stir in saffron. Arrange the lobster pieces, prawns, mussels and peas attractively with the pimentos. Continue cooking until rice is cooked and has absorbed most of the liquid, 15-20 minutes.

180 *Scampi*

The very large prawns, so often called scampi, have become popular in both hot or cold dishes. Dublin Bay prawns are often sold as 'scampi', and those that come from the Mediterranean.
When sold cooked they are peeled and used as ordinary prawns or instead of lobster in hot dishes (see Recipes 152-164).
Most scampi is sold deep frozen, and uncooked. It should be allowed to defrost sufficiently to separate the fish, then used in the following ways. NEVER RE-FREEZE THIS, as it can be very dangerous.

181 *Fried scampi*

Dry the fish and coat in batter (see Recipe 7) or egg and breadcrumbs carefully. Lower into hot deep fat and fry for 3-4 minutes only, then lift out and drain well on crumpled tissue paper or absorbent kitchen paper. Serve with lemon and tartare sauce (see Recipe 365).

182 *Devilled scampi*

Follow directions as for scampi Meunière, but work a little curry powder into the butter when darkening this with a few drops of Worcestershire sauce.

183 *Scampi bordelaise*

Make ½ pint tomato sauce (see Recipe 360) adding a little sherry to this. Put the uncooked scampi in the sauce and simmer steadily for 5 minutes. Serve at once with a border of boiled rice.

184 *Scampi meunière*

4 servings

3 oz. butter
about 18 large prawns,
   cooked or raw
seasoning
little lemon juice

1 dessertspoon chopped
   parsley
few capers if desired

To garnish:
lemon

Heat the butter and add the prawns. If using the already cooked prawns they need just be heated, but if using raw prawns, then cook steadily for about 4 minutes. Lift on to a hot dish and continue cooking the butter until it becomes dark brown, add seasoning, lemon juice, chopped parsley and capers and pour over the scampi. Garnish with lemon.

185 *Scampi Provençale*

4 servings

small onion
clove garlic
2 or 3 tomatoes
2 tablespoons olive oil
about 18 large prawns,
  cooked or raw

chopped parsley
seasoning
little white wine

To garnish:
little chopped parsley

Fry the chopped onion, garlic and tomatoes in the hot oil. If using raw scampi add these together with chopped parsley, seasoning and white wine to moisten. Cook steadily for about 5-6 minutes. If using cooked prawns then add white wine, parsley, seasoning to the onion mixture; get this very hot before heating the prawns for 2-3 minutes. Serve garnished with chopped parsley.

186 *Snails*

Most of the edible snails used are imported – ready frozen and stuffed with garlic butter, i.e. maître d'hôtel butter to which should be added a little crushed garlic or garlic juice. To prepare as a hot dish the snails should be washed·very well in cold water, then left to soak overnight in cold salted water to remove the slime. They can then be cooked as mussels for about 20 minutes, the flesh removed from the shells, and the black end taken away. The snails can then be served hot with maître d'hôtel butter (see Recipe 68) or returned to the liquid in which they were cooked.

187 *Frogs' Legs*

While these are an acquired taste, many people think they taste rather like chicken. Only the hind legs of the frog are used and these should be cut from the body, washed well in cold water, then skinned. Put into boiling water, bring the water to the boil then drain off the liquid and use the frogs' legs as follows:

To fry
Season well and fry in butter with finely chopped onion and/or bacon or coat in egg and breadcrumbs and fry.

To bake
Cover with white wine, add chopped onion, parsley and cook for approximately 15 minutes.

Fricassée
Toss the frogs' legs in butter, together with chopped onion, then add creamy white sauce, see Recipe 216, and simmer gently for approximately 15 minutes.

188 *How to recognise and cook fresh-water fish*

Fish and when in season

CARP
October-February

Unless a very small carp, this fish is too tough for grilling or frying. Is best baked rather slowly, preferably with onions and tomatoes in a covered casserole. Allow 8 oz. per person.

EEL
September-May

Must be purchased from a fishmonger who keeps them alive in a tank. He will cut and skin them. Stew, or make into a jelly. 6-8 oz. per person.

TROUT
April-September

Buy whole; grill, fry or bake. Delicious fried and served with brown butter sauce, i.e. meunière (see Recipe 192). Keep well basted when cooking as the fish is rather dry. Ideal to cook almost immediately after being caught.

PERCH
May-February

Generally small enough to serve 1 fish per person. Be careful of the spikes in the dorsal fin as they are very sharp. This fish is difficult to scale, so plunge for a minute in boiling water then scale. Delicious flavour. Best fried, and served with meunière sauce (see Recipes 184, 192).

SMELT
September-March

Becoming very rare. Can be poached, grilled, fried, baked or cooked in white wine or cider. To prepare remove the fins, but leave head on to cook.

BREAM see White Fish table
  (Recipe 12)

189 *Jellied eels*

Cut the eel into 2-inch lengths, having skinned it first. Put into cold water, adding a little salt, squeeze of lemon juice. Use enough water to JUST cover the fish. Simmer very gently for approximately 45 minutes to 1 hour until the flesh is very tender. Lift out the eel and arrange in mould or dish. Measure the liquid, and if a very firm jelly is required add 1 teaspoon powder gelatine to each ½ pint of stock. Strain over the eels and allow to set.
If the liquid is boiled down not only does it have a better flavour but you can omit the gelatine.
Bay leaf or spice can also be added to flavour.

190 *Eel with parsley sauce*

Skin the eel and cut into 2-3-inch lengths. Put into cold salted water, adding a sprig of parsley and 1 or 2 slices of lemon. Simmer gently for approximately 45 minutes, then drain and serve with parsley sauce (see Recipe 216) and garnish with lemon and parsley.

191 *Fried eel*

Skin the eel and cut into 2-3-inch lengths. Coat in seasoned flour, then in egg and breadcrumbs and fry steadily in hot fat until tender. Drain and serve with lemon.

192 *Trout meunière*

Trout should not be confused with salmon trout. It is a fresh-water fish (see fresh-water table Recipe 188) and can be grilled, baked or fried.
A simple but delicious way is to serve trout meunière. Heat about 2 oz. butter for each 2 fish in a large pan. Fry the fish steadily in this, then when cooked lift on to a hot dish; add a squeeze of lemon juice and seasoning to butter and cook until golden brown. Pour over fish, add chopped parsley and garnish with piped potatoes.

193 *Trout Grenobloise*

Recipe as trout meunière, but use rather more butter and when trout is cooked add finely chopped mushrooms and a few rather coarse breadcrumbs, fry in the hot butter, then pour over the trout.

194 *Baked trout with black grapes*

4 servings

4 medium trout	*Sauce:*
2 oz. margarine	1 oz. flour
4 tablespoons white wine	½ pint milk
6 olives	seasoning
1 lemon	
1 small bunch black grapes	

Clean the trout, but leave heads and tails on. Place the prepared trout in a baking dish, previously brushed with melted margarine. To keep in a circular shape during cooking place each trout in a corner of the tin. Brush with the remaining melted margarine, pour on the wine and cover with foil. Bake in the middle of a moderate oven (375°F. – Gas Mark 4) for 30-40 minutes.

To make the sauce:
Remove the fish liquor from the trout and place in a saucepan. Add the flour and stir well. Cook gently for 1 minute, add the milk and bring to the boil, simmer for 3 minutes, stirring all the time, season. Remove the trout to a serving dish, place in olives to represent eyes. Slice the lemon, place on the serving dish. Divide the grapes in half, cut one half into quarters and stir into the sauce. Garnish with rest of grapes.

Baked Trout with Black Grapes

195 Baked trout with caper and mushroom sauce

4 servings

4 medium-sized trout
4 oz. mushrooms
1 oz. table margarine
1 tablespoon capers
grated rind and juice of
  1 lemon

To garnish:
2 lb. potatoes, cooked
1 tablespoon milk
1 oz. table margarine
salt and pepper
cocktail onions to decorate

Sauce:
1 oz. table margarine
1 oz. flour
½ pint milk

Peel mushrooms and slice thinly. Wash and dry the trout and place tightly together in a baking tin, curving the bodies into an 'S' shape. Brush with melted margarine, sprinkle over the prepared mushrooms, capers, grated rind and juice of 1 lemon. Cover with foil. Bake in a moderate oven (375°F. – Gas Mark 4) on middle shelf for 30-40 minutes. Remove the fish liquid, mushrooms and capers to use for sauce.

Make sauce with margarine, flour and milk. Add fish liquid, capers and mushrooms and reheat. Cream potatoes with milk, margarine, salt and pepper. Pipe or pile on to a hot oval serving dish. Put the trout on top and place a cocktail onion in each to represent 'eyes'.

196 Trout in white wine

4 servings

4 trout
seasoning

white wine
flour for thickening

Take out the backbone of the trout; put into a casserole, season well and pour over enough white wine to cover. Bake in the middle of a moderate oven (375°F – Gas Mark 4) for 15 minutes or simmer gently in a large saucepan for 10 minutes. Serve on a hot dish, thicken the white wine slightly with flour and pour over.

197 Trout baked in cider

Clean fish and put into buttered dish. Pour over cider to cover. Season. Cover and cook as Recipe 196. Lift on to hot dish. Make a sauce using 1 oz. butter, 1 oz. flour to ½ pint of the cider. Serve with the fish.

198 Grayling

This fish is a member of the trout family and should be cooked like trout.

199 Gudgeon

This fish is a member of the carp family, and should be cooked like carp.

200 Canned fish

Canned fish provides an excellent basis for many dishes. There are innumerable types of canned fish, the following are the most usual and useful to store.

Fish	Use It For
Anchovies	Garnish on fish dishes – to put on top of scrambled eggs as Scotch Woodcock, on canapés for cocktail savouries. Since very salty, add seasoning sparingly to the main dish. Anchovy essence is used for flavouring, but pounded anchovies make an excellent anchovy butter or filling.
Crab	Sandwich fillings, salads, etc., as fresh crab.
Herrings	Savoury dishes – softer than fresh herring so suitable for fillings in pastry, etc.
Roes	Use as savoury on toast.
Salted	Use as savoury for cocktail canapés or hors d'oeuvres.
Lobster	Use as fresh lobster in salads, etc.
Pilchards	Use like fresh herrings, but as softer ideal for fillings, etc.
Prawns and Shrimps	Salads, savoury dishes, sauces, etc.
Salmon	Many people prefer this to fresh salmon. For salads choose the red salmon, which is the best quality, but the cheaper pink salmon is good in fish cakes, (see Recipe 19); use it instead of white fish. For sandwich fillings pound well and mix with mayonnaise.
Sardines and sild	Excellent sandwich filling or savoury on toast. Can be flavoured with grated cheese and browned under the grill. Almost essential as an ingredient in hors d'oeuvres, excellent with hard-boiled eggs in salads.
Tuna	Often called the chicken of the sea, because it has a firmer texture than most fish. Ideal in hot or cold fish dishes (see Recipes 205-207).

201 *Herring roll*

4 servings

1 can herrings
salt and pepper
lemon juice
6 oz. short crust pastry
  (Recipe 207)

To glaze:
egg and milk

Remove tails and centre bones and flake the fish. Add salt, pepper and lemon juice to taste. Roll the pastry to an oblong shape, spread the fish over it bringing it well to the edges. Damp the edges roll up and seal the ends. Brush the top with milk or beaten egg. Bake in a hot oven (425°-450°F. – Gas Mark 6-7) for 30 minutes.

202 *Scalloped herrings*

4 servings

2-3 cooked or canned
  herrings
½ pint white sauce (see
  Recipe 216)
salt and pepper
1 tablespoon lemon juice

4 tablespoons breadcrumbs
1 oz. butter or margarine

To garnish:
lemon and parsley

Remove skin and bones from the fish and flake it. Mix lightly with the sauce, season well and add lemon juice. Butter 4 scallop shells, line with breadcrumbs and divide the fish mixture among them. Cover with crumbs and sprinkle with melted butter. Bake in a hot oven (425°-450°F. – Gas Mark 6-7) or grill until golden brown. Garnish with a butterfly of lemon and a sprig of parsley. Serve with creamed potatoes.

Scalloped Herrings

203 *Vol-au-vent surprises*

6-8 servings

1 can Cornish pilchards
bunch chives
1 or 2 pickled cucumbers
dash of lemon juice

seasoning
6-8 vol-au-vent cases, bought
  or home made with flaky
  pastry (see Recipe 338)

Mash the pilchards and mix in the finely chopped chives, cubed cucumber, lemon juice and seasoning. Fill vol-au-vent cases with the stuffing. Serve hot or cold. If served hot, place in a moderate oven (375°F – Gas Mark 4) for 20 minutes. As a cold dish, the vol-au-vents will be lighter and more attractive if you put them in a hot oven (425°-450°F. – Gas Mark 6-7) for 5 minutes to crisp them before stuffing. A mixed salad of lettuce or chicory, tomatoes, spring onions and sliced cucumber is excellent with cold vol-au-vents.

204 *Mock scallops*

4 servings

½ green pepper
1 onion
½ oz. butter
2 medium tomatoes
8 oz. rice (cooked)
1 can Cornish pilchards
seasoning

To garnish:
parsley
lemon

Remove seeds from pepper and chop finely. Fry the finely chopped onion in the butter until it is gold and crisp. Add the chopped tomatoes, pepper and rice. Stir over a low heat until the rice is brown. Add the pilchards, roughly chopped. Add seasoning and dash of lemon juice. Reheat, then pile on hot scallop shells. Garnish with chopped parsley and lemon twists.

205 *Tuna amandine*

4 servings

1 small onion
1 oz. butter
1 oz. flour
1 pint milk
1 small can tomato purée
paprika
1 heaped dessertspoon
  Parmesan cheese

2 tablespoons cream
pepper and salt to taste
1 small can (3½ oz.)
  middle-cut tuna
2 oz. split roasted almonds
fried bread triangles

Chop onion finely and fry in butter until tender. Add flour and cook a few minutes, then add milk gradually, until smooth and creamy. Remove from heat and blend in the tomato purée, paprika, cheese, cream and seasoning. Flake tuna roughly and add. Turn into a casserole and sprinkle the top with almonds. Warm in a very moderate oven (350°F. – Gas Mark 3) for 7-10 minutes. Arrange the fried bread triangles around the tuna mixture. Serve with lettuce and gherkins.

Tuna Amandine

206 Crispy tuna cream

4-6 servings

1 oz. butter	pepper
1 oz. flour	salt
½ pint milk	2 or 3 slices of bread cut in
1 dessertspoon lemon juice	cubes
2 tablespoons grated cheese	2 oz. butter or oil for frying
1 egg yolk	paprika pepper
2 large cans tuna	

Melt butter in pan. Stir in flour and and cook for 1-2 minutes without browning. Gradually stir in milk and cook, stirring, until the sauce thickens. Add lemon juice, cheese, egg yolk and the tuna, divided into chunks. Cook very slowly for 5 minutes. Season. Turn into hot serving dish. Fry the bread until golden and crisp in hot oil or butter. Arrange in a ring over the creamed fish. Sprinkle the centre with paprika pepper.

207 Tuna baked roly

4-6 servings

6 oz. short crust pastry (see below) or flaky pastry (see Recipe 338)	1 tablespoon fruit chutney (optional)
7 oz. can middle-cut tuna in tomato	3 tablespoons finely chopped celery or other vegetables
1 small onion	seasoning
1 tablespoon chopped parsley	milk for glazing

Short crust pastry

8 oz. flour	cold water to mix – about 2
good pinch salt	tablespoons
4 oz. fat	

Roll the pastry to a rectangular sheet. Mix flaked tuna, chopped onion, parsley, chutney and celery. If needed, season further to taste. Spread filling over pastry and roll up as for Swiss roll. Mark with back of knife ready for slicing when cooked. Glaze with milk. Bake in a hot oven (450-475°F. – Gas Mark 7-8) for about 10 minutes. Reduce heat to moderate (375°F. – Gas Mark 4) and cook a further 20 minutes. Serve with hot vegetables and a creamy sauce with parsley and capers in it. Or a quick sauce can be made by heating soup from a 10 oz. can (mushroom or tomato) and sprinkling a tablespoon of semolina into it and bring it to the boil, stirring, until thickened.

Sieve flour and salt and rub in fat until mixture looks like fine breadcrumbs. Using first a knife and then the fingertips to feel the pastry, gradually add enough cold water to make the dough into a rolling consistency. Lightly flour the rolling-pin and pastry board. If a great deal of flour is necessary to roll out the pastry then you have undoubtedly made it too wet. Roll pastry to required thickness and shape, lifting and turning it to keep it light. Exact cooking times for pastry are given in the recipes but as a general rule it should be cooked in a hot oven (425°-450°F. – Gas Mark 6-7).

Crispy Tuna Cream

Tuna Baked Roly

208 Sour cream sauce

½ pint soured cream (or use fresh cream with 1 tablespoon lemon juice)

2 egg yolks
seasoning to taste
paprika pepper

Heat cream gently with egg yolks but on no account allow to boil. When hot, remove from heat and season. Transfer to sauce boat, sprinkle with paprika.

209 Using canned soups for sauces

Many people 'fight shy' of making fish dishes that require various sauces, but when one is busy the concentrated soups provide very good flavoured sauces to serve with fish, especially celery, mushroom, asparagus and tomato flavourings.

210 Quick tomato soused herrings

4 servings

4 herrings
seasoning
3 bay leaves

few peppercorns
can condensed tomato soup
6 tablespoons vinegar

Wash herrings and remove scales, heads and bones, take out roes. Lay herrings flat, place roes in centre of each fish, season and roll from tail. Place in a greased dish with bay leaves and peppercorns. Mix tomato soup with vinegar and pour over herrings. Cover with lid or greaseproof paper and cook in a very moderate oven (350°F – Gas Mark 3) for approximately 1 hour. Serve hot or cold.

211 Piquant celery sauce

This is quick for grilled or fried fish or fish cakes. Fillets of plaice or sole can be baked in it. Blend and heat together can cream of celery soup, ½ teaspoon tarragon or a pinch of thyme, 1 tablespoon mild mustard.

212 Frozen fish

There are many kinds of frozen fish available today, and it is an excellent idea for places where the quality of fresh fish is not all it might be. Follow the directions for cooking carefully. Some kinds of frozen fish may be cooked while still frozen. Others – particularly shell fish – must be defrosted carefully. Be very careful about storing frozen fish, since it will spoil just as quickly as fresh fish when once it has thawed out.

213 Fish creole

4 servings

Sauce:
1½ oz. chopped onions
4 oz. chopped celery
½ chopped green pepper
½ can sliced mushrooms OR 2-3 oz. sliced mushrooms
Either medium can whole tomatoes or 8 oz. skinned tomatoes
2 oz. butter
1 small can tomato purée and equal amount of water

dash chilli powder
dash Tabasco sauce (optional)

14 oz. frozen cod or haddock
water
squeeze of lemon juice
½ chopped onion
1 tablespoon chopped parsley
few peppercorns

To make the sauce, fry all the vegetables except canned tomato, if used, in hot butter. Then add tomato purée and water, seasonings. Simmer for 30 minutes. Meanwhile place fish in pan with canned tomatoes, just sufficient hot water to cover, add a squeeze of lemon, onion, parsley and peppercorns. Simmer gently for approximately 10-15 minutes until fish is tender. Remove from liquid. Keep hot. Coat with sauce and serve hot or cold.

214 Californian prawn cocktail

2 servings

1 small lettuce
tomato purée
mayonnaise
1 large grapefruit

1 packet frozen prawns, defrosted

To garnish:
parsley

Shred lettuce, add little tomato purée to mayonnaise. Serve ½ grapefruit per person. Cut grapefruit in half (serrate the edge as you cut), scrape out flesh carefully. Mix with chopped prawns (keeping some back for garnishing) and lettuce, then add enough mayonnaise to bind. Pile mixture into grapefruit halves and garnish with whole prawns and parsley.

215 Frozen trout with melted butter

Trout has been frozen very successfully, and can be cooked in any of the ways recommended (see Recipes 192-197). It can just be grilled or fried and served with melted butter and lemon, or browned almonds.

216 White sauce

1 oz. butter or margarine
1 oz. flour
¼ pint milk for coating consistency, i.e. sauce
⅛ pint milk for panada or binding consistency

1 pint milk for thin white sauce for soups
salt and pepper

Heat the butter gently, remove from the heat and stir in the flour. Return to the heat and cook gently for a few minutes, so that the *roux*, as the butter and flour mixture is called, does not brown. Again remove the pan from the heat and gradually blend in the cold milk. Bring to the boil and cook, stirring with a wooden spoon, until smooth. Season well. If any small lumps have formed whisk sharply.

Variation	Method	To accompany
Anchovy sauce	Stir in chopped anchovies or 1 teaspoon anchovy essence	Fish
Cheese sauce	Stir in 3-6 oz. grated cheese when sauce has thickened, and add little mustard	Vegetable, meat, fish and savoury dishes
Caper sauce	Use $\frac{1}{4}$ pint milk and $\frac{1}{4}$ pint stock. Add 2 teaspoons capers and a little caper vinegar	Boiled lamb. Can also be served with fish
Fish sauce	Use $\frac{1}{4}$ pint fish stock and $\frac{1}{4}$ pint milk.	Fish
Egg sauce	Add chopped hard-boiled egg	Boiled chicken
Onion sauce	Boil 3 onions, chop or slice and add to sauce – use little onion stock	Lamb, mutton or sausages
Parsley sauce	Add 1-2 teaspoons chopped parsley and squeeze lemon juice if wished	Fish – broad beans
Creamed tomato sauce	Whisk a thick tomato purée (which should be hot but not boiling) into hot white sauce. Do not boil together	Fish, meat and savoury vegetable dishes
Cucumber sauce	Whisk about $\frac{1}{4}$ pint thick cucumber purée into white sauce, add little lemon juice, green colouring and cream	Fish and vegetable dishes
Horseradish sauce (hot)	Whisk about 1 dessertspoon vinegar and 2 tablespoons grated horseradish into white sauce. Add small amount of cream and pinch sugar	Beef, hot trout
Mustard cream sauce	Blend $\frac{1}{2}$-1 tablespoon dry mustard with the flour. Proceed as white sauce, stirring in little extra milk or cream	Fish: herrings, mackerel, trout, etc., grilled lamb or steak
Béchamel sauce	Infuse pieces of very finely chopped onion, carrot, celery in milk, strain and make as white sauce	In place of white sauce as rich flavour
Economical Hollandaise sauce	Make white sauce, remove from heat and whisk in 1 egg, 1 dessertspoon lemon juice or vinegar. Cook gently without boiling for a few minutes	Fish or with vegetable dish
Maître d'hôtel sauce	As white sauce, but use half fish stock. Add 2 teaspoons chopped parsley and 3 tablespoons thick cream just before serving	Fish
Oyster sauce	Make white sauce, add about 12 oysters and little cream just before serving. Do not overcook	Fish

Prawn or shrimp sauce	Make white sauce, add about 2-3 oz. chopped prawns and a little anchovy essence just before serving. If using fresh prawns simmer shells and use ¼ pint stock instead of the same amount of milk.	Fish
Tartare sauce (hot)	Make white sauce, then whisk in 2 egg yolks, 1 tablespoon cream, 1 tablespoon capers, 1 teaspoon chopped gherkin, 1 teaspoon chopped parsley and a squeeze of lemon juice. Cook gently without boiling, for a few minutes	Fish, vegetable and some meat dishes; excellent with veal
Mushroom sauce	Cook 2 oz. chopped mushrooms in the milk, then use milk to make white sauce. Add cooked mushrooms and re-heat	Fish and vegetable dishes

217 *Hollandaise sauce*

2 egg yolks
pinch cayenne pepper
1-2 tablespoons lemon juice, vinegar or white wine

salt
pepper
2-4 oz. butter

Put egg yolks, seasonings and vinegar into the top of double saucepan. Whisk over hot water until sauce begins to thicken. Add the butter in very small pieces, whisking in each pat and allowing it to melt before adding the next. DO NOT ALLOW TO BOIL or it will curdle. If too thick, add a little cream.

Béarnaise sauce	Add finely chopped shallot and extra pepper to ingredients for hollandaise sauce. Add little chopped parsley and tarragon vinegar	Serve with steak
Mousseline sauce	Use only 1 oz. butter to the 2 egg yolks and add a little cream and grated nutmeg	Serve with asparagus, broccoli, other vegetables or salmon

218 *Chaudfroid of fish*

4 servings

1-1½ lb. cooked white fish
chaudfroid sauce (recipe 219)
savoury cream
lettuce

To garnish:
cucumber

Arrange fish on wire tray with plate underneath to catch any drips. Allow chaudfroid sauce to start to thicken and spread over fish with knife, dipped in hot water. When firm pipe with savoury cream, arrange on crisp lettuce, garnishing with cucumber.

Chaudfroid of Fish

219 *Chaudfroid sauce*

¼ pint aspic jelly

½ pint thick mayonnaise or salad dressing

Make aspic jelly, allow to cool and mix with mayonnaise.

220 *Lemon butter* — Beat a little lemon juice and grated rind into creamed margarine or butter.

221 *Mustard butter* — Add mustard and finely chopped watercress to creamed margarine or butter.

222 *Anchovy butter* — Add anchovy essence and pepper to creamed margarine or butter.

223 *Lobster butter* — Crumble the red coral (roe) of a female lobster, then work it into creamed margarine or butter. Add a little pepper, lemon juice and pinch of salt if wished.

224 *Fruit with fish* — You will find that fruit blends well in salads with fish. For example, a Tuna salad containing sliced banana, pineapple and/or grapefruit gives sharpness to the dish.

BEEF

225 *Beef* — The lean should be a clear bright red, and the fat firm and pale cream in colour. The very best joints MUST have a certain amount of fat on them.

Purpose	Cut to choose	Cooking time	Accompaniments
Roasting	Sirloin Ribs Fillet Aitch-bone (good quality) Topside Rump	15 minutes per lb. plus 15 minutes over. Well-done, 20 minutes per lb. plus 20 minutes over, or 40 minutes per lb. in very slow oven	Mustard Horseradish sauce Yorkshire pudding Roast potatoes Thin gravy
Grilling or Frying	Rump Fillet Sirloin Entrecote	5-15 minutes depending on thickness and personal preference	Chipped or mashed potatoes Salad Tomatoes Mushrooms
Stewing or Braising	Skirt or Chuck Bladebone 'Leg of Mutton' cut Brisket Flank	1½-3 hours (see also under Pressure Cooking Recipe)	Mixed vegetables Dumplings Thickened gravy
Pickling or Boiling	Brisket Shin or leg Silverside Flank Aitch-bone	1½-3 hours	Vegetables or salad
Stock for Soup	Neck Shin or leg Clod Marrowbone Oxtail Flank		

7. Scallop mayonnaise

8. Beef scone pie, Roast beef

226 To roast beef

If you like a very lean joint choose topside or rump or fillet. For a prime quality with a good distribution of lean and fat choose ribs of beef (for a large joint) or sirloin. Aitch-bone of first rate quality can be roasted, but is best roasted slowly.

If you like a crisp outside to the meat then DO NOT use a covered roasting tin. Instead put a little well clarified dripping (see Recipes 238-240) or fat on the meat, which can be seasoned lightly if desired. Either put meat in roasting tin or on trivet (rack) in the tin. Or the meat can be cooked on a turning spit.

Start in a hot oven (425°-450°F – Gas Mark 7). For joints under 4 lb. the heat need not be lowered a great deal. Follow times in Recipe 225, or in individual recipes.

For larger joints lower heat after first 1-1¼ hours to moderate (375°F – Gas Mark 4), or very moderate (350°F – Gas Mark 3), allowing longer cooking time. For a softer outside (and to keep the oven clean) use a covered roasting tin, or cover meat in foil. There is then no need to add fat to sirloin or ribs of beef, but add a little to topside of beef. Add about 10 minutes to cooking time, since it takes a little longer for the heat to penetrate through to the meat. It is easier to carve but many people think flavour is better ON the bone. (For boning meat: Recipe 638).

Roast Beef with Corn on the Cob

227 To cook Yorkshire pudding

4 oz. plain flour
good pinch salt
1 egg

½ pint liquid (½ milk and
   ½ water)
knob of fat, size of walnut

It may be necessary to raise heat of oven before putting Yorkshire pudding into cook and for first 5-10 minutes' cooking time; if you are afraid beef may get over-cooked, take it out for a few minutes.

Sieve flour and salt together into a basin, drop in the egg, then beat mixture well. Gradually beat in just enough liquid to make a stiff batter. Beat until smooth, leave for about 5 minutes, then gradually beat in the rest of the liquid. A batter like this can be left for some time before being cooked. Keep it in the coolest place possible. When ready to cook, put a knob of lard or dripping into a Yorkshire pudding tin (measuring 7 x 5 inches) and heat in oven for a few minutes. Pour in the batter and cook for about 30 minutes in a hot oven. In every type of cooker use the top of the oven which is the hottest position. To save cooking time you can cook the batter in small patty tins. Put a piece of fat (the size of a large pea) in each tin, heat this, then pour in the batter and cook for about 15-20 minutes at the top of a hot oven.

Another way of cooking Yorkshire pudding is in the meat tin. Pour away most of the fat, pour in batter, then stand meat on a trivet over the meat tin so juice from meat continues to drip in tin, flavouring the pudding. This method of cooking gives a flatter result.

228 Horseradish cream

1 tablespoon grated
   horseradish
½ teaspoon vinegar

2-3 tablespoons cream
seasoning

Mix all together. This cream is very strong.

229 Horseradish sauce

2 heaped tablespoons freshly grated horseradish
½ pint white sauce (see Recipe 216)

1 dessertspoon vinegar
good pinch salt
good pinch pepper
good pinch sugar

Wash some fresh horseradish, scrape the outside, rub against moderately coarse grater. Stir the horseradish into the hot sauce, then allow to simmer for 10 minutes. Cool, then whisk in vinegar and seasonings. Any grated horseradish left over can be stored in jars.

NOTE   There are many excellent horseradish creams and sauces to be bought, which will save the bother of preparing at home.

230 To make unthickened gravy

It is traditional to serve beef, lamb or mutton with the juice that runs out when the meat is carved, particularly with a roast such as underdone beef which provides plenty of its own juices. An alternative is to make a thin gravy. Once the meat is cooked, first pour away the fat, straining it into a basin. Keep it for use as clarified fat (see Recipes 238-240) as it has an excellent flavour, particularly in the case of beef. Once the fat has been removed, shake a very little flour into the meat juices and residue left in the roasting pan and brown over a little heat, finally adding either meat or vegetable stock. Bring to the boil, add seasoning and a few drops of gravy browning if desired. Allow about ½ pint thin gravy for 4-6 people.

231 Roast potatoes

If roasting round joint you need fair amount of hot fat with meat or use a separate tin. Dry potatoes, roll in hot fat in tin and allow approximately 50-60 minutes cooking. If preferred, first cook for 5-10 minutes in boiling salted water, drain, then roast. This produces potatoes that are floury on the inside.

232 California barbecued ribs of beef

6-8 servings

3-4 lb. ribs of beef
4 tablespoons fresh lemon juice
2 tablespoons chilli sauce (if available)
1 teaspoon horseradish sauce
1 teaspoon salt
dash Tabasco sauce
6 tablespoons fresh orange juice

2 teaspoons dry mustard
½ teaspoon paprika
2 tablespoons honey or brown sugar
1 clove garlic, finely chopped
1 tablespoon Worcestershire sauce
2 lemons, unpeeled and sliced

Cut ribs in pieces; place in roasting pan and brown in hot oven (450°F. – Gas Mark 7) for 50 minutes. Drain off fat. Combine remaining ingredients except sliced lemons, mix well and brush this sauce over ribs. Place a slice of lemon on each piece of meat. Reduce heat to (350°F. – Gas Mark 3) for 1 hour and baste frequently with sauce.

California Barbecued Ribs of Beef

233 Pot roasting

Pot roasting is very simple. Put a little fat in the bottom of a pan, which should be a good heavy one with a well-fitting lid. Brown your meat lightly then lift it out of the pan and insert either a small trivet or rack and lift the meat on to this. Put enough water in the pan to give about 1-inch but make sure it does not cover the meat as you do not want it to taste stewed. Season well and put on the lid. Allow approximately 40 minutes per lb.; add your vegetables during the cooking period so they get tender at the same time as the meat. When you dish up you will find the liquid at the bottom makes a delicious gravy. If by chance you have not a trivet then lift the meat on to a bed of vegetables but you must of course keep these in very big pieces so that they are not overcooked by the time the meat is ready.

234 Pot roast

6 servings

2-2½ lb. top rump of beef
1 oz. lard
2 medium onions (finely chopped)
1 can condensed vegetable soup

¼ pint cold water
1½ lb. potatoes (quartered)
½ teaspoon salt
pepper to taste
1 oz. flour
1 tablespoon cold water

Tie joint firmly with fine string. Heat lard in a large saucepan and lightly cook the onion. Add the meat and brown on all sides. Pour in the soup and water, cover and cook very slowly for 1½-2 hours. Add potatoes with the seasoning. Cover again and cook for a further 30 minutes. Remove meat and potatoes and keep hot on a serving dish. Mix flour to a paste with cold water, pour into the gravy and stir until thickened or, if liked, strain gravy, serve vegetables and thickened liquid separately.

The pot roast is quite suitable for oven cooking if cooked in a slow oven (300°F – Gas Mark 2) for 3 hours.

Pot Roast

235 Pot roasting in a pressure cooker

A pressure cooker can be used for pot-roasting. Any meat that can be roasted in the normal way is suitable, and if by any chance you have a less tender piece of meat, then try pot-roasting. The method is simple.

1 Put a little fat at the bottom of the cooker and heat this.

2 Brown the meat well in the fat, then lift the meat out of the cooker, insert the trivet, add the water.

3 Allow ½ pint of water for a joint that takes up to 15 minutes pressure cooking time, and add an additional ¼ pint water for each 15 minutes over this, e.g. for a joint taking 45 minutes you need 1 pint water.

4 Beef needs 10 minutes per lb. at 15 lb. pressure. Lamb, veal, pork need 12 minutes per lb. Roasting chicken needs 5 minutes per lb.

5 Allow pressure to drop at room temperature. You will find the liquid in the cooker makes excellent gravy.

6 If wished the pressure can be allowed to drop and vegetables put in at the right time, so that all the meal is cooked together in the one pressure cooker.

236 To make stock

Many of the recipes for sauces, gravy and casserole dishes mention stock. This is not difficult to make and it cannot be disputed that in many dishes a good stock will improve the flavour. It is however, considered quite dangerous to keep stock for a great length of time, unless stored in a refrigerator. Make the stock as freshly as possible; a pressure cooker enables you to do this quickly and easily. If it has been kept for several days it must be boiled well before being used. To make a good stock, cover the bones of beef (for a brown stock) or veal, poultry (for a white stock) with cold water, add bay leaf, seasoning and simmer gently for several hours.

237 Stock

(Pressure cooking time 45 minutes)

2 lb. bones, large marrow bones, if possible
2 pints water
1 carrot

1 turnip
1 onion
1 teaspoon salt

Break the bones and put into the cooker with all the other ingredients. Bring slowly to the boil and remove the scum from the top. Fix the lid and bring steadily to pressure. Reduce the heat and cook for 45 minutes. Allow ressure to return to normal before removing lid. When the stock is cold lift off any fat from top. Do not add potatoes or green vegetables to this stock as it will not then keep. In hot weather store in a refrigerator or re-boil every other day.

238 To make a good dripping

This is the fat that runs from meat or bacon during cooking. It is a valuable food and should not be wasted, for you will need it again to add to meat. It must be clarified before storing. To obtain still more dripping melt down very fatty pieces of meat (see Recipe 240).

239 *To clarify dripping*

This means cleaning, and the process is very necessary when using dripping. Cover the dripping with cold water in a rather deep saucepan, bring to the boil, then allow fat and water to cool. You will then be able to lift off the fat, leaving most of the impurities in the water.

Turn the piece of clarified dripping upside down on a plate, and scrape away any small particles of food adhering to the bottom with a sharp knife.

240 *To render down fat*

As explained under dripping, when additional fat is required, put fatty pieces of meat in a dish in a low oven and cook SLOWLY until all the dripping (or fat) has been obtained, and all that is left is a hard brown piece of gristle. Then clarify (see Recipe 239).

241 *To grill steak*

Steaks to Choose

MINUTE STEAK   Very thin slice of steak, so called because it only needs a minute on either side.

RUMP STEAK   Full of flavour, but less tender on the whole than fillet.

FILLET STEAK   Very tender indeed, very lean.

SIRLOIN STEAK   Cut from across the sirloin – excellent proportion of lean and fat.

ENTRECOTE   Cut from middle of ribs or sirloin. Tender, of good flavour.

POINT STEAK   Cut from the pointed end of the rump and most tender

PORTERHOUSE   Very large sirloin steak, up to 4 lb.

PLANKED STEAK   So called because it is served on wooden plank.

TOURNEDOS   Fillet steak tied into a circle with string, served with various garnishes (see Recipes 249-262).

Make sure the grill is really hot before steak is put underneath – times given in chart (see Recipe 225) for a gas or electric cooker. Brush the grill with plenty of oil or butter. Brush the steak also with oil or butter. Cook quickly on either side for 2 or 3 minutes. For an underdone or 'rare' steak that is probably enough, and it can be served at once. For a medium steak lower heat and cook for a further 5 or 6 minutes. For a well-done steak, lower the heat as much as possible, so steak cooks gently through to the centre. Continue cooking for about 10 minutes without scorching on the outside.

Serve with any of the following: grilled mushrooms, grilled tomatoes, fried onions, or to give a pleasant touch of sharpness with rings of lemon, capers. Many people like a crisp green salad with grilled steak and béarnaise sauce (see Recipe 217).

Grilling with Infra Red Grills

The modern infra red grill must, of course, be used with care, following manufacturers' instructions. Keep grill well brushed with oil; heat it up before use, and remember that once it is hot cooking time is a matter of seconds only.

242 *Grilled steak and mushrooms*

Illustrated is grilled rump steak and grilled mushrooms. The mushrooms are prepared and cooked in the grill pan in hot butter while steak is cooked as described on the grid. Just cut the bottom off stalks of small mushrooms and wash well. You need not skin them.

Grilled Steak and Mushrooms

243 *To fry steak*

Choose same quality and cuts of steak as for grilling. Heat a good knob of butter or olive oil in the pan and put in the steak. Fry quickly on either side to seal in the flavour. Lower the heat and cook gently for about 10-12 minutes for well done steak, about 6-8 minutes for medium, and 3-4 minutes for underdone. French or English mustard are the usual accompaniments. Some people like Worcestershire sauce. Tomatoes, mushrooms, watercress are the best garnish, or fried onion rings.

Fried Steak

244 *To fry onions*

Peel and cut onions into rings. Separate rings, dip in milk and seasoned flour. Shake off surplus flour and fry in shallow or deep fat.

245 *To make steak tender*

If in doubt as to whether steak is tender either beat with a rolling pin (or a special meat 'hammer') or put into a marinade of equal parts of well seasoned oil and vinegar or use the following recipe.

246 *Steak tenderiser*

Blend 2 teaspoons of dry mustard with 2 tablespoons vinegar. Sprinkle over steak before grilling and leave in a cool airy place for 30 minutes, not in the refrigerator.

247 *Mixed grill*

A mixed grill can be made from a variety of ingredients, but your grill is made or marred by the way it is served. Have the various grills attractively arranged on the plate, with a suitable garnish to add colour and variety. Watercress is the most usual garnish for a mixed grill, particularly if it includes steak, but try also potato crisps, cucumber slices, green peas, uncooked quartered tomatoes or thinly sliced red pepper. For the grill itself, choose from the following:

There is no reason why veal or pork chops, or cutlets could not be used instead of lamb, but a lamb chop is the most general choice. The secret of a good mixed grill is to time the cooking carefully, i.e. do not put all ingredients under the grill at the same time; start with food that takes the longest cooking, then gradually add the other ingredients. Do make sure grill is really hot before cooking and keep kidneys, steak and liver well basted with butter. Remember kidneys are easily over-cooked, so add these towards the end. Sausages on the other hand require a fair amount of cooking.

With most grills, tomatoes and mushrooms can be cooked in the grill pan, while the meats are cooked on the grid. It is advisable to put the pan with mushrooms and tomatoes underneath for a few minutes to give then a 'start', before covering with the grid and meat. Serve with vegetables, or a crisp green salad.

248 *Savoury mixed grill*

Choose steak, etc. and other ingredients as in preceding recipe. Prepare all the meats in usual way but to bring out flavour sprinkle with liquid meat seasoning* before cooking.

*obtainable from grocers.

249 *Tournedos of steak*

Buy fillets of steaks and ask the butcher to tie into rounds to form tournedos. If you prefer to use small skewers you can do so. To keep outer edge of meat very moist put fat bacon round this. Fry or grill as preferred. Serve on rounds of fried bread.

250 *Tournedos of steak Africaine*

Grill or fry the steaks, garnish with fried banana, serve with horseradish sauce.

251 *Tournedos of steak Arlésienne*

Fry the steak, garnish with rounds of aubergine, tomatoes and/or celery. Top with rings of fried onion.

252 *Tournedos of steak Belle Hélène*

Fry the steak, garnish with asparagus and truffle.

253 *Tournedos of steak Baronne*

Grill the steak, top with mushrooms and serve with tomato purée and béarnaise sauce (see Recipe 217).

254 *Tournedos of steak Calcutta*

Fry the steak and serve with curry flavoured rice. To make this, boil the rice then drain. Fry a little curry powder in butter and toss rice in this. Serve with brown sauce flavoured with chutney.

255 *Tournedos of steak chasseur*

Grill steak. Serve with chasseur sauce (see Recipe 356).

256 *Tournedos of steak Dumas*

Grill steak. Cover with onion sauce (see Recipe 216) sprinkle with cheese and brown under grill, top with ham slices and serve with potato croquettes.

257 *Tournedos of steak ménagère*

Grill the steaks, serve with border of duchesse potato (see Recipe 54) and garnish with tiny pieces of carrot, turnip and onions. Serve with good brown or espagnole sauce (see Recipe 356).

258 *Tournedos of steak Othello*

Grill or fry steak and top with fried or poached egg.

259 *Tournedos of steak d'Orsay*

Grill steak and garnish with olives and mushrooms.

260 *Tournedos of steak Parisienne*

Grill or fry steak and garnish with asparagus tips and béarnaise sauce (see Recipe 217).

261 *Tournedos of steak Pompadour*

Grill or fry steak and top with tomato purée and slice of grilled or fried ham and truffle (or mushrooms).

262 *Tournedos of steak Rossinel*

4 servings

4 large tomatoes
2 tablespoons breadcrumbs
little chopped parsley
pinch mixed herbs
seasoning
butter

4 fillet steaks (tied in rounds– the butcher will do this for you)
mushrooms
4 eggs

Halve the tomatoes, scoop out the centre pulp, chop this and mix with the crumbs, parsley, herbs, seasoning and about 1 oz. melted butter. Pile this mixture back into the tomato cases and put in the grill pan. Brush the steaks with melted butter, heat the grill, put the steaks on the grid of the grill pan and cook until tender and as desired. Meanwhile fry the mushrooms and eggs. Take string off steaks and serve with the stuffed tomatoes and mushrooms and top with eggs.

*This recipe is not to be confused with the very luxurious Tournedos Rossini, which are garnished with foie gras and truffles, or failing that with mushrooms.

263 *Steaks with sherry and tomato sauce*

4 servings

4 small sirloin steaks
1 oz. butter
1 small onion (finely chopped)
1 can condensed tomato soup or tomato sauce (see Recipe 360)

2 tablespoons cold water
3 dessertspoons sherry
salt
pepper
2 tablespoons cream

To garnish:
watercress sprigs

Fry steaks in hot butter for 8-10 minutes, turning half-way through cooking. Remove from pan and keep hot. Fry onion gently until tender. Add soup, water, sherry and seasoning, and heat, stirring frequently. Just before serving stir in cream. Arrange steaks on hot dish, pour over sauce, garnish with watercress.

Steak with Sherry and Tomato Sauce

264 *Steak Diane*

Fry minute steaks (i.e. very thin steaks) in hot butter. A little finely chopped shallot and parsley together with a few drops of Worcestershire sauce, or brandy, can be added to the butter before putting in the meat.

265 *To stew or braise beef*

Allow slow cooking time, unless you are using a pressure cooker (see time-table for meats, Recipe 225). Season meat well, and do not try to hurry the cooking. On the other hand, do not continue cooking for too long a period as this takes away all the flavour.

266 *Braised topside*

Coat the beef with a fairly thick layer of well-seasoned flour. Brown gently in hot lard or hot dripping in a large pan. Lift the meat out of the pan, add stock, bring to the boil and cook until sauce is smooth, but not too thick. Taste and re-season if desired. Put meat into a baking tin or large casserole. Pour over the sauce and cover with a lid or with plenty of foil. Cook in a very moderate oven (350°F – Gas Mark 3) allowing approximately 25 minutes per lb. To serve lift out of the liquid (serve this separately). Surround the meat with freshly cooked young carrots, sprinkled with chopped parsley, turnips, sprinkled with red pepper, broad beans and new potatoes tossed in butter and chopped parsley.

Braised Topside

267 *Braised steak and onions*

4 servings

1 lb. approximately, stewing steak	salt
2 oz. lard	pepper
3 large onions	pinch dry mustard
1 oz. flour	good pinch mixed herbs
1 pint stock or water flavoured with beef or yeast extract	4 carrots

Cut the steak into neat fingers. Heat the lard in the saucepan first, then fry the sliced onions and steak until a pale golden colour. Lift into a casserole. Blend the flour with the remaining fat and cook for several minutes, then gradually stir in the cold stock or flavoured water. Bring to the boil and cook until thickened. Season well, adding the herbs and sliced carrots. Pour over the beef and onions. Put the lid on the casserole and cook in a slow oven (275°-300°F – Gas Mark 2) for 2½-3 hours.

268 *Stewed steak*

4-6 servings

	1 onion
1-1½ lb. beef steak	2 cloves
salt	½ bay leaf
pepper	nutmeg or mixed herbs
1-1½ oz. lard or dripping	½ pint water

Cut the meat into neat squares or fingers. Season with salt and pepper. Brown the meat on both sides in the fat. Add sliced onion and flavourings and ½ pint water. Cover pan and stew slowly for 2 hours adding little extra liquid if required. Two teaspoons vinegar can be cooked with this stew or for a thicker stew roll the meat in seasoned flour instead of just salt and pepper.

269 *Stewed steak and vegetables*

As above but add approximately 1 lb. mixed root vegetables, cut into neat pieces, halfway through cooking.

270 *Dutch stew*

As stewed steak (see Recipe 268), but when meat is tender spread a small slice of crustless bread with little mustard. Add to liquid and cook for about 10 minutes then beat hard with wooden spoon.

271 *Stew and dumplings*

Cook the steak as in Recipe 268 and approximately 20 minutes before serving drop in the dumplings and cook fairly briskly. It is important to check you have plenty of liquid in the stew since the dumplings absorb a great deal.

272 Dumplings

4 oz. flour (with plain flour
  1 teaspoon baking powder)
good pinch salt

2 oz. shredded suet or
  margarine
water to mix

Sieve dry ingredients, add suet or rub in margarine, mix to a sticky dough with water, roll in balls with lightly floured hands. Cooking time varies according to size, from 15-25 minutes.

273 Beef stew Provençale

4-5 servings

2 tablespoons olive oil
2 large onions
3 rashers bacon
1¼ lb. chuck steak, cut into
  neat fingers
1 oz. flour
seasoning
¼ pint cheap white wine
little water

3 or 4 tomatoes
bunch mixed herbs (or good
  pinch dried herbs)

To garnish:
olives
cooked rice

Heat the oil in the pan and fry the sliced onions, and diced bacon, add the meat coated with well-seasoned flour and toss in the oil for a few minutes. Add all the other ingredients, adding approximately ½ pint water. Bring to the boil and cook for a few minutes until a fairly thick liquid, taste and re-season. Reduce the heat, put a lid on the pan and simmer gently for 3 hours. Remove the herbs if fresh and pour on to a hot dish, garnish with olives and boiled rice.

274 Beef casserole Provençale

4 servings

1 lb. stewing beef
1 tablespoon cornflour
seasoning
2 oz. fat
2-3 small onions

3-4 small carrots
1 clove garlic
2 tablespoons red wine
½ pint stock or water
few black olives

Cut meat into small pieces. Coat with seasoned cornflour and brown in the hot fat in a stewpan. Remove the meat and put into a casserole. Put the onions, carrots and garlic into the stewpan with any remaining cornflour and cook for a few minutes until the vegetables are lightly browned. Add the wine and about ½ pint stock or water and bring to the boil, stirring. Pour over the meat in the casserole, cover tightly and cook in a slow oven, for about 2 hours. Just before serving, add the olives.

275 Curried beef steak

4 servings

Curry:
1 oz. pure cooking fat
1 large onion
½ oz. curry powder
1 lb. rump steak
2 oz. sultanas
½ pint stock or water
seasoning

Rice:
1 oz. pure cooking fat
1 medium onion
6 oz. Patna rice
1 pint boiling water
1 level teaspoon salt

Accompaniments:
2 green and red peppers,
  sliced
2 bananas, sliced
1 lemon
2 medium tomatoes, sliced
1 medium onion, sliced
1 oz. pure cooking fat
6 poppadums
mango chutney
carrots
celery

Curry

Melt the cooking fat in a frying pan. Peel and chop the onion; fry until tender. Add the curry powder; fry for 1-2 minutes. Wash, trim and cut the beef into cubes. Add with the sultanas, fry for 1-2 minutes. Pour in the stock and season well. Simmer over low heat for 20-25 minutes.

Rice

Melt the cooking fat in a saucepan; chop the onion and fry until tender. Add the washed, well drained rice and fry until the grains become white, stirring all the time, about 5 minutes. Add the boiling water, gradually. Season. Allow to simmer, with the lid on, until the rice has absorbed all the water, about 20 minutes. When cooked, pile the rice in the centre of a hot dish and pour over the curry.

Accompaniments

Serve the following individual bowls with the curry:

1 Wash the peppers, remove the pips. Slice finely and place in a bowl.
2 Peel and slice 2 bananas. Place in a bowl. Squeeze half the lemon over. Cut the remaining half lemon in chunks and arrange on the banana.
3 Sliced tomatoes and onion in layers in a bowl.
4 Melt 1 oz. pure cooking fat and fry the poppadums, one at a time, until crisp. Drain on kitchen paper. (Poppadums are wafer thin Indian pancakes made with brown Urd flour. These may be bought in many delicatessen and food halls.)
5 Mango chutney.
6 Small whole boiled carrots and heads of celery.

Curried Beef Steak

9. Beef casserole provencale, Lancashire hot pot

10. Spaghetti with meat sauce

11. Italian meat balls with mixed vegetables and
    mashed potatoes

12. Steak and kidney pie

276 *Curried stewing steak*

Method as Recipe 275 but when using stewing steak allow 1 pint of water or stock and simmer for 2-3 hours.

277 *Quick curried steak*

There is a great advance in de-hydrated, ready prepared dishes and while the instructions should be followed for the basic cooking you can give them individual touches by garnishes.

278 *Tomato beef curry casserole*

Using a package of ready prepared beef curry, use tomato juice instead of water.

279 *Beef and prune hot-pot*

4 servings

2 oz. prunes
few olives
12 oz. lean stewing beef
1 oz. cornflour
salt and pepper

8 oz. potatoes
1 large onion
1 beef cube
chopped parsley

Soak prunes overnight in cold water to cover, then remove stones and stuff prunes with olives. Trim the meat and cut into strips and coat with cornflour to which salt and pepper has been added. Peel and slice potatoes and onion. Put a layer of sliced potatoes into the bottom of a casserole, cover with a layer of meat, then add the onion, the remaining meat, potatoes and prunes. Take water in which the prunes were soaked and make it up to ¾ pint with boiling water. Dissolve beef cube in this liquid and pour it over ingredients in the casserole. Cover tightly and cook in a slow oven about 2-2½ hours or until meat is tender (275°-300°F. – Gas Mark 2-3). Sprinkle with parsley before serving.

Beef and Prune Hot Pot

280 *Spiced beef casserole*

4-5 servings

1-1½ lb. stewing beef
½ teaspoon curry powder
½ teaspoon paprika pepper
½ teaspoon mixed spice
seasoning
1 oz. flour
2 oz. fat

¾ pint stock
1 tablespoon
   Worcestershire sauce
1 tablespoon vinegar
8 small onions
8 oz. diced celery
1 clove garlic (optional)

Cut the meat into 1-inch squares. Mix flavourings with the flour and roll meat in this. Fry in hot fat for a few minutes then lift into a casserole. Add stock, and garlic, if used, sauce, and vinegar to residue of fat and flour left in the pan. Bring to the boil and cook for several minutes. Put onions, celery, into casserole and cover meat and vegetables with the sauce. Cover and cook for 3 hours in a slow oven (300°F – Gas Mark 2)).

281 *Using ready mixed soups*

The excellent canned soups and soup mixes of today provide first class sauces in meat dishes. Follow the directions for blending and add to all types of meat.

282 *Tomato steak*

4 servings

1 lb. stewing steak
salt and pepper
2 level tablespoons flour
1 oz. dripping
1 can condensed tomato soup
½ pint water
6 small onions
3 potatoes

Dumplings:
3 oz. plain flour
1 level teaspoon baking
   powder
¼ teaspoon salt
pinch mixed spice
pepper
1 oz. lard or margarine
cold water

Cut meat into 1-inch cubes, removing excess fat. Season with salt and pepper and toss in the flour. Melt the dripping in a pan, add the meat and brown. Pour in the can of condensed tomato soup and water. Stir well and allow to simmer for 1½ hours. Add whole onions and the potatoes cut into four and simmer for a further 20 minutes.

Dumplings
Sieve flour, baking powder, salt, spice and pepper into a basin, rub in the fat and mix to a firm dough with water. Divide into 8 and drop into the stew. Simmer for a further 15 minutes with the lid on.

283 Twentieth century casserole

4-5 servings

1 level tablespoon flour
1 packet French onion soup
1¼ lb. stewing beef, cut into
   1-inch cubes
½ pint water
2 medium sized carrots,
   diced
a little diced turnip, swede or
   celery

To garnish:
peeled and quartered
   tomatoes and/or a few
   cooked peas

Mix together in a casserole the flour and dry soup powder. Add the cubed meat and turn until evenly coated with the mixture, then stir in ½ pint cold water and the diced vegetables. Cover closely and cook in a very moderate oven (350°F – Gas Mark 3) for 2-3 hours. 10 minutes before serving put the tomatoes and/or peas on top and allow to heat through.

Twentieth Century Casserole

284 Beef olives

4 servings

1 lb. stewing beef – cut very
   thinly
2 oz. dripping
¾ pint brown sauce (see
   Recipe 350) or brown
   gravy
bay leaf

For the stuffing:
2 oz. fine breadcrumbs
1 oz. suet or fat
¼ teaspoon mixed herbs
few drops lemon juice
yolk of 1 egg
seasoning
½ teaspoon chopped parsley

Cut the meat into neat squares. Mix all ingredients for the stuffing together; then divide this between the pieces of meat and spread over. Form into rolls or, if the squares of meat are sufficiently large, gather up into a dumpling shape and secure with thin string or cotton. Heat the dripping in a pan and fry the 'olives' in this until just brown on the outside. Cover with a brown sauce, add the bay leaf. Put a lid on the saucepan and simmer gently for 1½ hours or put into covered casserole for 2 hours in a moderate oven (350°F – Gas Mark 3). To serve, arrange on a dish with a border of piped mashed potato and as many mixed vegetables as possible, cut into small dice before serving.

285 Steak and mushroom tournedos

4 servings

1 lb. stewing beef
1½ oz. dripping
1 oz. flour
¾ pint good brown stock
seasoning

4 oz. mushrooms
bay leaf
rounds of fried bread
Parisienne potatoes or
   creamed potatoes

Although tournedos are generally associated with fillet of steak grilled, this recipe will make stewing beef a much more attractive dish. Cut the beef into neat rounds about 2-inches in diameter. Heat the dripping and toss the meat in this until just brown on either side. Arrange in a casserole. Work the flour into the remaining dripping and cook for several minutes, until just turning brown. Remove pan from the heat and gradually stir in the stock, bringing to the boil and cooking until the sauce just thickens. Season well, pour over the pieces of beef, adding chopped mushrooms and bay leaf. Cover the casserole and cook in the middle of a very moderate oven (350°F – Gas Mark 3) for 2 hours. Just before serving, cut rounds of bread and fry until crisp and brown. Lift the pieces of meat out of the sauce and put on the bread, pour the sauce around and arrange Parisienne or creamed potatoes all round the outside.

286 Potatoes Parisienne

Use a vegetable scoop and insert the scoop into the raw potato and push and turn quite firmly. With a little practice you will find you get an almost perfect ball. Dry and roast in oil or fat in the oven or cook in deep fat.

287 Paprika beef stew with cheese

4 servings

1 lb. stewing beef
1 oz. butter
8 oz. thinly sliced onions
2 crushed cloves of garlic
1 level tablespoon paprika
1 level tablespoon plain flour
1 level tablespoon tomato
   purée

pinch caraway seeds
   (optional)
good pinch salt
scant ½ pint stock or water
2 oz. finely grated Cheddar
   cheese

Dice the beef and brown in the hot butter, add the onions and garlic, and continue to cook for a few minutes. Stir in the paprika, flour and tomato purée. Add the caraway seeds if used, salt and the stock or water. Bring to the boil, stirring, cover and simmer for about 1½ hours, or cook in a pressure cooker under 15 lb. pressure for 30 minutes. Stir in the grated cheese, and serve the stew with potato dumplings or buttered noodles sprinkled with grated cheese, and with a green vegetable.

Paprika Beef Stew with Cheese

288 *Beef stroganoff (1)*

4 servings

1 lb. lean beef
generous sprinkling of salt,
   pepper, mustard
pinch curry powder
   (optional)
1 very large onion
2 oz. butter or margarine
1 tablespoon flour

1 pint water or stock (water
   to be flavoured with beef
   extract)
1 oz. extra butter or
   margarine
2 tablespoons tomato juice
   or purée
2 tablespoons cream
   (preferably soured)

Cut the meat into small pieces or fingers, sprinkle lightly with salt, pepper, mustard and curry powder. Fry the thinly sliced onion in butter until soft, then work in the flour. Cook gently for a few minutes, gradually stir in the stock, bring to the boil and allow to thicken. Heat the other butter, fry meat until golden brown, add to sauce with other ingredients and simmer gently. If using fillet steak it will only take about 15-20 minutes, but stewing steak could be used and will take about $1\frac{1}{2}$ hours to become tender. Serve on hot rice. For very special occasions add little brandy before serving.

289 *Beef stroganoff (2)*

4-5 servings

1 onion
4 oz. butter
4-8 oz. mushrooms
$1\frac{1}{4}$ lb. lean fillet steak
seasoning

$\frac{3}{8}$ pint soured cream or use
   fresh cream and lemon
   juice
4-8 oz. mushrooms

Fry chopped onion in half the butter and mushrooms in the rest. Cut steak into strips, season, fry in the onion flavoured butter, season well. Add warmed cream, heat together gently then add mushrooms and serve at once.

290 *Hungarian goulash*

4 servings

1 lb. stewing beef
1 oz. dripping
8 oz. thinly sliced onions
1 clove garlic (optional)
1 tablespoon paprika pepper
seasoning

1 tablespoon plain flour
$\frac{1}{2}$-$\frac{3}{4}$ pint stock or water
3 tablespoons tomato
   chutney
$\frac{1}{4}$ pint yoghourt

Cut meat into 1-inch cubes and brown quickly in the hot dripping. Remove, and fry lightly the sliced onions and crushed garlic. Add the paprika pepper, seasoning and flour and stir and stir over low heat. Pour in the stock and bring slowly to the boil, stirring. Return the meat, add the tomato chutney and simmer gently for $1\frac{1}{2}$-2 hours. Just before serving stir in the yoghourt and serve the goulash with buttered noodles or mashed potatoes and sauerkraut if liked.

Hungarian Goulash

291 Spicy bean mince

4 servings

1 small onion, finely
  chopped
½ oz. dripping
1 lb. minced beef
2 large tomatoes, skinned
  and chopped
½ teaspoon cayenne pepper

¾ teaspoon salt
1 can condensed bean with
  bacon soup

To garnish:
small triangles of toast
parsley

Fry onion gently in dripping until tender and golden brown. Stir in meat, tomatoes and seasoning. Cook over low heat for 30 minutes, stirring occasionally. Add the condensed bean with bacon soup and heat gently for a further 15 minutes. Serve meat mixture in a shallow dish and garnish with triangles of toast and parsley. Serve at once.

292 Beef pancakes (France)

4 servings

For the pancakes:
4 oz. plain flour
1 teaspoon baking powder
good pinch salt
1 egg
½ pint milk or milk and water
fat or oil for frying

For the beef mixture:
1 tablespoons dripping or fat
1 small onion
4 oz. cooked beef
seasoning
butter
parsley

Sieve the flour, baking powder and salt together. Make a well in the centre and beat in the egg and enough milk to make a firm batter. Beat well, then leave for 10 minutes. Add the remainder of the milk and beat again.

For beef mixture
Heat the dripping in a pan and fry the onion, which should be cut finely, until soft, then add the cooked beef (which should also be cut very finely or minced) and the seasoning. Toss together with the onion until well mixed. Add this to the pancake mixture and stir thoroughly. Heat enough oil or fat in the frying pan to give a shine (see there is no loose fat in the pan) and wait until a faint haze is seen. Pour in spoonfuls of the batter mixture, cook quickly until crisp and brown on the under side, then toss or turn and cook on the upper side. Take the hot pancake out of the pan, spread with butter, sprinkle with chopped parsley and roll tightly. Instead of frying in the pan, pancakes can be cooked on a greased girdle or hot plate.

293 Bobotee (South Africa)

4-6 servings

1 oz. dripping or fat
2 sliced onions
1 good tablespoon curry
  powder
1 teaspoon salt
2 teaspoon sugar
1 tablespoon vinegar or
  lemon juice

thick slice of bread weighing
  about 4 oz.
½ pint milk
1½ lb. minced beef
1 large or 2 small eggs
1 oz. chopped almonds
  (optional)

Heat the fat in a frying pan and cook the onions until soft, then add the curry powder, salt, sugar, vinegar or lemon juice and mix thoroughly. Put the bread into a dish, pour over the milk, let it stand for 15 minutes, then pour off and keep any milk that the bread has not absorbed. Beat the bread until very soft then add this to the fried onion mixture together with the meat and 1 of the eggs or half the beaten egg if using 1 only. Put this mixture into the bottom of a well-greased dish. Pour the milk left from soaking the bread over the rest of the egg, cover the meat mixture with this custard and top with almonds. Put the dish into the middle of a moderately hot oven (400°F – Gas Mark 5) and cook for 30 minutes, after this time reduce heat (350°F – Gas Mark 3) for a further 30 minutes.
This dish can be made with cooked meat, although it is not so full of flavour. In this case cook for 25 minutes only.

294 Chili con carne (Mexico)

4 servings

2 oz. butter
1 large onion
1 green pepper
2 sticks celery
12 oz.-1 lb. minced or diced
  beef
either 8 oz. tomatoes or
  ½ pint tomato pulp
8 oz. cooked kidney beans
  (soaked and cooked
  haricot beans)

1 tablespoon chilli powder
½ teaspoon salt
cayenne pepper
2 teaspoons paprika
  pepper
¼ pint water

Heat the butter in a saucepan. Chop the onion, pepper and celery. Cook in the butter until just tender, then add the other ingredients. Bring just to the boil, lower the heat and cook gently for approximately 55 minutes or 1½ hours if diced meat used. Stir halfway during the cooking, and add a little more water if necessary. This is very hot.

NOTE: Some people like to add 2 oz. cooked rice to this recipe.

295 Spaghetti and meat sauce

4 servings

8 oz. chopped onion
2 oz. butter
1 lb. minced beef
2 crushed cloves garlic
8 oz. skinned, seeded
  tomatoes
2 tablespoons tomato purée

pepper
salt
¼ pint water
12 oz. spaghetti
2 oz. melted butter
bowl finely grated Cheddar
  cheese

Lightly brown onions in butter, add beef and garlic; cook 5 minutes, stirring. Add tomatoes, purée, seasoning and water, cover and simmer 2 hours. Cook spaghetti in boiling salted water (about 15 minutes), drain, toss in melted butter and serve with meat sauce poured over. Hand round the bowl of grated Cheddar cheese separately.

Spaghetti and Meat Sauce

296 *Mince collops or savoury minced beef*

4 servings

1 onion
1½ oz. fat
1 oz. flour
½ pint brown stock

pinched mixed herbs
12 oz.-1 lb. minced beef
seasoning

The mince is a much better flavour and texture if it is NOT fried first but added to the brown sauce. Chop the onion finely and toss in the fat, work in the flour and cook for several minutes. Add stock, bring to the boil and cook until thickened. Add the herbs, the beef, seasoning and stir well. Continue stirring until the meat is completely broken in small pieces, then lower the heat and simmer gently for 1 hour, stirring frequently.

297 *Moussaka (Greece)*

4-6 servings

2 oz. margarine
8 oz. onions
2 lb. potatoes
1 lb. minced beef
8 oz. tomatoes
seasoning
parsley

Sauce:
1 oz. margarine
1 oz. flour
½ pint milk or milk and
    water
seasoning
1 egg
2 oz. grated cheese

Heat the margarine in a saucepan and fry the sliced onions until just soft, but not broken. Remove onions from the pan, then slice the potatoes and toss these in the margarine. Make the sauce by heating 1 oz. of margarine in a pan, stir in the flour and cook for a few minutes until a dry *roux*. Take the pan from the heat and add the milk. Return to the heat and stirring all the time, bring to the boil; then cook until slightly thickened. Add the seasoning then allow the sauce to cool slightly and stir in the well-beaten egg and the cheese. Do not cook again. Arrange a layer of sliced potatoes at the bottom of a deep casserole, then a layer of the meat, a layer of the onion, then sliced tomatoes. Season each layer and continue filling the casserole in this way, ending with a layer of potato and using small quantities of the sauce to pour over each layer. Put the lid on the casserole and bake for 1½ hours in the middle of a very moderate oven (300°-350°F – Gas Mark 2-3). Take off the lid, sprinkle with chopped parsley and serve at once.

298 *Tomato mince*

4 servings

2 oz. lard
1 onion, finely chopped
1 lb. minced beef
1 can condensed tomato soup
  or ½ pint tomato sauce (see
  Recipe 360)

1 rounded tablespoon
  oatmeal
salt
pinch of cayenne pepper

Melt the lard and gently fry onion until tender. Add the meat and cook gently, stirring continuously, until brown. Pour in the tomato soup, add oatmeal, salt and pepper. Cover and simmer gently for 30 minutes. Serve with toast or mashed potatoes.

Tomato Mince

299 *Swedish casserole*

4-6 servings

Meat balls:
1 lb. minced beef
4 heaped tablespoons fresh
  breadcrumbs
pinch of dried herbs
  (optional)
1 tablespoon sliced onion
1 level teaspoon salt
pepper
1 egg

1 oz. flour to coat

Sauce:
1 oz. dripping
2 rashers streaky bacon
1 medium-sized carrot
3 tomatoes
1 large can butter beans
1 tablespoon sliced onion

Mix the beef, crumbs, herbs, onion and seasoning and bind with beaten egg. Shape into 12 balls and toss each in flour. Heat the dripping in a saucepan, add the meat balls and fry gently until evenly browned then remove from the pan. Add the chopped bacon, carrot and tomatoes and fry gently until browned. Stir in the entire contents of the can of butter beans and sliced onions. Bring to the boil, then turn into a 2-pint casserole. Arrange the meat on top, cover and bake in a moderately hot oven (400°F – Gas Mark 5) for 30 minutes.

300 *Beef ring*

4-6 servings

½ onion
2 eggs
2 oz. beef dripping
2 oz. flour
¼ pint stock
1 lb. minced beef
¼ pint double cream
seasoning

Worcestershire sauce

To garnish:
freshly cooked carrots, peas,
  mushrooms
½ pint brown sauce (see
  Recipe 350)

Chop the onion finely, beat eggs well. Melt the dripping, add the flour and cook 1 minute. Add the stock, cook 3 minutes. Add all the other ingredients and place the mixture in a greased ring mould. Cover with greased greaseproof paper and stand in a saucepan of boiling water so that the water comes halfway up the sides of the mould. Boil gently with the lid on for 1 hour. Turn on to a hot dish and decorate with some freshly cooked vegetables and a little brown sauce or gravy. Serve hot.

Swedish Casserole

Beef Ring

301 *Beef and oatmeal loaf*

4-6 servings

1 lb. minced beef
2 large onions (minced)
8 oz. fine oatmeal
1 teaspoon mixed herbs

salt
pepper
1 can condensed vegetable
  soup

Put all the ingredients into a large bowl and mix thoroughly. Pack into a well greased 2 lb. loaf tin and bake in a moderate oven (375°F – Gas Mark 4) for 1¼-1½ hours. Serve hot with vegetables or cold with salads or as a substantial sandwich filling.

302 *Galantine of beef*

4-6 servings

1 oz. dripping
1 oz. flour
¼ pint stock or water with a
  little beef extract added
12 oz.-1 lb. beef minced finely
  or 8 oz. minced beef and
  8 oz. sausage meat
2 oz. fine breadcrumbs
1 egg

seasoning

To coat:
aspic or chaudfroid sauce
  (see Recipe 219)

To garnish:
small pieces cooked
  vegetables

Heat the dripping in a pan, stir in the flour and cook for several minutes. Add the cold stock gradually, bring to the boil and cook gently until thickened. Mix this sauce with the other ingredients. Put into a greased tin or mould and steam for 1½ hours. If no suitable tin available, form into a neat roll and wrap in greased paper then cloth. It is very important to cover with greased paper to keep the galantine as dry as possible when cooking. Turn out carefully and allow to cool. Coat either with aspic or a chaudfroid sauce. Allow this to cool, and when just beginning to set, spread over the cold galantine with a palette knife dipped in hot water. Decorate with brightly coloured pieces of vegetables putting these into position before the jelly is quite firm.

303 *Hamburgers*

4 servings

1 chopped onion
1 oz. whipped-up cooking fat
12 oz. minced raw steak
2 oz. fresh breadcrumbs
salt
pepper
1 egg
seasoned flour

To garnish:
mashed potato
rings of fried onion
baked or grilled tomatoes

Chop the onion finely and fry until golden brown in the melted whipped-up cooking fat. Stir in the minced steak, breadcrumbs and seasoning, and bind with the beaten egg. Divide into 4 even portions and shape into round flat cakes. Coat well with seasoned flour and bake near the top of a hot oven (425°-450°F – Gas Mark 6-7) for 30 minutes or fry in shallow whipped-up cooking fat, allowing 8-10 minutes on each side. Serve the hamburgers on a hot dish garnished with mashed potato, rings of fried onion and baked or grilled tomatoes.

Hamburgers

304 *Rissoles*

These are an ideal way of using left-over cooked meat. Mince the meat and follow either the recipe for Durham cutlets (see Recipe 617) or Hamburgers (see preceding recipe). Form the mixture into flat round cakes, coat with beaten egg and crumbs and fry.

305 *Viennese steaks*

6-8 servings

1½-2 lb. minced beef
1 dessertspoon chopped
   parsley
little grated nutmeg
1-2 tablespoons tomato
   ketchup
black pepper

salt
½ level teaspoon finely
   crushed dried mixed herbs
2 eggs
flour
butter or oil for frying
1 or 2 onions

Mix the minced meat with parsley, nutmeg, ketchup, seasonings and mixed herbs to taste. Separate 1 egg and set white aside. Beat yolk with another whole egg and use to bind meat mixture. Divide into portions and shape each with floured hands to look rather like large slices of fillet steak. Dredge with flour on all sides. Fry in heated butter or oil until well browned on both sides, then drain and keep hot. Peel and slice onion. Coat with flour, dip into beaten egg white then into flour again and fry until golden and crisp. Serve as a garnish. Or cook a larger quantity and serve round the steaks. Serve brown sauce (see Recipe 350) separately.

306 *Boiled silverside or brisket of beef*

8-10 servings

piece of salted beef about
   3-4 lb.
4 small carrots
4 small onions
good pinch pepper
mustard

To garnish:
dumplings
freshly cooked vegetables

It is a good idea to buy enough brisket to allow for a cold meal, for it is delicious with salad. Soak the beef in COLD water for 1 hour or 2. If the butcher says it is very salted soak overnight. Put the beef into a large saucepan with the vegetables, and half cover with cold water. Add a good pinch pepper and mustard. Bring quickly to the boil. Remove any scum that comes to the top. Put the lid on the saucepan, lower the heat, and simmer gently, allowing about 30 minutes per lb. and 30 minutes over, i.e. a 4 lb. piece will take 2½ hours to cook. If wished dumplings can be cooked with this, allowing them about 15 minutes quick cooking. Do not thicken the liquid. To serve the meat put it on a large hot dish, with the vegetables and stock round, then garnish with dumplings (see Recipe 272) and a few freshly cooked vegetables.

307 *Wet pickle for beef or ox tongue*

10-12 servings

To 4-6 lb. silverside of beef
   or whole ox tongue use
1 lb. salt

1 gallon water
6 oz. moist brown sugar
½ oz. saltpetre

Put all the ingredients for the pickle into a large pan, bring to the boil and boil for 5 minutes. Skim well. Strain into a large basin or pickling jar and leave until quite cold. Remove any discoloured parts from the meat and wipe thoroughly with damp cloth. Put into cold pickle, cover and keep in cool larder 10-14 days. Turn the meat every day. Cook as for boiled brisket (see Recipe 306).

308 *Dry pickle for salt beef*

To 5-6 lb. brisket or flank of
    beef use
1 oz. saltpetre
2 lb. common salt
1 lb. moist brown sugar
1 shallot or small onion

2 bay leaves
1 small teaspoon herbs
1 small teaspoon crushed
    peppercorns
1 small teaspoon spice
    (allspice, mace and cloves)

Remove any discoloured parts from the meat and wipe very thoroughly with a damp cloth. Pound the saltpetre and mix all the ingredients in the pickle jar. Put in the meat and rub well with the salt mixture. Cover and keep in a cool larder for 10-14 days – rub and turn the meat daily. Remove from the pickle, wash and scrape and cook as for boiled brisket (see Recipe 306).

309 *Pressure cooking of meat and poultry*

You will find details of pot roasting in a pressure cooker under Recipe 235, but most of the dishes in this book can be cooked in the pressure cooker. Use 15 lb. pressure.

Stewed meats
STEAK   Approximately 20 minutes
LAMB   Approximately 15 minutes
OX TAIL   Approximately 20 minutes
OX TONGUE   Approximately 45-55 minutes
MINCED BEEF   Approximately 10-15 minutes

Boiled meats, etc.
BRISKET   Approximately 12-15 minutes per lb.
POULTRY   Approximately 7 minutes per lb.

In the case of stews, because there is little evaporation during cooking use only half the quantity of liquid given in the recipes in this book. The stew can either be thickened at the end of cooking or the meat can be rolled in seasoned flour and cooked in a little hot fat at the bottom of the pan. The liquid is then added, the lid put on, brought to pressure and cooking time commences from then on.

310 VEAL

Be very critical, particularly in hot weather, as veal does not keep well. There is little fat to see, but what there is should be firm and white; the lean must look dry and be a pale pink.

Purpose	Cut to choose	Cooking time	Accompaniments
Roasting	Shoulder		
	Breast	25 minutes per lb. plus	Sausages
	Best end of neck	25 minutes over	Veal stuffing or other
	Loin		well-flavoured stuffing.
	Fillet		
	Chump end of loin		
Grilling	Chops from loin	15-20 minutes	Chipped potatoes
or	Fillet		Tomatoes
Frying	Best end of neck chops		Mushrooms
	Thin slices from leg	5-6 minutes	
Stewing	Breast	1½-2½ hours	Mixed vegetables
or	Fillet		Various sauces
Braising	Knuckle		
	Middle and scrag end of neck		
Boiling	Head	1½-2½ hours	Mixed vegetables or salads
	Feet		
	Breast		
Stocks	Feet	1½-2½ hours	
for Soups	Knuckle		

311 *Stewing or braising veal*

You often see stewing veal described as pie veal. Choose breast, fillet, knuckle, middle and scrag end of neck. Tomatoes, paprika, mushrooms are all suitable for flavouring.

13. Glazed forehock

14. Stuffed shoulder of veal

312 *Blanquette of veal*

4-6 servings

1 lb. veal
2 onions
bouquet garni (see Recipe 638)
1 chicken bouillon cube
1 pint water
2½ oz. butter
2 oz. flour

1 small can evaporated milk
1 or 2 egg yolks
juice of 1 lemon

To garnish:
bacon rolls
lemon butterfly slices
parsley

Put veal, onions and herbs into pan with chicken bouillon cube and water. Simmer gently until tender (1½ hours). Strain, keep the meat hot. Make a sauce with the butter, flour, and 1 pint stock, cook 2 minutes. Add the evaporated milk and re-heat. Stir in the egg yolk and lemon juice but do not re-boil. Pour over the veal and garnish with bacon rolls, lemon butterfly slices and parsley.

313 *Fricassée of veal*

Made just like blanquette of veal if using fresh veal. Cooked veal can be re-heated in a white sauce, using partly stock and partly fresh or evaporated milk. The mixture can be flavoured with bouquet garni (see Recipe 638) or little lemon.

314 *Braised veal and ham*

4-6 servings

1 onion
3 tomatoes
2 oz. lard
12 oz. stewing veal
1 oz. flour

¾ pint stock (or water flavoured with yeast extract)
seasoning
6 oz. boiled bacon or ham

Fry the sliced onion and skinned sliced tomatoes in the hot lard until tender. Cut veal into neat fingers, roll in seasoned flans and add to pan. Gradually cook until golden coloured, then stir in the stock. Bring to the boil and cook until thickened and smooth. Season well. Simmer gently for 1 hour, then add fingers of the boiled bacon or ham and cook for a further 45 minutes.

315 *Barbecued veal*

4-6 servings

1¼-1½ lb. stewing veal – cut into neat pieces, or use veal chops instead
seasoning
good pinch dry mustard
2 bay leaves
good pinch mixed herbs
1 or 2 oz. margarine
3 large onions
1 oz. flour

2 teaspoons sugar
2 tablespoons lemon juice or vinegar
2 eating apples
3 tablespoons cooking Burgundy (optional)

Cut the veal into small pieces, wash and dry well. Put into a saucepan, just covering with cold water, add seasoning, mustard, bay leaves and mixed herbs, bring to the boil and skim thoroughly. Lower heat and cook gently for 1½ hours. Remove veal from liquid and measure off 1 good pint of stock. Heat margarine in saucepan and when very hot fry onions, cut into neat rings, until softened but neither broken or browned. Mix in the flour. Take saucepan off the heat and gradually add 1 pint of the veal stock, stirring the whole time. Bring the sauce to the boil and stir until slightly thickened. Add seasoning, sugar, lemon juice or vinegar. Put pieces of veal into the sauce and cook very slowly for 15-20 minutes. Cut the apples into rings, taking out the cores and pips but leaving them with the skins still on, particularly if these are a bright colour. Simmer for 5 minutes only. Lastly stir in the Burgundy, although the dish still has a good flavour if this is left out. Arrange the veal on a dish with the sauce and the rings of apple and onion on top.

316 *Tomato rolls*

4 servings

4 thin slices of veal from the leg
1 oz. butter
seasoning
1 finely chopped onion
little chopped parsley
little grated lemon rind

Sauce:
1 small onion
tiny piece eating apple
1 oz. butter or margarine
1 rounded teaspoon cornflour
generous ½ pint water
1 small can tomato purée
seasoning

Spread each slice of veal with butter and sprinkle with seasoning, onion, parsley and lemon rind. Roll firmly with the onion mixture inside – secure with skewers. To make the sauce: Grate the onion and apple and toss in butter for a few minutes, taking care they do not brown. Blend cornflour and water, pour into saucepan, add tomato purée. Bring to boil and cook until clear and smooth. Season well. Put the veal rolls into casserole – cover with sauce and lid or foil. Cook for approximately 2 hours in slow oven (300°F. – Gas Mark 2). Serve with boiled rice.

317 *Veal birds*

4-5 servings

1½ lb. veal steak, cut very thinly and pounded
made mustard
flour
salt and pepper
1½ oz. fat
¼ pint stock or tomato juice

Orange stuffing:
6 tablespoons soft breadcrumbs
½ level teaspoon mixed herbs
grated rind 1 small orange
½ beaten egg
sprinkling salt and pepper

Divide the veal into 8 to 10 even-sized oblong pieces. Mince any trimmings and add to the stuffing. Lightly spread veal with made mustard. Mix the stuffing, spread on veal, roll and secure with fine string or wooden picks. Roll in seasoned flour and brown in a little hot fat. Place in casserole and add stock. Cook slowly in covered casserole in centre of very moderate oven (300°-325°F – Gas Mark 2-3) about 45-60 minutes. Serve with rice and chopped peppers.

318 *Veal marengo*

4 servings

good 1 lb. neck of veal
little flour
seasoning
3 oz. butter or 3 tablespoons
  oil
2 finely diced onions or
  shallots
½ pint white stock or water

8 oz. skinned tomatoes
2 oz. mushrooms

To garnish:
4 slices bread
fat for frying
parsley
lemon

Cut the meat into neat pieces, coat with a thin layer of seasoned flour and fry until pale golden brown in the hot butter or oil. Add finely diced onions and fry until transparent, then add stock, chopped tomatoes and mushrooms. Season well. Simmer gently for approximately 1 hour. Serve garnished with triangles of fried bread, parsley and lemon.

319 *Veal rolls*

4 servings

4 thin slices veal
1 oz. flour
seasoning
2 oz. fat or dripping
¾ pint stock
approximately 1 lb. mixed
  root vegetables

Mushroom stuffing:
2 oz. margarine
1 small onion
4 oz. mushrooms
4 oz. soft breadcrumbs
2 teaspoons chopped parsley
seasoning

To make the stuffing heat margarine and fry finely chopped onion in this. Add finely chopped mushrooms (stalks as well), crumbs, parsley, seasoning. Work together and spread on slices of meat, roll firmly and tie with cotton. Roll in the seasoned flour and fry in the hot fat. Put into casserole. Add remaining flour to fat in pan and the stock. Bring to the boil and cook until thickened. Season well. Arrange vegetables in casserole round the meat and pour over gravy. Cover and cook for 2 hours in very moderate oven (350°F – Gas Mark 3).

320 *Veal and bacon rolls*

Spread stuffing on veal and roll, then roll a rasher of bacon round each stuffed piece of veal. Tie, and continue as before. If bacon is reasonably fat you can reduce the dripping to 1 oz.

321 *To roast veal*

For roasting veal choose: shoulder, breast, best end of neck, loin, fillet, chump end of loin. The perfect way to roast veal is to use a larding needle and the thin strips of fat from bacon. Insert these through the meat so that it is really moist during cooking. Otherwise use plenty of greased foil or paper when cooking and remember that veal needs cooking well.

322 *Roast veal with creamed sauce*

joint of veal (approximately
  3 lb.)
seasoning
fat or bacon fat or butter
greaseproof paper or foil

2 tablespoons cream (or top
  of milk)
¾ pint thin white sauce (see
  Recipe 216)

Season veal and cover with plenty of fat (or insert strips of fat as described before), and paper or foil. Allow 25 minutes per lb. and 25 minutes over in a moderately hot oven (400°F – Gas Mark 5). Half an hour before the end of cooking time take joint out of oven, remove paper and pour off most of the fat from the tin – leave about 1 tablespoon. Blend cream with sauce, pour into meat tin, then baste joint with this. Continue cooking as before, but lower heat to moderate, basting several times with the sauce.

323 *Harlequin rice with veal*

4 servings

4 veal chops
1 oz. flour
2 teaspoons salt
¼ teaspoon pepper
2 oz. fat
1 clove garlic

2 medium-sized tomatoes
1 lb. sliced onions
12 tablespoons apple-juice or
  stock
2 oz. cooked rice
4 oz. sliced ripe olives

Dredge chops in a mixture of flour, 1 teaspoon of the salt and pepper. Brown in hot fat with the split garlic in a heavy frying pan. Remove garlic. Skin tomatoes and chop coarsely. Add to meat together with onions, apple juice and remaining 1 teaspoon salt. Bring to the boil, lower heat. Cover and simmer about 30 minutes. Remove chops to dish. Add rice and olives to ingredients in pan. Replace chops on top of rice. Cover and simmer until rice is hot.

Harlequin Rice with Veal

324 *Italian meat balls*

4 servings

12 oz. minced pie-veal
1 medium onion, finely
   chopped
1 teaspoon mixed, dried
   herbs
seasoning
3 slices white bread
¼ pint milk
1 egg

4 tablespoons water
flour
4 oz. fat or oil to fry
1 can condensed tomato
   soup or ¼ pint tomato
   sauce

To garnish:
4 black olives (optional)
1 lemon

Mix veal, onion, herbs and seasoning. Remove crusts from bread and soak it in a little milk for 30 minutes. Squeeze bread gently between palms of hands to remove excess milk. Add to veal mixture. Beat together the egg and water. Add the egg and water to veal mixture a little at a time, beating thoroughly and using sufficient to make firm, light mixture. Roll into 2-inch balls. Dust in flour and brown in hot fat or oil. Put in ovenproof dish. Pour over the tomato liquid, cover with lid. Cook in a moderate oven (375°F – Gas Mark.4), for 20 minutes. Serve with black olives and quarters of lemon.

325 *For frying or grilling veal*

Choose: Chops from loin, fillet, best end of neck, thin slices from leg. Keep moistened with plenty of fat while frying. Coating with egg and crumbs or flour keeps flavour in the meat. When grilling, brush with oil or plenty of melted fat or butter.

326 *Grilled veal cutlets*

4 servings

4 cutlets of veal (cut from
   loin)
little melted butter or
   margarine

mushrooms
tomatoes

To garnish:
watercress

Heat grill, brush cutlets with melted butter and cook steadily under the grill, standing meat on grid. Cook the mushrooms and tomatoes in grill pan at the same time, garnish with watercress.

327 *Escalopes of veal*

Buy thin slices of veal (cut from leg), beat gently with rolling pin to flatten even more. Coat with seasoned flour, then dip into beaten egg and cover with fine crumbs. Fry steadily in shallow fat, oil or butter or butter and oil mixed, until golden brown on both sides. Garnish with wedges of lemon, or for a more elaborate garnish, top rings of lemon with freshly chopped hard-boiled egg and parsley, or egg and capers. Excellent with green salad.

328 *Veal escalopes in cheese*

4 servings

4 thin slices veal (approx.
   12 oz.)
beaten egg
1 oz. plain flour
3 oz. finely grated Cheddar
   cheese
salt and pepper

2 oz. butter
¼ pint vegetable or meat
   stock
3 tablespoons sherry

To garnish:
lemon fans
parsley sprigs

Trim the veal slices if necessary, and dip in beaten egg. Mix the flour and grated cheese thoroughly, season with salt and pepper, and use to coat the veal. Fry the veal on both sides in hot butter until nicely crisped and golden brown, taking about 10 minutes. Arrange down the centre of an entrée dish. Add the stock and sherry to the pan, and bring to the boil. Pour over the veal and serve at once garnished with lemon fans and parsley.

329 *Escalopes of veal with fried egg*

Fry the escalopes of veal and top with fried egg. Serve with mushroom or tomato sauce (see Recipes 216, 360) if desired.

330 *Escalopes of veal with ham and cheese*

Fry the escalopes of veal then put a slice of cooked ham on top of each fillet, top with a slice of Gruyère or Cheddar cheese and heat under grill.

331 *Escalopes of veal Hongroise*

Fry the escalopes of veal and serve with a white sauce (see Recipe 216) flavoured with paprika. Garnish with mushrooms and tomatoes.

332 *Escalopes of veal in Madeira sauce*

Do not coat the veal but fry in butter until just tender. Serve with Madeira sauce (see Recipe 356).

333 *Escalopes of veal Milanaise*

Fry escalopes of veal and serve in a border of cooked macaroni or spaghetti with tomato sauce (see Recipe 360). Mushrooms can be added as well.

MEAT PIES AND PUDDINGS

334 *Veal and ham pie*

6 servings

12 oz. raised pastry*
1 lb. fillet veal
6 oz. ham
salt and pepper
½ level teaspoon grated lemon
  rind
1-2 hard-boiled eggs

7 tablespoons water or bone
  stock
beaten egg for glazing
1 level teaspoon gelatine
½ level teaspoon meat
  extract

*½ quantity given for raised
  pastry crust (see Recipe
  341)

Make pastry and keep warm in basin until ready to use. Remove
pastry from basin and with two-thirds of the dough line a 6-
inch cake tin or 1 lb. loaf tin. Wash and dry the meats, removing
any skin, and cut into 1-inch cubes. Roll the meats together in
salt and pepper and lemon rind. Place half the meat in the
bottom of the pastry-lined tin, cut the eggs into halves, place on
top of the meat, cover with remaining meat. Pour into the pie 3
tablespoons of the water or stock. Turn the top edge of pastry-
lining in over the meat, damp it all round, roll out remaining
third of pastry to make a lid. Press down well all round the edge
and cut at ½-inch intervals with a sharp knife to secure. Make a
hole in the centre, brush with beaten egg. Place in centre of a
moderate oven (375°F – Gas Mark 4) for 2-2¼ hours. Leave to
cool. Melt the gelatine in remaining water or stock and stir in
the meat extract. When the pie is cool and the gelatine mixture
just setting, pour into the pie through the hole in the centre and
leave to set before serving.

Veal and Ham Pie

335 *Beef scone pie*

4-6 servings

1 medium onion, finely
  chopped
1 oz. lard or dripping
1½ lb. minced beef

1 can condensed oxtail soup
salt
pepper
8 oz. scone dough (see below)

Scone Dough

8 oz. self-raising flour or
  8 oz. plain flour with
  4 level teaspoons baking
  powder added

salt
1-2 oz. margarine or cooking
  fat
milk

Gently fry onion in melted lard until tender. Add the minced beef and, stirring,
cook until brown. Pour in the condensed oxtail soup, season and mix thoroughly.
Place mixture in deep casserole, roll out scone dough ½-inch thick and make
8 small scones. Place on top of mince and bake in a very hot oven (475°F – Gas
Mark 8) for 20-25 minutes until scones are cooked and golden brown. Serve at
once.

Sieve flour with good pinch of salt, rub in fat. Mix to a fairly soft dough with
milk, roll out and cut into rounds.

Beef Scone Pie

336 *Beef shells*

4 servings

12 oz. minced stewing steak
seasoning
6 oz. short crust pastry (see
   Recipe 207)
1 onion
1 oz. dripping
8 oz. tomatoes

1 tablespoon flour
1 teaspoon curry powder
1 teaspoon Worcestershire
   sauce

To garnish:
wedges of tomatoes

Simmer stewing steak gently in water to cover, seasoning well, until just tender. Drain and save some of the stock. Line scallop shells with thin pastry and bake 'blind' until crisp and golden brown. Fry the chopped onion in dripping, add the steak, most of the tomatoes, chopped, the flour and curry powder. Cook gently for several minutes. Add the stock, bring to the boil and cook until thoroughly smooth and thick. Add the sauce and any extra seasoning desired. Fill scallop shells with the beef mixture. Serve hot or cold garnished with wedges of tomato.

337 *Cornish pasties*

4 servings

8 oz. short crust pastry
   preferably made with
   dripping (see Recipe 207)
8 oz. raw beef steak
4 oz. kidney or liver
   (optional)

2 raw potatoes
1 onion
seasoning

Roll out the pastry and cut into large rounds about the size of a large saucer or tea plate. Chop meat and liver or kidney finely. Peel potatoes and onion, and slice thinly, cutting into small pieces. Mix together with salt and pepper. Place mixture along centre of pastry rounds, sprinkling sparingly with water and seal edges of pastry across the top, fluting with the fingers for decoration. Cook in a hot oven for 15 minutes, then lower the temperature a little and continue to cook for a further 30-35 minutes. It is important to seal the pastry completely as the contents of the pasty cook in their own juice and no steam must escape.

338 *Steak and kidney pie*

12 oz.-1 lb. stewing steak
2 lamb's or sheep's kidneys
   or about 4 oz. ox kidney
1 level teaspoon flour
good pinch pepper

$\frac{1}{2}$ teaspoon salt
water or stock
6 oz. short crust (see
   Recipe 207) or flaky pastry
   (see below)
little milk

Cut the steak and kidney into small pieces and roll in the seasoned flour. Stand a pie support or egg cup in the centre of the pie dish to support the pastry. Put the meat into the dish, seeing that the kidney is well distributed. Pour over enough water or stock to come halfway up the meat, any more will boil out in cooking. Roll out the pastry and cover the pie. If you have any scraps of pastry left, form them into leaves and a rose to decorate the pie; it is traditional in cookery to ornament savoury pies in this way and not sweet ones. To make leaves, roll out the pastry to a strip, then cut leaf shapes (approximately diamond) marking the 'veins' with the point of a knife. To make a rose, cut a narrow strip, then roll this round, and with your finger-tips depress at intervals to give a petal shape. Brush the top of the pie over with a very little milk, sticking the leaves and rose into position. Make a tiny slit in the pastry over the pie support or egg cup, to allow the steam to escape. Bake in the centre of a hot oven (450°F – Gas Mark 7) for about 25 minutes to give the pastry a chance to rise, then put a piece of paper over the top and lower the heat to very moderate (350°F – Gas Mark 3) to make sure the meat is cooked. Give it about a further 1$\frac{1}{2}$ hours. When serving, have a sauce boat of hot stock available to pour into the pie to make extra gravy if you wish.

Another way of cooking this is to simmer the meat and kidney first until nearly tender, tossing in the seasoned flour and frying as in stewed steak (see Recipe 268). Put in pie dish, allow to cool slightly. Cover with the pastry and bake for 30-40 minutes.

Flaky pastry

8 oz. plain flour
pinch salt

5-6 oz. fat
water to mix

Sieve flour with salt. Divide fat into 3 portions. Rub 1 portion into flour in usual way and mix to rolling consistency with cold water. Roll out to oblong shape. Now take the second portion of fat, divide it into small pieces and lay them on surface of $\frac{2}{3}$ dough. Leave remaining $\frac{1}{3}$ without fat. Take its 2 corners and fold back over second $\frac{1}{3}$ so that the dough looks like an envelope with its flap open. Fold over top end of pastry, so closing the 'envelope'. Turn pastry at right angles, seal open ends of pastry and 'rib' it. This means depressing it with the rolling-pin at intervals, so giving a corrugated effect and equalising the pressure of air. This makes it certain that the pastry will rise evenly. Repeat the process again using the remaining fat and turning pastry in same way. Roll out pastry once more, but should it begin to feel very soft and sticky put it into a cold place for 30 minutes to become firm again before rolling out. Fold pastry as before, turn it, seal edges and 'rib' it. Altogether the pastry should have 3 foldings and 3 rollings. It is then ready to stand in a cold place for a little while before baking, since the contrast between the cold and the heat of the oven makes the pastry rise better.

To bake, use a very hot oven (475°F – Gas Mark 8) for the first 15 minutes, after this lower the Gas Mark to 5 or 6, or turn the electric oven off to finish cooking for remaining time at a lower temperature.

339 *Steak and mushroom pie*

Ingredients as in previous recipe, but use small button mushrooms in place of kidneys.

340 *Steak and kidney plate pie*

4-6 servings

6 oz. flaky or rough puff
   pastry (see Recipe 338)

Filling:
1 lb. stewing steak
4 oz. kidney

1 rounded tablespoon well
   seasoned flour
1 small onion
1 oz. fat
½ pint water
1 teaspoon made mustard
egg or milk to glaze

Cut meat into small pieces and toss in seasoned flour. Fry sliced onion slowly until brown. Move to one side and brown the meat lightly in the fat. Add the water; cover and simmer very gently for 1½-2 hours. Stir in mustard and correct seasoning to taste.

Roll the pastry to a thin sheet, about ¼-inch thick. Cut a strip and line moistened edge of 9-inch pie plate. Turn hot filling into the plate. Cover with pastry, trim and cut up edges, using flat of finger along edge of the pastry while slitting into pastry with the flat knife blade. Decorate with pastry leaves and slit centre. Brush top with beaten egg or milk. Bake in a hot oven (450°F – Gas Mark 7) for 10-15 minutes. Reduce heat to moderate (375°F – Gas Mark 4) and bake a further 15 minutes until the pie is golden and flaky. Serve hot, with hot green vegetables, jacket potatoes and mustard.

341 *Raised pork pie*

8-10 servings

Hot water pastry:
10 oz. lard
10 oz. water (½ pint)
1½ lb. plain flour
little egg to glaze

Filling:
8 oz. streaky bacon rashers
3 lb. pork
salt
pepper
ginger
2 tablespoons water
2 pig's trotters or 2 pig's ears
1 onion
8 black peppercorns
1 bay leaf
1 quart water

First make your hot water paste by boiling the lard and water together. Pour in flour and stir until it leaves the pan cleanly. Allow to cool and then knead it. Mould it into a ball and then shape it into a pie with your hands. Be sure to leave about a third of the paste for lid. You can mould the pie round a suitable tin or saucepan which you have greased slightly. If using a cake tin cut 2 rounds of pastry for the top and bottom, the same diameter as the cake tin, and a strip the circumference of the tin. Line the pie mould with bacon rashers. Dice pork and sprinkle with salt, pepper and ginger and fill the pie. Add only 2 tablespoons of water. Turn the sides of the pie inwards and place on the lid. Decorate to taste, but there must be a central vent left for you to pour in the pie jelly after. This is traditionally camouflaged with a 'rose' made of pastry. Brush over with beaten egg and bake in centre of a moderate oven (350° – Gas Mark 3) for about 2½ hours. Allow to cool, meanwhile place trotters, chopped onion, peppercorns and bay leaf in a quart of water and simmer without the lid for 1½ hours. Reduce the water to ⅓ pint in this way. Strain off and allow to cool. This is your pie jelly. Just before it sets, pour it into the cold pie a little at a time. When the pie is full, set in the refrigerator or very cool place.

Raised Pork Pie

342 *Lamb pie*

6 servings

1½-1¾ lb. (6 cutlets) best end
   neck lamb
1½ lb. sliced potato
8 oz. sliced onions
1 clove garlic (chopped)
1 teaspoon mixed herbs

1 teaspoon chopped parsley
salt and pepper
¼ pint stock or water
8 oz. flaky pastry (see
   Recipe 338)
egg for glazing

Trim the ends of the cutlet bones leaving 1½-inches free from meat. Arrange in a large pie dish so that the bones stand up in a line down the middle of the dish. Fill up with the sliced potatoes, onions, chopped garlic, herbs and parsley and add seasoning and stock. Roll out the pastry to cover the pie dish. Cut a strip approximately ½-inch wide to fit round the edge of the pie dish. Damp with a little water. Make a slit down the middle of the pastry so that the bones stand upright. Cover the pie dish with pastry, pressing the edges firmly together. Trim with a sharp knife. Knock up and scallop the edge. Roll out the pastry scraps, cut into leaves and decorate the pie crust round the slit. Glaze the pie with a little egg. Bake near the top of a very hot oven (475°F – Gas Mark 8) for 15-20 minutes, then place in the middle of the oven, lower the heat to moderate (375°F – Gas Mark 4) and continue cooking for approximately 40 minutes. For serving, place a small cutlet frill on the top of each bone.

343 *Sage cobbler of lamb*

2 lb. lamb (meat from
    shoulder, neck or breast)
1 oz. well seasoned flour
2 medium onions
1 oz. cooking fat, lard or
    dripping
about 12 oz. chopped
    celery or turnips
1 pint water
2 level tablespoons tomato
    purée
¼ teaspoon salt

Topping:
8 oz. plain flour
2 rounded teaspoons
    baking powder
1 level teaspoon salt
2 oz. butter or margarine
½ teaspoon sage
6 tablespoons milk (or 1 egg
    and 2 tablespoons milk)

Divide the meat into 1-inch pieces and coat with seasoned flour. Slice onions thinly. Melt fat in pan, add vegetables and fry over medium heat until light gold. Move to one side and fry meat. Transfer to a 2 or 3 pint casserole dish then pour over water mixed with the tomato purée and salt. Cover with lid and cook in the centre of the oven (350°F – Gas Mark 3) for 2 hours.

To make the Topping:
Sift flour, baking powder and salt. Rub in fat, add sage, then mix to a soft, but not sticky dough with milk. Turn out on to lightly floured board and knead quickly. Roll into a round, ½-inch in thickness. Cut into 6 equal triangles with sharp knife. Remove casserole from oven, uncover then arrange the scone triangles on top of meat. Brush with milk, return casserole to oven and bake (425°F – Gas Mark 6) for 20 minutes.

344 *Steak and kidney pudding*

4-6 servings

8 oz. suet crust pastry (see
    below)
12 oz.-1 lb. stewing steak

4 oz. ox kidney
2 tablespoons seasoned flour
2 tablespoons stock or water

Suet Crust Pastry

8 oz. flour (self-raising flour,
    or plain flour with 2 level
    teaspoons baking powder)

pinch salt
2-4 oz. finely shredded suet
water to mix

Turn suet crust pastry on to a lightly floured board. Roll out two-thirds and with it line a well greased 1½ pint pudding basin. Put in the steak and kidney (cut into small pieces and rolled in the seasoned flour) and add the stock or cold water. Roll out the remaining pastry to form a topping, cover the pudding and seal the edges with cold water. Cover with greased paper or aluminium foil and steam 3½-4 hours.

Sieve flour, baking powder if used and add suet. Mix to rolling consistency with cold water. Roll out thinly, as this pastry rises. Line a pudding basin with the dough, leaving some over for the cover. Fill with fruit, meat or vegetables, add the seasoning and put on the pastry cover. Put a piece of greased greaseproof paper on cover and wrap in pudding cloth. Steam or boil rapidly for 2-3 hours, or even longer, depending on the filling. For a good result, make sure that the water is boiling rapidly when the pudding goes in, and always replenish with boiling water.

Sage Cobbler of Lamb

Steak and Kidney Pudding

SAUCES

345 *To make thick gravy*

Pour off most of the fat from the roasting tin, leave just about 1 oz. and the sediment from the meat or poultry. Work into this 1 oz. of fat, 1 oz. of flour. Cook together for several minutes then add ½-¾ pint of stock (vegetable stock with flavouring can be used instead). Bring to the boil and cook until thick and smooth. Strain if desired. Some people prefer to use 1 pint liquid.

346 *All-round sauce*

1 onion
½ lemon
½ pint ale
½ pint good stock or bouillon
   from cube
salt
pepper

1 garlic clove (whole)
2 cloves
½ pint wine vinegar
sprig thyme
bay leaf
1 tablespoon flour

Slice the onion and lemon thinly and put into a pan with all the other ingredients except the flour. Simmer for 30 minutes then allow to cool and skim off the fat. Work a little of the sauce into the flour, then add this to the whole, so that it does not go lumpy and re-heat before serving. This sauce is good with the cuts of any joint, hot or cold, also with poultry.

347 *Apple sauce*

1 lb. apples
water

1 oz. margarine or butter
2 tablespoons sugar

Peel apples and slice thinly, then put into small saucepan adding about ¼ pint water, the margarine and the sugar. Allow to simmer steadily until a smooth mixture. Beat well with wooden spoon when apples are cooked to give good appearance.

348 *Bigarade Sauce*

Add rind of 1 orange (bitter or Seville if possible) to brown sauce (see Recipe 350). Strain and re-heat with orange and lemon juice and add a little claret or port wine. Add sugar and seasonings. Serve with duck, goose or pork.

349 *Bread sauce*

1 small onion
2 or 3 cloves (optional)
½ pint milk

2 oz. breadcrumbs
1–2 oz. margarine
salt, pepper

Peel the onion and if you are using cloves stick these firmly into the onion. Put this into the milk together with the other ingredients. Slowly bring the milk to the boil. Remove from the heat and stand in a warm place for as long as possible. Just before the meal is ready, heat the sauce gently, beating it with a wooden spoon. Remove onion before putting into sauce boat.

350 *Brown sauce*

Coating consistency:
1 oz. cooking fat or dripping
1 oz. flour
½ pint brown stock
salt and pepper

Panada sauce:
as above but ¼ pint brown
   stock

Thin sauce:
as above but 1 pint brown
   stock

Heat the fat or dripping in a pan. For a better flavour fry a little chopped onion, celery, carrot, in which case use 2 oz. fat. Add the flour and cook steadily in the fat until brown in colour. Be careful not to over-brown this. Add stock, carefully stirring all the time, bring to the boil, season and cook until thick and smooth. If vegetables have been used, strain.

351 *Cider sauce*

½ pint dry cider
¾ pint brown sauce (see Recipe
   350) or good brown gravy
2–3 cloves

1 bay leaf
salt
pepper

Put all the ingredients in a pan and simmer for about 15 minutes until slightly reduced. Strain and re-heat before serving, checking the seasoning. This is a good sauce with ham or gammon, pork or duck or goose, either served hot or cold.

352 *Cranberry sauce*

8–12 oz. cranberries
¼ pint water

2–3 oz. sugar
knob of butter

Simmer the cranberries in the water. Rub through a sieve, add sugar to taste and a little knob of butter. For an unsieved sauce make a syrup of water and sugar. Drop in the cranberries, cook until a thick mixture, add butter.

353 *Curry sauce*

1 medium-sized onion
1 cooking apple
1 oz. butter
1 level tablespoon curry
   powder
1 teaspoon curry paste
1 level tablespoon cornflour
½ pint stock or water

1 dessertspoon chutney
1 tablespoon dessicated
   coconut
1 dessertspoon sultanas
1 teaspoon lemon juice
salt
1–2 tablespoons milk or
   cream (can be omitted
   with meat curries)

Chop the onion and cooking apple and sauté in the butter. Then add curry powder, paste and cornflour. Stir until blended, cook a few minutes and then stir in stock. Bring to the boil, stirring all the time. Add chutney, coconut and sultanas. Cover and simmer for at least 1 hour. Stir in the lemon juice, add seasoning and the milk or cream.

354 *Economical Spanish sauce*

1 oz. dripping
1 sliced onion
1 oz. flour
1 pint stock or water
1 sliced carrot

2 oz. mushrooms stalks
pinch ground mace
celery, salt, pepper
1 tablespoon tomato ketchup

Melt the dripping and fry the onion slowly to a golden-brown, add the flour and cook until lightly browned, stirring occasionally. Pour in the stock carefully and bring to the boil, stirring, add the carrot, mushroom stalks, mace, celery salt and pepper, cover and simmer for 30–40 minutes, stirring now and then. Strain the sauce, stir in the tomato ketchup and re-heat. Use as required.

355 Espagnole sauce

Add a few mushrooms, piece of bacon, onion and carrot to brown sauce (see Recipe 350). Simmer until tender and sauce very thick. Sieve and re-heat with little smooth tomato pulp and sherry. Serve with meat dishes.

356 Variations on Espagnole sauce

(1) Madeira sauce

Serve with meat, especially ham but add Madeira instead of sherry.

(2) Hunter sauce or sauce chasseur

Follow directions for making espagnole sauce, but do not sieve vegetables.

357 Mandarin orange sauce

1 can mandarin oranges
2 tablespoons butter
2 oz. chopped celery
1 level tablespoon cornflour
2 tablespoons wine vinegar
1 teaspoon soy sauce

Drain mandarin orange segments, reserving syrup. Melt butter in frying pan and sauté celery. Add orange syrup and cornflour, stirring until transparent. Add vinegar, soy sauce and orange sections. Heat. Serve in separate bowl as sauce for fritters and ham.

358 Orange and port wine sauce

Peel 2 oranges and remove white pith from the skin. Cut this into very narrow ribbons. Simmer in a little water until tender. Make brown sauce with stock from giblets but add a little port wine and the orange strips.

359 Poivrade sauce

Ingredients as either brown sauce (see Recipe 350) or better still espagnole sauce (see Recipe 355) but to give the pepper taste, simmer approximately 12 peppercorns in the sauce and flavour with brandy.

360 Tomato sauce

1 oz. butter
1 small onion
1 carrot (optional)
1 rasher bacon
5 large fresh or canned tomatoes
bay leaf
½ oz. flour
½ pint stock or liquid from can of tomatoes
salt and pepper
good pinch sugar

Heat the butter and toss the diced onion, carrot and bacon in this. Do not brown. Add tomatoes and bay leaf, and simmer (for a few minutes with canned tomatoes and rather longer with fresh tomatoes). Blend the flour with the stock, add to the ingredients and simmer gently for about 30 minutes. Stir from time to time. Rub through a sieve, add seasoning and sugar and re-heat.

361 Classic mayonnaise

1 egg yolk
good pinch salt, pepper and mustard
2-4 tablespoons olive oil
1 dessertspoon vinegar
1 dessertspoon warm water

Put the egg yolk and seasonings into a basin. Gradually beat in the oil, drop by drop, stirring all the time until the mixture is thick. When you find it creamy stop adding oil, for too much will make the mixture curdle. Beat in the vinegar gradually, then the warm water. Use when fresh. If using an electric blender, put egg, seasonings and vinegar into goblet. Switch on for a few seconds, then pour oil in steadily.

362 French dressing

1 dessertspoon vinegar
1 tablespoon salad oil
pinch sugar, salt and pepper
1 tablespoon finely chopped parsley or chives.

Mix the ingredients for the dressing together in a basin.

363 Green mayonnaise

Add finely chopped parsley, chives, sage and thyme to mayonnaise. Or use finely chopped mint to serve with lamb.

364 Salad cream

1 oz. flour
1 teaspoon sugar
½ teaspoon salt
good pinch pepper and dry mustard
½ pint milk
1 oz. butter or 1 tablespoon of oil
1 egg
2 tablespoons vinegar

Mix the flour, sugar and seasonings together with a little of the cold milk. Bring the remainder of the milk to the boil, pour over the flour, stirring thoroughly. Put the mixture into the saucepan, adding the butter or oil and beaten egg and cook very slowly until the sauce coats the back of a wooden spoon. Remove from the heat and whisk in the vinegar. Pour at once into a screw-topped bottle. This will keep for some days if stored in a cool place.

365 Tartare sauce

Make any of the mayonnaises and add little chopped parsley, gherkins, capers. If available add also a very little chopped fresh tarragon, or a few drops tarragon vinegar.

NOTE: Other sauces under individual recipes. A complete list will be found in the index.

366 Apple and onion stuffing

3 good-sized cooking apples
4 good-sized onions
1 oz. butter
8 oz. cooked potatoes
½ teaspoon grated lemon rind
½ teaspoon dried sage
pinch thyme
pinch salt and pepper

Peel the apples and chop very finely. Chop the onion and cook for a few minutes in butter. Mix all ingredients together and season well. Use for goose.

367 Chestnut stuffing (1)

1 lb. chestnuts
stock
8 oz. chopped cooked ham
   (optional)
little milk
2 oz. breadcrumbs
butter

Split the chestnuts and boil for about 10 minutes in water. Strain. Remove the skins, and simmer the nuts in stock to cover, until very tender. Rub through a sieve, and add to all the other ingredients. This stuffing can be varied by adding chopped onion, mixed herbs or parsley, but do not use too strong flavours to obscure the delicious chestnut taste. Use for turkey.

368 Chestnut stuffing (2)

1 lb. chestnuts
2 oz. breadcrumbs
seasoning
1 or 2 oz. margarine
2 tablespoons milk

Boil the chestnuts until soft, remove shells and rub nuts through a sieve. Add to the breadcrumbs, together with seasoning, margarine and milk.

369 Cranberry rice relish

12 oz. cooked rice
6 tablespoons Sauternes wine
1½ lb. fresh cranberries
2 oranges
8 oz. canned pineapple
8 oz. sugar
8 oz. mincemeat
8 oz. walnuts or pecan nuts

Allow rice to soak in Sauternes for about 3 hours. Chop or mince cranberries and oranges. Add chopped pineapple, sugar, mincemeat and chopped nuts. Let stand and chill while rice marinates. Combine cranberry mixture with marinated rice. Serve with turkey.

370 Forcemeat stuffing

8 oz. sausage meat
chopped parsley
1 egg
mixed herbs

Mix all ingredients thoroughly. If desired the finely chopped cooked giblets of the poultry can be added.

371 Fried crumbs

Make large crumbs from the bread and fry in butter until crisp and golden brown. This can be done the day before and the crumbs re-heated gently in the oven.

372 Giblet stuffing

As for veal stuffing (see Recipe 377) but instead of parsley use the finely chopped cooked giblets of the bird.

373 Ham and rice stuffing

(for turkey)

8 oz. rice
8 oz. celery or large onion
2 oz. butter
chopped cooked liver of the
   bird
4-6 oz. chopped ham or
   bacon
2 teaspoons chopped parsley
1 teaspoon mixed herbs
1 egg
seasoning

Boil the rice in salted water until just tender. Chop celery or onion finely and fry in the hot butter, add to the rice (which should be well drained), together with the other ingredients. This gives enough for a 12 lb. bird.

374 Oat stuffing

4 oz. breadcrumbs
4 oz. margarine
4 oz. quick-cooking rolled
   oats
4 teaspoons mixed herbs
seasoning
8 tablespoons stock or water

Fry breadcrumbs in margarine until golden-brown. Add oats and other dry ingredients. Moisten with stock or water.

375 Sage and onion stuffing

2 large onions (peeled)
½ pint water
1 oz. suet or butter
good pinch salt and pepper
2 oz. breadcrumbs
1 teaspoon dried sage
1 egg

Put the onions into a saucepan, adding ½ pint water. Simmer steadily for about 20 minutes when the onions will be partly cooked. Remove from water on to chopping board and chop into small pieces. Transfer to a basin then add all other ingredients. Add a little onion stock if wished. This is sufficient for a duck. For a large goose use about 3 times the quantity.

376 Toasted rice stuffing

3 oz. fine breadcrumbs
3 oz. rice
1 pint water
salt and pepper
3 tablespoons butter or
   margarine

1 tablespoon onion, minced
1 tablespoon parsley, minced
3 oz. celery, minced
1 egg, well beaten
1 teaspoon thyme or poultry
   seasoning, as desired

Toast the breadcrumbs. Spread the raw rice in a shallow pan and place in a moderately hot oven (400°F – Gas Mark 6). When the grains turn slightly yellow, stir well. Continue to stir and roast until a good light brown colour is obtained. Watch carefully to keep from burning. Put toasted rice in saucepan, add cold water, and ½ teaspoon salt. Cover with a tight-fitting lid. Set over a hot heat until it boils vigorously. Then reduce the heat as low as possible and simmer for 14 minutes. Remove the lid to permit the rice to steam dry. Melt butter or margarine, add onion, parsley and celery. Sauté until tender. Combine with toasted breadcrumbs and toasted rice. Add egg and seasonings. For all poultry.

377 Veal stuffing

2 oz. shredded suet or melted
   margarine
½ teaspoon mixed herbs
grated rind and juice of
   ½ lemon

4 oz. breadcrumbs
1 egg
seasoning
2-3 teaspoons chopped
   parsley

Mix all the ingredients together thoroughly. The cooked meat from the giblets can be added to make a rich stuffing, if wished. Make 2 or 3 times this quantity for a large turkey.

378 Veal stuffing with bacon

Add 2 or 3 finely chopped rashers of bacon to veal stuffing (see Recipe 377). This is particularly good with veal since the bacon provides moistness as well as flavour.

379 Veal stuffing with gherkins

Ingredients as veal stuffing (see Recipe 377) but add 6 finely chopped gherkins and a few capers. This is particularly good in bacon olives (see Recipe 610).

380 Bacon rolls

Cut streaky bacon into half lengths, roll firmly and thread on a skewer. Either bake in the oven, grill or fry until crisp.

381 Orange salad

lettuce
2 large oranges
small teaspoon mustard

good pinch salt and pepper,
   sugar
1½ tablespoons oil
1½ tablespoons vinegar

Wash and dry lettuce and arrange on small plates. Peel oranges and remove outside pith then, using a very sharp knife, cut sections from the orange. Arrange on the lettuce. Put the mustard on to a flat plate, add the seasonings and gradually blend in the oil and vinegar. Pour over the salad.

OFFAL

382 Bones

Bones of meat, poultry, etc., provide the basis for first class stock (see Recipe 236). The marrow from beef bones can be taken out and served as a savoury on toast.

383 Brains

The brains from calves', pigs' or sheep's heads can be served in a thick sauce on toast or as a sauce. They are very nutritious.

384 Chitterlings (fraise or crow)

This is the name given to the small intestines of a calf. They are sold ready prepared in some pork butchers. Served cold or they can be fried in a little hot butter.

385 Feet

The feet of calf and pig contain a great deal of gelatine and are used to help set moulds and brawn.

386 Ears

Not so popular today, but once considered a great delicacy. The traditional recipe in old country houses was to boil them until tender and serve cold.

387 Faggots

These are made from pigs' offal. Can be bought ready made. For preparing them yourself see Recipe 404.

388 Head

The head of calf is considered the most delicate in flavour but both sheep's and pigs' heads can be used in exactly the same way. For preparing calf's head see Recipe 402, for brawn, Recipe 403 and 495.

389 Heart

The small heart of sheep, calf or pig can be stuffed and roasted (see Recipes 405-406). Ox heart is inclined to be tough and can be casseroled slowly.

390 *Kidneys*

These can be used in a number of ways (see Recipes 407-410), as a savoury dish, served either as a main dish or served on toast as a savoury, with or without fried bacon. The kidneys from pig, calf or lamb are all very tender and can be cooked fairly quickly. All that is needed is to remove the gristle and skin. Ox kidney on the other hand, is much tougher and should be used in recipes with prolonged cooking.

391 *Lights*

These are the lungs of the animal. In some parts of the world they are considered a great delicacy when cooked slowly in a thickened sauce. They are generally bought for animal consumption.

392 *Liver*

This is a very important food and has a rich source of food values, particularly for young children and invalids. Calves' liver has the highest quality. Liver gets tough with over-cooking.

Liver

393 *Melts*

This is the spleen of the animal. It can be baked or stewed for stock. Sold very rarely today.

394 *Pig's fry*

This is the term given to a selection of offal from pig. Directions for cooking it, Recipe 492.

395 *Suet*

This is the hard internal fat from sheep and ox. It provides a first class basis in many recipes. Obtainable today already shredded.

396 *Sweetbreads*

These are considered a great delicacy and an ideal food for invalids since they are easily digested. They come both from the pancreas, throat and heart breads of a young calf, the pancreas being the less fine quality. They must be used when very fresh and directions (see Recipes 421-423) show that before final cooking they are blanched in boiling salted water.

397 *Tail*

It is the tail of an ox which is used in cooking and this provides a first class meal (see Recipe 417), but oxtail can be used in a number of casserole dishes.

398 *Tongue*

Small tongue from calf, sheep or pig can be used in exactly the same way as ox tongue. For cooking and pressing these see Recipes 418-420, but the tongue when once boiled and skinned can be heated in a brown or Madeira sauce (see Recipes 350, 356) and served with vegetables as a hot meal.

399 *Tripe*

Whilst many people dislike this intensely it is a first class food at a very economical price. It comes from the stomach of the animal (see Recipes 424-427).

400 *Trotter*

This is merely another word for feet of the animal. Used generally to describe pigs' feet. They are very good served hot with sauce (see Recipe 494).

401 *Udder*

This is an offal that is very rarely seen and if available is generally smoked when it tastes rather like a smoked ham.

402 Calf's head with brain sauce

6-8 servings

1 small calf's head
parsley
mixed herbs
bay leaves
water to cover

To garnish:
toast snippets

Brain sauce:
brain from calf's head
½ pint white sauce
(see Recipe 216)

Split head down centre. Wash carefully, and remove brains. Put head, parsley, herbs and bay leaves into a pan of cold water, just covering the head. Bring just to boil, remove any scum, then put on lid and simmer gently for about 3 hours. When done, take out meat, chopping neatly. The tongue can be served separately or cut into fingers, and added to cooked meat when serving. To serve, arrange meat from the head on to a hot dish. Pour over brain sauce, and garnish with toast. Soak the brain in cold water, to which should be added a few drops vinegar or lemon juice to whiten it. Simmer 15 minutes in salted water, then strain, chop and add to white sauce.

403 Calf's head brawn

6-8 servings

1 small calf's head
small bunch parsley
pinch mixed herbs

seasoning
8 oz. stewing steak
juice of ½ lemon

Cook as in preceding recipe, but simmer for 1½ hours. Remove all the meat from the bones, cutting this meat into neat pieces, then return this to the stock, together with diced steak and lemon juice. Simmer gently for a further 1½ hours. Put the meat into a basin or mould, strain the liquid over it, and leave to set. NOTE: If desired, half the head may be served as a hot dish, half as brawn.

404 Faggots

1 large onion
4 oz. belly of pork
12 oz. pigs' liver
1 pig's heart or 1 pig's kidney
2 oz. breadcrumbs

good pinch sage
good pinch thyme
1 egg
good pinch seasoning

To make proper faggots you should ask your butcher for a pig's caul if possible.

Slice onion, pork and rest of the offal and simmer in a little water until just tender. Mince thoroughly then mix with the crumbs, herbs, egg and seasoning. Form into balls and wrap in a piece of caul. Put into a greased baking tin and bake for approximately 1 hour in the centre of a moderately hot oven (400°F – Gas Mark 5). If you cannot get a caul for covering, bake in a greased dish, mark into squares, cover with greased foil.

Serve with creamed potatoes, pease pudding or frozen or canned peas.

405 Baked stuffed hearts

4 servings

2-3 sheep's hearts
1 teaspoon salt

sage and onion stuffing (see Recipe 375)
2-3 oz. dripping or lard

Put the hearts into cold water with a teaspoon salt for about 20 minutes. This draws out the blood. Dry the hearts well, then fill with the stuffing. If you find it difficult to get the stuffing into the centre of the hearts, cut them in halves, then put together again and tie firmly with cotton. Put into roasting tin with the dripping and cook in a moderately hot oven (400°F – Gas Mark 5) for about 50 minutes. To serve cut into slices.

406 Braised hearts

4 servings

2-3 sheep's hearts or 12 oz. ox heart
1 oz. lard
1 onion
1 oz. flour

1 pint stock or water flavoured with bouillon cube
salt
pepper

Wash the hearts thoroughly, then cut into slices about ½-inch thick. Heat the lard, fry the sliced onion and heart for a few minutes. Stir in flour and cook for about 5 minutes. Gradually stir in the cold stock or water and bouillon cube, bring to the boil and cook until thickened slightly. Add salt and pepper. Put lid on pan and simmer gently for about 1½ hours. Dish up garnished with macedoine of vegetables.

407 Kidneys with parsley stuffing

4 servings

4 calves' kidneys
seasoning

4 sprigs parsley
2 oz. butter or margarine

Split kidneys lengthwise, without completely severing them. Trim off a little of the fat, leaving a thin coating round each kidney. Season well with salt and pepper. Stuff each kidney with sprig of parsley, close, and secure with string. Either fry the kidneys in the butter or margarine for 20-25 minutes, or lightly brown them in fat, then transfer them to casserole in a moderate oven for 1¼-1½ hours adding a little boiling stock or water.

408 Devilled kidneys

4 servings

2 oz. dripping
2 sliced onions
2 skinned tomatoes
½-1 teaspoon curry powder
1 level teaspoon flour
½ pint stock
6-8 kidneys or 12 oz.-1 lb. kidney

1 tablespoon chutney
squeeze of lemon juice
seasoning
1-1½ lb. creamed potatoes

To garnish:
2 hard-boiled eggs

Heat the dripping then fry the sliced onion and tomatoes until very soft. Stir in the curry powder and flour and cook slightly, gradually adding stock. Bring to boil, add the sliced and halved kidneys, chutney, lemon juice and seasoning. Cook until tender. Make a border of mashed potatoes, put the kidney mixture in centre, garnish with sliced hard-boiled eggs.
This recipe has the advantage that either lamb or ox kidney may be used.

409 *Kidney goulash*

4-5 servings

8 oz. steak
1 or 2 kidneys
4 oz. pork or veal
1½ tablespoons olive oil
2 onions
1 oz. flour

1 beef bouillon cube
1 tablespoon tomato soup
   powder
1 dessertspoon vinegar
½ pint water
dumplings (see below)
little red wine (optional)

Cut meat into cubes and fry in oil until brown. Stir in sliced onions, flour, bouillon, soup powder, vinegar and water, bring to the boil. Simmer 2 hours. Add dumplings and wine. Cook 30 minutes. Serve with cooked carrots.

Dumplings

6 oz. flour (with plain flour
   use 1½ level teaspoons
   baking powder)
water
3 oz. suet, finely chopped
1 tablespoon Romany soup

powder, or flavour
liberally with finely
chopped herbs
including chives or a little
garlic

Mix dry ingredients. Add water to make a slightly sticky dough. Roll into balls and add to goulash 30 minutes before serving.

410 *Stewed kidneys*

4 servings

2 onions
1½ oz. margarine or fat
2 or 3 rashers bacon
4 lambs' kidneys
1 oz. flour
½ pint brown stock (or water
   with a little beef or yeast
   extract)

seasoning
½ tablespoon concentrated
   tomato purée (or use 2
   tomatoes)
cooked rice

To garnish:
parsley

Slice the onions very thinly – fry in the hot margarine together with the diced bacon (care should be taken NOT to brown the onions). Remove fat from kidneys and cut into neat pieces or halve. Add the diced kidneys to the onions and cook for several minutes. Blend in the flour and when this has been thoroughly absorbed, gradually add the stock. Bring to the boil, stirring well and cook until smooth. Season, add tomato purée and simmer for 10 minutes. Serve in a border of cooked rice or on rice. Garnish with parsley.

411 *Liver, fried or grilled*

When frying or grilling liver, do remember that it should never be overcooked, otherwise instead of being moist and tender it becomes hard and dry.

412 *Liver casserole*

4 servings

½ oz. dripping
4 rashers streaky bacon cut
   into strips
1 packet French onion soup
1 level tablespoon flour

1 lb. liver, cut into portions
   for serving
½ pint water

To garnish:
chopped parsley
triangles of toast

Melt the dripping in a large pan, add the bacon and fry for a few minutes. Meanwhile, mix the French onion soup powder and flour together and coat the pieces of liver with the mixture. Add the liver to the pan and fry lightly on both sides. Stir in the remaining soup powder, then the water and bring to the boil, stirring all the time. Turn into a casserole, cover and cook in a moderate oven (375°F – Gas Mark 4) for about 40 minutes. Before serving garnish with a little chopped parsley and triangles of toast.

413 *Liver with orange slices*

4 servings

12 oz. calves' liver
seasoned flour (flour with
   salt, pepper, pinch
   mustard, cayenne added)
1 oz. butter or margarine
1 onion (chopped finely)
2 cloves garlic
1 tablespoon chopped parsley
pinch salt

4 tablespoons stock
2 tablespoons red wine
   (could be omitted in which
   case add about 1
   tablespoon vinegar)
1 large orange
little olive oil
brown sugar

Prepare the liver in the usual way. Slice thinly. Dip in the seasoned flour. Melt half the butter or margarine in a frying pan and sauté the liver quickly on both sides. Remove to the hot serving dish. Add the remaining butter or margarine and fry the onion and finely chopped garlic. Cook until soft. Add parsley, pinch of salt, stock and wine. Bring to the boil and pour over the liver. Cut the orange into thin slices allowing 1 per person, brush with olive oil and sprinkle it with brown sugar, and brown quickly under the grill. Serve with cauliflower and potatoes.

414 *Liver scallops*

4 servings

mashed potatoes
8 oz. calves' liver
¼ pint white sauce (see
   Recipe 216)
little lemon juice
margarine

To garnish:
4 oz. cooked peas

Pipe a border of mashed potato round 4 scallop shells. Mix chopped or minced liver with the sauce and pile into centre of the shells, adding just a squeeze of lemon juice. Brush the potato with melted margarine and put into a hot oven (450°F – Gas Mark 7) for 10 minutes. Garnish with the hot green peas, which should be well drained and tossed in margarine.

415 *Stuffed liver*

4 servings

8 oz. calves' liver
2 oz. breadcrumbs
1 tablespoon evaporated milk
1 teaspoon mixed herbs
salt and pepper
beaten egg
fine breadcrumbs
fat for frying

To garnish:
4 oz. mushrooms
parsley

Cut liver into slices and dry on kitchen paper. Soak breadcrumbs in evaporated milk and stir in herbs and seasoning. Spread between slices of liver. Dip in beaten egg then fine breadcrumbs and fry in fat, being careful not to overcook liver. Remove to a serving dish and keep hot. Slice mushrooms and fry. Place on top of liver. Garnish with parsley and serve with new potatoes and peas.

Stuffed Liver

416 *Liver tournedos and bacon moulds*

6 servings

Tournedos:
12 oz. liver
1 tablespoon seasoned flour
dripping
1 teaspoon cornflour
½ beef bouillon cube
¼ pint water
browning

Bacon moulds:
8 oz. thinly sliced bacon
6 rounded tablespoons
  breadcrumbs
3 rounded tablespoons
  chopped or grated apple
onion soup powder
1 beaten egg

To serve:
12 oz. creamed potato
cooked whole carrots and
  peas

Cut liver in 3-3½-inch rounds. Line 6 greased individual moulds with the bacon. Bind the breadcrumbs, apple and onion soup powder together with the egg. Divide this between the moulds, cover with greased paper and steam 15-20 minutes. Dip the liver in the seasoned flour, fry in the dripping 7-10 minutes. Pipe the hot potato in 6 rounds on to a hot meat dish, top with the liver and keep hot. Strain off the surplus dripping and mix the cornflour, bouillon cube and water in the frying pan, bring to the boil and colour with browning. Turn out the bacon moulds, on to the meat dish between the liver, pouring some of the gravy around. Garnish with carrots and peas.

417 *Oxtail hot pot*

4-5 servings

2-2½ lb. oxtail cut into neat
  joints
seasoning
celery salt
flour
little fat
1 small can tomatoes or
  2 large fresh tomatoes
1 teaspoon made mustard
  (French or English)
2 teaspoons chopped parsley

To be added later
2 or 3 leeks or onions
2-3 carrots
2 oz. mushrooms
small cauliflower
2 sticks celery
little lemon juice

Roll pieces of oxtail in seasonings mixed with the flour, and fry in a little hot fat until rich dark brown. Put into casserole, add tomatoes (skinned and chopped), the mustard, parsley and enough water to COVER ONLY. Put on tightly fitting lid and cook for about 2½ hours in centre of a very moderate oven (300°-350°F – Gas Mark 2-3).
If you find oxtail rather rich, cool, and remove fat before proceeding further. Add diced vegetables and lemon juice and cook for about 40 minutes longer. Do not overcook.

418 *Pressed ox tongue*

Ask for a salted tongue and soak for several hours, or overnight, in cold water. If it is not possible to obtain a salted tongue then cook at once, adding salt to taste. The colour is never as good, though, as when salted or pickled. Put into cold water, bring to the boil, add onion, carrot, bay leaf. Simmer very gently in covered pan allowing 40 minutes per lb.
At the end of this time lift tongue out of stock and allow to cool until you can handle it. Meanwhile, boil stock in open pan until only about ¼ pint.
Remove skin of tongue and any tiny bones at the root of the tongue. Lift into a round cake tin or saucepan, curling it round to give a good shape. It needs to be a fairly tight fit. Dissolve 1 level teaspoon powder gelatine in the stock, strain over the tongue. Put a plate or weight over top to press into shape and leave until cold. Remove weight, etc., dip base of tin or saucepan into hot water for ½ minute to loosen the jelly round the meat and turn out.

Oxtail Hot Pot

Pressed Ox Tongue

419 *Pressed pigs' tongues*

4 servings

4 salted pigs' tongues (if
  using unsalted tongues add
  salt to cooking water)
2 trotters
1 large onion
8 crushed peppercorns

juice 1 lemon
1 bay leaf
salt
pepper
pinch ginger

Wash the tongues and trotters well and place in a saucepan. Cover with water, bring to the boil and skim. Add other ingredients and simmer until tender. Remove the tongues and allow to cool. Trim and skin the tongues and pack into a glass bowl. Pour the strained cooking liquor over to cover. Place a plate on the tongues a little smaller than the diameter of the bowl and stand a heavy weight on the plate to press the tongues. Stand for 24 hours in cold place, or overnight in a refrigerator to set. Turn out to serve.

Serve the trotters separately if wished, hot with parsley sauce, cold with vinaigrette dressing.

420 *Tongue rolls*

4 servings

2 teaspoons chopped parsley
2 teaspoons finely chopped
  onion or shallot
4 fillets anchovy
8 capers

few drops vinegar –
  preferably tarragon
4 slices cooked tongue
4 rashers bacon

Mix together the parsley, onion, chopped fillets of anchovy, capers and the few drops of vinegar. Press together so they form a fairly firm stuffing. Spread over the pieces of tongue; roll the tongue, then roll a rasher of bacon round the outside. Wrap in greaseproof paper and place in a covered dish. Bake for a good 10 minutes near the top of a very hot oven (475°F – Gas Mark 8). Unwrap and serve at once with creamed potatoes and peas.

421 *Creamed sweetbreads*

4 servings

12 oz.-1 lb. sweetbreads
6 tablespoons white stock or
  white stock and milk
little lemon juice

seasoning
1 oz. flour
1 tablespoon milk
2 tablespoons cream

First soak the sweetbreads in cold water for 1 hour. Put into a saucepan and cover with more cold water, then bring the water to the boil and throw it away. This process is known as 'blanching' the sweetbreads and whitens them. Return the sweetbreads to the saucepan with the stock, lemon juice, and seasoning. Simmer gently for about 15-20 minutes. Remove sweetbread and take off any skin. Blend the flour with 1 tablespoon cold milk, add to stock, then bring to the boil and cook until thickened. Lastly stir in the cream.

422 *Fried sweetbreads with capers*

4 servings

2 calves' sweetbreads
3 oz. plain flour
salt and pepper
1 tablespoon olive oil
¼ pint warm water

1 egg white
fat for frying
2 oz. butter or margarine
2 tablespoons vinegar
1 tablespoon capers

Soak the sweetbreads in water for 1 hour, changing the water frequently. Remove skin and membrane and all trace of blood. Blanch (see Recipe 421). Stew the sweetbreads for 30 minutes and then cut into slices. Make a batter by sieving the flour and seasoning into a basin, adding olive oil, and water and mixing to a smooth paste. Fold in the whipped egg white. Dip sweetbreads in batter and fry in hot fat until golden-brown. Drain. Melt the butter and let it burn brown, add vinegar and capers. Serve the sweetbreads with crisp bacon rashers, creamed spinach and the caper sauce.

423 *Fried sweetbreads*

4 servings

12 oz.-1 lb. sweetbreads
1 egg
crisp breadcrumbs
butter for frying
parsley

To garnish :
parsley

First soak the sweetbreads in cold water and blanch them (see Recipe 421), then simmer in salted water for about 15-20 minutes. Skin and if wished press between 2 plates then slide this on the saucepan or dry well, then brush with egg and roll in crisp breadcrumbs. Heat the butter and fry sweetbreads until golden brown. Drain on kitchen paper and serve garnished with finely chopped parsley.

15. Steak with orange salad

16. Grilled liver and bacon

424 *Baked tripe*

4-5 servings

1½ lb. tripe
sage and onion stuffing (see
  Recipe 432)

To garnish:
1 lb. diced mixed vegetables
½ pint brown sauce
  (see recipe 350)

Blanch the tripe as directed in Recipe 425, and spread with the stuffing. Roll firmly, skewer or tie and put into a casserole and bake in the centre of a very moderate oven (350°F – Gas Mark 3), for 1½ hours. Serve garnished with the vegetables, and brown sauce.

425 *Creamed tripe*

4 servings

1 lb. tripe
lemon juice
4 small onions
seasoning

1 oz. flour
½ pint milk
little cream
1 oz. butter

Cut the tripe into neat fingers and put to soak in cold water for 1 hour. Blanch by putting in a saucepan, just covering with cold water, and then bringing the water to the boil and simmering for 1 minute. Throw the water away. Blanching both whitens the tripe and gives it a better flavour. Add just enough water to cover the tripe, little lemon juice, and the onions. Season well and simmer gently for 1 hour. By this time the liquid will only be half covering the tripe. Blend the flour with the milk, add to tripe, bring to the boil and cook until thickened. Stir in cream and butter. The tripe may be removed on to a hot dish and the sauce boiled until it has thickened further.

426 *Creamed tripe and onions*

4-5 servings

1½ lb. tripe
½ pint milk
½ pint water
2 large onions
seasoning
1 oz. flour
1 oz. butter or margarine

To garnish:
parsley
paprika pepper

This makes one of the most economical of all meals and is really delicious if carefully cooked.

Cut the tripe into neat pieces. Put into a pan of cold water, bring to the boil, throw away the water. This improves the colour of the tripe. Put the tripe with ¼ pint milk and ½ pint water, the thinly sliced onions and seasoning into a pan and simmer gently until tender; this takes about 1 hour. Blend the flour with the remainder of the milk, add to the tripe, bring to the boil and cook until smooth. Add the butter and a little extra seasoning if required. Garnish with chopped parsley and paprika pepper.

427 *Tripe mornay*

4 servings

12 oz.-1 lb. tripe
2-3 oz. grated cheese
½-¾ pint white sauce (see
  Recipe 216)

seasoning
2 or 3 tomatoes

Blanch and simmer the tripe (see Recipe 425), then put at the bottom of a small dish. Add half the cheese to the sauce and a little extra seasoning. Pour over the tripe. Cover with the rest of the cheese and the skinned sliced tomatoes. Bake for 15 minutes near the top of a moderately hot oven (400°F – Gas Mark 5).

LAMB AND MUTTON

428 *Lamb and mutton*

See that the lean is dull red, but very firm. The fat should be white in colour. You can differentiate between lamb and mutton – lamb is paler in colour, but in many recipes either can be used. Mutton, naturally, needs longer cooking time in stewing.

Purpose	Cut to choose	Cooking time	Accompaniments
Roasting	Leg Loin and Saddle Best end of Neck (lamb) Shoulder Breast, stuffed and rolled	20 minutes per lb. plus 20 minutes over	Mutton, redcurrant jelly Lamb, mint jelly or mint sauce Fresh peas
Grilling or Frying	Loin chops Gigot chops Cutlets	10-15 minutes	Chipped potatoes Tomatoes Mushrooms Peas Salads
Stewing Braising or Boiling	Neck Breast Leg Shoulder	1½-2½ hours	Mixed vegetables Creamed potatoes
Soups or Stock	Scrag end of neck Head Trotters		

429 *Roast lamb or mutton*

Choose shoulder, leg, loin, breast or saddle.

Give a leg of lamb a new flavour by cutting the skin and inserting just 1 clove of garlic before cooking. Crush the clove slightly before adding to meat.

Try also roasting best end of neck of lamb. The flavour is particularly 'sweet' and the meat extra tender.

430 *Roast stuffed shoulder of lamb*

1 shoulder of lamb

Stuffing:
1 onion
2 rashers bacon (or use 2 oz. bacon fat)
2 oz. soft breadcrumbs
2 oz. chopped celery (or use diced raw potato when celery unobtainable and add ½ teaspoon celery salt)
good-sized grated carrot
1 tablespoon chopped parsley
seasoning

Ask the butcher to bone the shoulder and use the bone for stock. Wipe meat, sprinkle with salt and pepper into pocket where bone was.

Fry finely chopped onion with chopped bacon or bacon fat and then add all other ingredients. Mix well and press into pocket of meat, roast and serve with roast potatoes and braised onions.

431 *Stuffed leg of mutton*

good-sized leg of mutton
4 oz. breadcrumbs
4 oz. rather fat bacon
2 oz. chopped mushrooms
1 large finely chopped onion
little chopped mint or parsley
beaten egg
seasoning

Either get your butcher to bone the leg, or slit it down the side and remove bone. Mix the crumbs with the finely chopped bacon, mushrooms, onion, mint and egg. Season well and press into the slit or cavity where the bone was. Tie securely. Roast in the usual way.

432 *Saddle of lamb*

2 loins of lamb

Saddle of lamb is 2 loins joined together. They can be rolled slightly to give a neat shape and will be roasted (see Recipe 429). If, however, you like the outside to be very crisp do not roll it underneath. This is not so neat in shape but for many people is more appetising.

433 *Honey glazed lamb*

1 leg lamb (the small New Zealand lamb ideal for this dish)
salt and pepper
4-5 tablespoons honey
1 tablespoon chopped mint

NOTE: This is an ideal joint to use over a barbecue fire and so the directions given below apply to that. On the other hand it can be equally well roasted by the usual methods, glazing with the honey mixture at the end of the cooking time.

Wipe leg of lamb over with a damp cloth and trim. Season with salt and pepper and place on spit bar. Heat up fret for 5 minutes. Sear lamb for 10 minutes approximately until lamb changes colour then lower heat. During the last 15 minutes of roasting pour off fat from drip pan, place honey and mint in pan, mix well together and baste joint frequently with this glaze.

434 *Roast crown of lamb with apple and raisin stuffing*

1 crown roast of lamb about 12 loin chops

Stuffing:
1½ rounded tablespoons onion soup mix
1 lb. sour apples
4 oz. seedless raisins
½ teaspoon cloves
½ tablespoon chopped parsley
½ clove garlic, chopped
6 oz. soft breadcrumbs
2 oz. melted butter or margarine
½ teaspoon salt, pepper
½ teaspoon sage
½ teaspoon mace
½ teaspoon nutmeg

For this you need at least 12 loin chops (allow 2 chops per serving). Ask the butcher to chine and roll them into a crown (see pictures, Recipes 474, 475). Crown roast can have stuffing put in before baking; the fillings for crown roast pork (see Recipes 474, 475) are equally suitable for lamb. Roast as in Recipe 428. If you haven't put stuffing in the centre, the joint looks very attractive filled with mixed vegetables, cauliflower or creamed potatoes and each bone should have a cutlet frill on top.

Cook the apples in a little water and sieve. Heat the raisins in a little water until plump then drain. Mix all ingredients for stuffing. Have the loin of lamb trimmed and formed into a crown by butcher. Cover the tip of each rib bone with a raw cube of potato to prevent burning during cooking. Rub the meat well with salt. Fill the centre with the apple and raisin stuffing and roast in a moderate oven (375°F – Gas Mark 4), for 30-35 minutes to the lb. Remove the cubes of potato from the ribs before serving and replace with paper frills.

(Illustrated in colour on the jacket.)

435 *To bone breast of lamb*

To bone and stuff a breast of lamb, follow the step-by-step instructions below. This is a very good method of roasting breast of lamb, as it enables you to use stuffing, which absorbs some of the fat, and also makes the meat go further.

Boning

Stuffing

Rolling and Tying

The Finished Dish

436 *Stuffed breast of lamb*

4 servings

1 breast of lamb (about 2 lb.)
salt
pepper
lemon juice or garlic
2 tablespoons flour

Stuffing:
½ oz. dripping or butter
1 cooking apple
8 oz. sausage meat
2 tablespoons chopped parsley
rosemary
1 teaspoon finely chopped mint or ½ teaspoon mixed herbs

Bone the lamb (see preceding recipe). Prepare the stuffing. Melt the dripping or butter and lightly sauté the apple, peeled, cored and chopped and the sausage meat. Cook for 2-3 minutes then stir in the other ingredients. Wipe the lamb, sprinkle the inside with a little salt, pepper and lemon juice or rub with garlic.

Spread with the stuffing, roll it up and tie with string or secure with metal skewers. Mix a pinch of salt and pepper with flour and rub this into the surface of the lamb. Place in a shallow baking dish and cook (300°F – Gas Mark 2) for about 2 hours. Serve accompanied by duchesse or creamed potatoes, peas and apple sauce.

437 *Stuffed roll of lamb*

4-6 servings

8 oz. pork sausage meat
1 teaspoon anchovy essence
½ leg lamb small shank end, boned

dripping
green salad
3-4 hard-boiled eggs
mint flavoured mayonnaise

Mix the sausage meat with the anchovy essence. Spread this on the boned lamb which should then be rolled up firmly and secured with string. Place in a roasting tin with dripping spread evenly over it and roast in a hot oven (450°F – Gas Mark 7) for 20 minutes to the lb. of meat when stuffed; the heat can be reduced after the first hour. When ready, wipe off dripping with absorbent kitchen paper, remove outer skin, and press meat between two large plates with a weight on top. When cold, serve cut into thin slices with green salad, slices of hard-boiled egg and mint flavoured mayonnaise (see Recipe 363).

438 *Chops en papillote*

4 servings

2 hard-boiled eggs
1½ oz. fresh breadcrumbs
1 small clove garlic
  (chopped in little salt)
½ teaspoon salt

pinch pepper
1 tablespoon chopped parsley
1½ oz. melted butter
4 loin chops lamb

Chop the hard-boiled eggs finely, and mix with the breadcrumbs, garlic, seasoning, parsley and melted butter. Coat each chop with this mixture, wrap in a piece of aluminium foil or greaseproof paper, and bake in a hot oven (425°-450°F – Gas Mark 6-7) for 25-30 minutes. Remove to grill pan. Open the foil and grill the chops until golden brown. Serve with seasonal vegetables.

439 *Cutlets in aspic*

4 servings

1½-2 lb. best end of neck of
  lamb (boned and rolled
  lightly)
1 can condensed consommé
1 level teaspoon gelatine
salt and pepper

½ teaspoon Worcestershire
  sauce
1 teaspoon sherry
cucumber slices
2 stuffed olives

Place rolled meat in greased ovenproof casserole and bake in a moderate oven (375°F – Gas Mark 4) for 1-1¼ hours. Remove from casserole and allow to cool. Cut into 3-inch slices. Blend ½ can of the condensed consommé with gelatine and allow to soften. Heat remaining soup and stir into gelatine mixture, add seasoning. Worcestershire sauce and sherry. Pour enough consommé mixture into a round tin or dish to cover bottom. Arrange rolled cutlets in dish with overlapping cucumber slices up the sides of the dish, and sliced stuffed olives in centre, forming a flower pattern. Allow to set. Pour on remaining consommé soup. When firmly set turn out on to a large serving dish and garnish with cucumber slices. Serve with crisp salad.

Cutlets in Aspic

440 *Lamb with raisin stuffing*

4-5 servings

1 best end neck of lamb
  (boned)
butter

Stuffing:
1 large cooking apple
4 oz. seedless raisins
1 tablespoon chutney
2 oz. white breadcrumbs
salt and pepper
1 small egg

Peel, core and finely dice apple, mix well with seedless raisins, chutney, breadcrumbs and seasoning. Bind with beaten egg. Spread stuffing on lamb, roll lightly and tie with fine string. Place joint in roasting tin, cover with a little butter and roast in moderately hot oven (400°F – Gas Mark 5) allowing 20 minutes to the lb. plus 20 minutes over. Serve with salad.

Lamb with Raisin Stuffing

441 *To fry or grill lamb*

Since lamb contains a reasonable amount of fat no extra fat need be added when frying or grilling. Fry steadily rather than too quickly to give a pleasant crispness to the outside fat of lamb. Have the grill hot to begin with and brown the meat on either side, then lower to moderate to cook through to the centre. Generally speaking mutton is not suitable for grilling or frying.

442 *Cinnamon pot roast*

4-6 servings

1 half-leg lamb (shank end)
1 clove garlic
1 tablespoon flour
1 teaspoon cinnamon
pepper
salt
8 oz. carrots
few strips white part of celery
8 oz. small onions

Stuffing:
1 small onion
fat or oil for frying
2 tablespoons brown
    breadcrumbs
4 oz. pork sausage meat
rosemary (optional)
salt
pepper
1 egg yolk

Chop onion and fry in a little fat until soft. Add crumbs, sausage meat, rosemary, seasoning and bind with egg yolk.

Ask butcher to bone the shank. Open up the meat and spread with stuffing. Roll up and tie in shape with thin twine. Peel and slice clove of garlic and insert slivers under the skin here and there. Rub joint all over with mixture of flour, cinnamon, pepper, and salt. Shake off surplus flour and, using a thick cooking pan, fry joint all over in hot fat until it is evenly browned. Add vegetables and sufficient water and stock to half fill pan. Cover and cook in moderate oven (375°F – Gas Mark 4) for about 2-2½ hours keeping joint moving to prevent sticking and adding more liquid if necessary. Mix a little flour, cinnamon and seasoning with cold water to make a thin cream and strain in liquid from pan. Cook in a separate pan for 6-7 minutes then pour over joint. Transfer from pan to serving dish and arrange vegetables around meat. Serve liquid in sauce boat.

443 *Grilled lamb chops with garlic butter*

4 lamb chops   little melted butter

Garlic butter
1 oz. butter
½ clove garlic (crushed in
    little salt)

Brush the chops with a little melted butter, and put on to the grill pan. Heat the grill till red hot and grill the chops allowing 5-7 minutes on each side. Place a pat of garlic butter on each chop, and serve with baked jacket potatoes and tomatoes.

Soften the butter and mix in the chopped garlic – divide into four portions, and leave to harden.

444 *Cushion chops*

4 servings

4 large lamb chops, boned
4 oz. mushrooms
1 oz. bacon
3 oz. veal
1 tablespoon minced onion
salt

pepper
1 egg
dripping or shortening
flour
dried breadcrumbs

Trim the chops of any excess fat and tie them into neat rounds. Wipe or wash mushrooms. Remove bacon rinds. Put the mushrooms, bacon, veal and onion through the mincer twice or chop finely. Season with salt and pepper and mix in enough egg, lightly beaten, to make the mixture bind. Fry one side of each chop slowly in the dripping to a light brown. Remove the string, spread the cooked sides evenly with the stuffing mixture and leave until cold. Dip the chops in seasoned flour, brush with the rest of the egg and coat thoroughly with breadcrumbs. Fry in deep fat (320°F.), or in a fry-pan (stuffed side down first) for 4-6 minutes each side. Serve with sautéed mushrooms, and asparagus or other green vegetables.

Cushion Chops

445 *Noisettes of lamb garni*

4 servings

1½ lb. best end neck lamb
4 large firm tomatoes
1½ lb. hot mashed potatoes

small knob fat
1 can peas or cooked fresh
    peas
little flour

Divide the lamb into cutlets and remove the bone. Curl the end around the edge of the cutlet and secure with a small skewer. Cut the tomatoes in half and scoop out the centres, keeping the tomato pulp on one side to use in the gravy. Pipe or spread a layer of potato down the centre of an ovenproof dish, surround with tomato shells and place the dish in a moderate oven (375°F – Gas Mark 4-5) for about 15 minutes. Grill or fry the noisettes of lamb about 6-8 minutes on each side, then arrange on the potato. Meanwhile, heat the peas, drain and use the liquor for the gravy, thickening with flour in the usual way. Add dripping from cooking noisettes and the tomato pulp. Pile the peas into the tomato shells and serve.

446 *Saffron steaks of lamb*

6 servings

½ teaspoon saffron
½ pint double cream
juice of 1 lemon
2 lb. lamb from the shoulder
   or leg
2 grated onions

1 teaspoon fresh ground
   black pepper
1 clove grated garlic
   (optional)
little oil
1¼ teaspoons salt

Dissolve the saffron in a little hot water and mix with the cream and lemon juice. Cut the lamb into individual steak sizes. Rub the meat with grated onion, black pepper and garlic. Cover the lamb steaks with the cream and saffron mixture, rubbing well into the meat with the back of a serving spoon. Leave the meat on one side for an hour so that it will absorb the spices. This dish has a better flavour if left overnight. Heat the grill and put a little oil into the grill pan, to prevent the meat from sticking. Place the lamb with its marinade sauce under the grill. Cook with a medium heat and turn once so that both sides are browned. Sprinkle with a little salt before serving.

447 *Kebabs or skewer cooking*

This is a most attractive way of serving foods. Arrange a mixture of foods – kidneys, bacon, sausages, diced steak or tender lamb, mushrooms, tiny onions, tomato halves, pineapple cubes, etc. on to metal skewers. Brush with plenty of melted butter and cook under the grill, turning the skewers to make sure that the food is well cooked. The food can be slipped from the skewer quite easily on to serving plates. Serve with vegetables or cooked rice.

Skewer Cooking

448 *Curried lamb kebabs*

6 servings

6 lamb cutlets from best end
   of neck
salt and pepper
1 large onion
little butter
1 teaspoon curry powder

1 teaspoon sugar
1 level teaspoon cornflour
4 tablespoons vinegar
4 rashers streaky bacon
12 prunes soaked and stoned

Cut each cutlet into 3 pieces, season well. Chop onion finely and fry gently in the butter, adding the curry powder, sugar, cornflour and vinegar to make the coating sauce. Cool, pour over the meat, mix well and leave overnight. Skewer the meat alternately with the bacon and prunes. Grill gently turning frequently for about 15-20 minutes.

449 *Shashlik*

This is another name for kebabs of lamb. As described above the lamb is cut in squares and cooked on skewers. Alternate squares of bacon can be used with the lamb.

450 *To stew lamb or mutton*

There are many recipes in which lamb is stewed and, so that the meat does not make the stew too fat, it is a good idea to add potatoes to the vegetables. A little rosemary or mint are excellent flavourings.

451 *To braise lamb or mutton*

The meat is first fried in fat and this can be obtained by removing and cooking the surplus fat.

452 *To boil lamb or mutton*

Boiling is a particularly good way of cooking lamb (see Recipe 463). Because there is a reasonable amount of fat on lamb it does keep the lamb moist providing cooking is done slowly. If preparing lamb for an invalid the method of steaming meat (see Recipe 454) is particularly suitable. (Mutton should not be substituted.)

453 *To casserole lamb or mutton*

Hotpots containing lamb are extremely popular and to give a good blending of flavour both onion and potato should be used.

454 *To steam lamb*

Cut off any fat from the meat. Put on a plate with seasoning. Cover with a second plate and steam over a pan of boiling water for about 20 minutes until tender. Transfer to a second hot plate in case any fat has melted on to bottom plate.

455 *American lamb casserole*

4 servings

8 scrag end chops of lamb
seasoning
little flour
2 large onions

4 skinned tomatoes
1-1½ lb. potatoes
2 or 3 tablespoons stock
fat or margarine

Fry the lamb chops (after coating with seasoned flour) for a few minutes then lift out of pan. Fry thinly sliced onions and tomatoes for a few minutes. Fill casserole with layers of meat, onion and tomatoes and thinly sliced potatoes, ending with potatoes. Add seasoning and stock and put small amount of fat or margarine over top layer of potatoes. Cover and cook for about 2 hours in a very moderate oven (350°F – Gas Mark 3). Take off lid and allow 15-20 minutes to brown.

456 *Haricot mutton*

4 servings

6 oz. haricot beans	pepper
1 oz. lard or dripping	few potatoes
1 large onion	
1 lb. stewing mutton	*To garnish:*
1 oz. flour	parsley
1 pint cold stock or water	
4 small carrots	
salt	

Soak haricot beans overnight in cold water leaving plenty of room in the container for the beans to swell. Heat the lard in the saucepan and fry the sliced onions and meat, cut into neat pieces, for a few minutes. Stir in the flour and cook this gently for about 5 minutes, stirring all the time. Gradually add the cold stock or water, bring to the boil, stir well until the stock has boiled and thickened slightly. Add the carrots, salt and pepper, and haricot beans, well drained. Simmer gently for nearly 2 hours. Slice the potatoes on top of the mutton stew, adding a good pinch of salt and pepper. Cook for a further 25 minutes until the potatoes are tender. To dish up lift the sliced potatoes carefully from the stew, put these on to a hot dish, pour the haricot mutton on top. Garnish with sprigs of parsley.

457 *Spiced minced lamb*

6-8 servings

4 oz. butter	$\frac{1}{2}$-inch stick of cinnamon
4 medium sized onions	1 small jar unflavoured
2 lb. lean minced lamb	yoghourt
(young New Zealand lamb	1 teaspoon salt
is excellent)	1 clove garlic (optional)
1 tablespoon turmeric	2 medium sized tomatoes
2½ teaspoons ground	
coriander	*To garnish:*
1 teaspoon ground ginger	cooked rice
½ teaspoon fresh ground	2 tablespoons chives
black pepper	
6 cloves	

Melt the butter in a heavy saucepan, put in the minced onions and cook gently until the onions are browned. Add the minced lamb to which the turmeric, coriander, ginger and black pepper have been added. Stir and cook for 7-8 minutes. Add the cloves and cinnamon, yoghourt, salt and the crushed or grated garlic. Peel the tomatoes and stir into the meat mixture which should now be brought to the boil. As soon as it boils, turn down the heat and simmer with the pan covered for about 20 minutes. Serve on a bed of hot rice and garnish with a little chopped chives. If you use curry powder instead of all the fresh spices listed above, you will need to use 1¼-1½ tablespoons of it together with the cloves, cinnamon and chives.

Spiced Minced Lamb

458 *Lancashire hot pot*

4 servings

1½ lb. middle or best end	about 8 oz. onions (or
lamb	chopped leeks)
2 kidneys (optional)	1 lb. peeled and sliced
pepper and salt	potatoes
1 or 2 carrots	½-¾ pint water
1 piece turnip	dripping

Cut meat into neat pieces, dust with pepper and salt. Put into casserole layers of meat and vegetables with such extra seasonings required. Finish with a layer of thickly sliced potatoes, overlapping. Pour in water, sufficient to come about one third of the way up the casserole, and cover top with little dabs of dripping. Cover casserole and put into a fairly slow oven (275°-300°F – Gas Mark 1-2) for about 3 hours. Uncover casserole about half an hour before, raise oven heat and brown the top layer of potatoes. Serve with pickled red cabbage

Lancashire Hot Pot

459 Lancashire hot pot with cheese

A very delicious flavour is given to the previous recipe if a layer of grated Lancashire cheese is put on the potato about 30 minutes before serving and melted.

460 Irish stew casserole

6 servings

2½ lb. middle neck of mutton
about 2½ lb. potatoes
4 oz. shallots or very small onions or 1 large onion

black pepper
salt
chopped parsley
1 pint water

Trim meat and cut into pieces, rejecting excessive fat. Peel and slice potatoes. Peel onions and slice. Line a casserole with sliced potatoes, then cover with a layer of meat (seasoned) a sprinkling of chopped parsley and sliced shallots or onions. Fill up dish with further layer of potatoes and meat, etc. Boil water and add carefully to casserole. Cover and place in moderate oven (375°F – Gas Mark 4) until contents begin to simmer. Lower heat, cook gently about 1½ hours.

461 Irish stew

4 servings

12 oz.-1 lb. scrag or middle neck of lamb
1 lb. potatoes
8 oz. onions
about ¾ pint water

salt
pepper

To garnish:
cooked peas and carrots

Cut meat into neat pieces. Cut 2 new potatoes in halves, or 1 old potato into small slices. Slice the onions. Put the meat, half the pieces of potato and the sliced onions into the pan, adding about ¾ pint water and seasoning. Bring slowly to the boil, remove any scum, lower the heat, and simmer gently for just over 1½ hours. Add the rest of the potatoes, seasoning, and continue cooking for about 40 minutes. Pile the meat and stock in the centre of the hot dish with the potatoes round and a garnish of the freshly cooked peas and carrots.

462 Braised mutton Bretonne

4 servings

1 oz. whipped-up cooking fat or dripping
1 lb. middle neck mutton
1 carrot
1 onion
1 turnip
2 sticks celery
1 clove garlic (if liked)

1 bay leaf
1 heaped teaspoon chopped parsley
½ pint stock or water
salt
pepper
4 oz. haricot beans

Melt cooking fat in a pan or casserole and, when hot, brown meat well and then set aside. Add the vegetables, thickly sliced, and chopped garlic and brown lightly. Lay the meat on the bed of vegetables, add the herbs, stock and seasoning. Cover tightly and simmer gently, or put into the centre of a moderate oven (375°F – Gas Mark 4) for 1½-2 hours. Cook the beans in boiling, salted water for 1 hour while the meat is cooking. (It is best to soak these overnight in boiling water to which a pinch of bicarbonate of soda has been added.) Dish the meat in a bean border and serve with onion sauce (see Recipe 216) if liked.

Braised Mutton Bretonne

463 Boiled mutton and caper sauce

4 servings

1-1¼ lb. scrag or middle neck of mutton (for a large family a leg of lamb can be used, as shown in picture)

carrots
onions
seasoning
caper sauce (see Recipe 216)

Put the meat into the pan with the vegetables, cover with cold water, bring to the boil, skim. Add seasoning, lower the heat and simmer gently for approximately 1½-2 hours. Lift meat and vegetables on to a hot dish and make the caper sauce, using half milk and half the mutton stock. Extra mutton stock can be served separately.

464 Boiled mutton and quick caper sauce

Quickly-made and delicious caper sauce can be prepared by adding capers to thick mayonnaise and warming gently. Serve over the mutton or hand it round separately and garnish the dish with boiled root vegetables.

17. Braised topside, Stuffed breast of lamb

18. Kidney kebabs

19. Lamb and apple curry, as recipe for Chicken curry

20. Sweet and sour pork, Roast pork with apple and raisin sauce

Boiled Mutton and Quick Caper Sauce

465 *Curried mutton cutlets*

3-4 servings

1 lb. middle neck mutton
  (3 or 4 cutlets)
2 oz. whipped-up cooking fat
1 onion, chopped
1 rounded tablespoon curry
  powder
1 rounded tablespoon plain
  flour
1 apple, chopped
1 skinned tomato (optional)
1 oz. sultanas
¾ pint stock or water
1 rounded teaspoon salt

½ teaspoon lemon juice
1 teaspoon black treacle
1 dessertspoon chutney

Boiled rice:
6 oz. Patna rice
1 pint water
½ teaspoon salt

To garnish:
lemon fans
parsley sprigs

Wipe and trim the cutlets. Melt the whipped-up cooking fat in a pan and, when hot, brown the meat on both sides. Lift on to a plate. Fry the onion to a golden brown in the hot fat, then stir in the curry powder and flour and continue cooking for a few minutes. Add the apple, tomato, sultanas, stock and the salt. Bring to the boil, stirring. Replace the cutlets, cover tightly and simmer gently for 1½-2 hours. Before serving add the lemon juice, treacle and chutney. Wash the rice thoroughly and add to the boiling salted water, keeping it on the boil. Cover and cook over gentle heat 20-30 minutes until tender. If the rice becomes too dry add little extra boiling water. When the grains have swollen to capacity uncover the pan and continue to cook over very low heat to dry rice. This is for about the last 5 minutes of cooking. Shake the pan from time to time to separate the grains and use a fork to fluff up. Arrange the cutlets down the centre of the dish, pour the sauce over and serve with border of the carefully cooked rice. Garnish with lemon fans and parsley sprigs.

Curried Mutton Cutlets

466 *Braised lamb and curried rice*

4 servings

Braise the lamb (see Recipe 462), but omit the haricot beans. For the curried rice, boil rice in salted water until just tender but not over-soft. Strain and mix with a little fried curry powder and onion.

467 *Spring lamb mirabelle*

4-6 servings

1 leg lamb	freshly ground pepper
1 or 2 carrots	1 tablespoon cornflour
piece turnip	1 small can evaporated milk
1 onion	1 dessertspoon capers
strip of celery	1 dessertspoon caper vinegar
small bouquet garni (see Recipe 638)	1 packet frozen mixed vegetables
salt	½ oz. butter

Chop shank end of lamb from joint and put into lower compartment of steamer. Add roughly chopped flavouring vegetables, herbs and seasonings. Add about 1½ pints water. In the top part of steamer place remainder of joint. Sprinkle with a little seasoning. Cover pan and steam joint for about 1 hour per lb., adding a little more boiling water, if required, to maintain approximately 1½ pints liquid. Remove pan from heat. Mix cornflour with 2 tablespoons diluted evaporated milk and water, making a thin cream. Stir in about ¼ pint flavoured liquor from lamb, gradually, following with remaining milk from can. Simmer together until sauce is smooth and creamy. Season to taste and stir in capers and vinegar. Re-heat to simmering point. Cut lamb into slices and arrange on a hot dish overlapping. Trickle some of the sauce over, serving remainder separately. Meanwhile cook frozen vegetables, toss in butter. Serve with lamb. Chopped parsley may be stirred into sauce if liked. Save remaining stock in pan (with knuckle end of joint) for soup.

PORK

468 *Pork*

The lean part of the meat must look pale pink, and the fat white and dry. Pork must never be served under-done. Try to avoid serving pork in very hot weather.

Purpose	Cut to choose	Cooking Time	Accompaniments
Roasting	Loin Leg Bladebone Spare rib	25 minutes per lb. plus 25 minutes over	Sage and onion stuffing Mustard Apple sauce Orange salad
Frying or Grilling	Chops from loin Spare rib chops	15-20 minutes	Apple sauce Apple rings Sage and onion stuffing Tomatoes Mushrooms
Boiling	Head Hand and spring Belly Cuts given for roasting	2½ hours	Salads Mixed vegetables

469 *When roasting pork*

Choose loin, leg, shoulder, bladebone, spare rib. To give pork a delicious flavour when roasting, mix a little finely chopped onion with salt, pepper and dry mustard, then rub the meat with lard or olive oil and sprinkle the onion mixture over this.

If roasting in a covered roasting tin or in foil remove the lid or foil a good 30-45 minutes before serving to allow the crackling to become crisp.

Always rub fat of pork with lard or oil and season before roasting to give a good crackling, see below.

Start in a really hot oven and allow time shown in table above OR reduce the heat after first 30 minutes to moderate and cook more slowly allowing about 35 minutes per lb.

470 *Roast loin of pork*

See that the loin is deeply and evenly scored. Rub over lightly with lard and sprinkle liberally with salt. Roast as table (see Recipe 468).

Serve with sage and onion stuffing or apple sauce. Make stuffing little stiffer than usual, form into balls. Put into halved peeled dessert pears and put round pork. Roast for the last 45 minutes of cooking time.

471 Stuffed boned loin of pork

8 servings

3-4 lb. piece of loin of pork
lard or oil
salt

For stuffing:
8 oz. fine white breadcrumbs
1 teaspoon sage
1½ oz. chopped walnuts
1 tablespoon chopped parsley
1 teaspoon grated lemon rind
salt
pepper
1 egg
milk to bind

Make sure your butcher scores the rind deeply and evenly as this is half the secret of good crackling. Mix all the stuffing ingredients together thoroughly and stuff the loin. Roll and tie securely in 3 places. Rub the joint over lightly with lard or oil and sprinkle generously with salt. This is the other half of good crackling. Place in the middle of hot oven (450°F – Gas Mark 7) and roast as table.

---

472 Roast pork with apple and raisin sauce

6 servings

3 lb. loin pork
little melted fat or oil
seasoning
¼ pint cider
1 lb. small onions or shallots

For the sauce:
1 lb. cooking apples
1 tablespoon sugar
2 oz. stoned raisins
juice ½ lemon
¼ teaspoon powdered ginger

Score the fat and brush with fat or oil and sprinkle very lightly with salt. Weigh and allow 45-50 minutes per lb. and 50 minutes over (for slow roasting at a higher temperature, weigh after stuffing meat). Stand on rack in the roasting tin and pour the cider into the tin. Boil the onions for 25 minutes in well seasoned water, drain, add to meat tin 30 minutes before end of cooking time. Peel, core and slice the apples and simmer with the other ingredients needed for the sauce. Serve the pork sliced with the onions and the sauce.

---

473 Pork with green pea stuffing

8 servings

3-4 lb. loin of pork with
   kidney

Stuffing:
kidney from loin
1 can condensed green pea
   soup
2 oz. breadcrumbs
1 egg yolk
salt and pepper
2 oz. lard

Bone pork and score rind. To make stuffing, remove core from kidney and chop the kidney finely. Mix the condensed green pea soup with breadcrumbs, egg yolk and seasoning, kidney and lard. Spread on inside of meat, roll tightly and secure with string or skewers. Place meat in roasting tin and cook as Recipe 468.

Pork with Green Pea Stuffing

---

474 Fruited rice filled crown roast of pork

1 crown roast of pork 16-24
   ribs
   (allow 2 ribs per serving)
salt and pepper

Stuffing:
12 oz. cubed, pared apples
5 oz. chopped celery
5 oz. chopped onion
2 oz. dripping
6-8 oz. cooked rice

3 oz. raisins
1 teaspoon grated lemon peel
1 teaspoon salt
pinch, thyme, rosemary,
   marjoram and pepper

To garnish:
parsley

Ask butcher to prepare crown roast of pork. Wipe with damp cloth. Season inside and out with salt and pepper. Place roast on roasting dish. If desired rib ends may be covered with pieces of bacon or aluminium foil. Bake (350°F – Gas Mark 3) for about 2½-3 hours, or until meat is tender. Sauté apples, celery and onion in meat dripping until tender but not brown. Add cooked rice, raisins, lemon peel, seasonings and herbs. Mix well. About 45 minutes before the roast is done, remove from oven and fill centre of roast with rice dressing. Cover with aluminium foil (this is to prevent rice from becoming too dry) and return to oven to finish cooking. Garnish with parsley.

Fruited Rice-Filled Crown Roast of Pork

Crown Roast of Pork with Orange Cranberry Dressing

475 *Crown roast of pork with orange cranberry dressing*

6 lb. crown roast of pork
(14-16 chops)
(allow 2 ribs per serving)

orange cranberry dressing
(see below)
preserved oranges filled with
cranberry sauce (see below)

Place roast, rib-ends up, on rack in shallow roasting pan. Fill centre with orange cranberry dressing. Cover rib ends with aluminium foil during roasting. Roast in slow oven (325°F – Gas Mark 2-3) about 3½ hours (35 minutes per lb.) or until meat thermometer registers 185°.

NOTE: If dressing browns too quickly, cover with foil also. Garnish with filled preserved oranges.

476 *Orange cranberry dressing*

2 tablespoons grated orange
peel
1 orange, peeled, diced
6 oz. fresh or frozen
cranberries, chopped
8 oz. bread cubes
2 tablespoons grated onion

1 clove garlic, minced
2 oz. butter
2 oz. sugar
½ teaspoon marjoram
¼ teaspoon thyme
1 teaspoon salt
freshly ground pepper

Combine orange peel, diced orange and chopped cranberries. Sauté bread cubes, onion and garlic in butter for 10 minutes. Add orange and cranberry mixture and remaining ingredients. Toss lightly and fill centre of roast.

477 *Preserved oranges filled with cranberry sauce*

6 medium oranges
cold water
5 tablespoons salt
juice 1 lemon

2 pints water
2 lb. sugar
2 tablespoons ground ginger
cranberry sauce (Recipe 352)

Wash oranges; grate peel from oranges (about 50 per cent of surface). Cover with cold water. Stir in salt until dissolved. Allow to stand 5 to 6 hours or overnight. Drain off salt water; cover with fresh cold water and let stand for 30 minutes. Drain. Cut large hole in stem end of oranges with sharp knife or apple corer. In another saucepan bring to the boil the lemon juice, 1 quart water, sugar and ginger. Add drained oranges. Bring to the boil and simmer uncovered 1 hour, until oranges are tender and clear. Leave oranges in syrup to cool. Drain and fill cavity with chilled cranberry sauce.

478 *Baked Creole chops*

4 servings

4 loin pork chops
1 oz. lard
1 large onion
1 green pepper

1 can condensed tomato soup
or tomato sauce (see
Recipe 360)

Trim chops and fry in melted fat until golden brown. Cut 4 rings from onion and chop remaining pieces. Blanch green pepper, cut 4 rings and chop remaining pieces. Put chopped onion and green pepper in base of ovenproof dish. Place 4 chops in dish and arrange an onion and green pepper slice on top of each. Pour condensed tomato soup over chops. Cover and bake in a moderate oven (375°F – Gas Mark 4) for 45 minutes.

479 *To grill pork*

Make sure grill is hot. Pork chops or cutlets have the bone trimmed to look more attractive. They are cut from the loin. They need little basting, since there is generally a good distribution of fat and lean. Once the outside of the meat has been sealed, turn the heat low to make sure the chops are well cooked through to the centre. Serve with apple sauce (see Recipe 347), orange salad (see Recipe 381), sage and onion stuffing (see Recipe 375) or with grilled tomatoes, mushrooms.

480 To fry pork

Pork should be fried steadily so that you draw the fat from the meat and no extra fat is then required. Brown it on both sides lightly in the pan then lower the heat and cook steadily through to the centre.

481 Fried pork and green beans

4 servings

12 oz. lean pork (from hand and spring)
1 oz. lard
1 sliced onion or shredded leek

1 lb. green beans (fresh or frozen)
1 tablespoon soya sauce* or Worcestershire sauce
pepper

*soya sauce is stocked by leading grocers.

Cut the pork into thin strips. Fry in the lard with the onion or leek for 5 minutes over moderate heat. Add the beans and toss together 5-6 minutes more. Pour in the soya sauce and season with pepper. Serve very hot. This is delicious with boiled or fried rice or noodles.

Fried Pork and Green Beans

482 Grilled peppered pork chops

6 servings

6 thin pork chops
melted lard
salt

¼ oz. black peppercorns, crushed

Brush the chops over with melted lard and sprinkle with salt. Put the crushed peppercorns evenly over the chops and grill thoroughly, about 5 minutes each side, over a glowing charcoal barbecue or under moderately hot grill.

483 Mixed pork and bacon grill

4 servings

4 small trimmed pork chops
seasoning
2 pig's kidneys
4 pork chipolata sausages

4 rashers streaky, rolled and skewered bacon
2 tomatoes
4 large mushrooms
1 oz. lard

Season the chops and start to grill. After grilling the chops for 3 minutes each side, season the kidneys, split into 2 and add them and the sausages to the grill pan. After a further 2 minutes each side add the curled bacon rashers, tomato halves and mushrooms seasoned and brushed over with melted lard. After 1½ minutes each side the mixed grill should be done to a turn.

484 Sweet-sour pork

4-6 servings

1 lb. pork fillet from leg
½ oz. flour
seasoning
6 tablespoons oil
1 clove garlic, crushed
2 tart eating apples
1 medium can pineapple pieces OR cubes
1 green pepper
1 red pepper

For the sauce:
1 level tablespoon cornflour
1 dessertspoon soya sauce*
3 tablespoons vinegar
2 tablespoons sugar or honey
¼ pint chicken or white stock
¼ pint pineapple juice
6 oz. long grain rice

*soya sauce is stocked by leading grocers

Cut pork into 1-inch cubes, mix with flour and seasoning. Heat oil, add garlic, pork and fry until lightly browned on all sides. Lower heat, add cored and sliced apples, chopped and sliced pineapple (reserving juice for sauce), green and red pepper. Continue cooking over gentle heat for 10 minutes, or until tender. For sauce, blend all ingredients together in a basin, put into saucepan, boil for 2-3 minutes, stirring well until sauce is transparent. Pour over meat mixture and serve with boiled rice.

Sweet and Sour Pork

485 Grilled pork chops with braised pineapple

4 pork chops

4 rings pineapple

Forcemeat balls

8 oz. breadcrumbs
salt and pepper
1 teaspoon crushed mixed
  herbs
paprika pepper
1 teaspoon minced parsley

2 oz. butter
2 teaspoons minced onion
1 crushed clove garlic
little milk
few toasted or browned
  breadcrumbs

Grill the pork chops under a moderate grill for 15-20 minutes, turning at half time to ensure steady, even cooking. Take 1 pineapple ring to each pork chop, brush sides with melted fat from pork chops, place under the grill with the chops for the last 5 minutes of cooking. Serve with forcemeat balls.

Mix the breadcrumbs with rest of the ingredients except crumbs, bind together with a little milk to a fine consistency, form into balls, roll in toasted breadcrumbs and fry in pork fat.

486 Nasi goreng

4-5 servings

6 oz. pig's liver
12 oz. lean pork (from the
  hand and spring)
½ onion
1 oz. lard

2 oz. shrimps (optional)
2 oz. sultanas
1 tablespoon soya sauce*
2 eggs

*soya sauce is stocked by leading grocers.

For fried rice:
12 oz. rice
½ onion finely chopped
1 oz. lard
salt

This is a Malayan-Chinese dish – the name means, simply, 'fried rice'. Famous as a Sunday lunch dish in Singapore and Malaya.

Boil rice in salted water, rinse in cold water, then allow to cool and dry. Cut the liver and pork into very thin strips and fry them quickly, with ½ onion finely chopped, in ½ oz. lard for about 5 minutes. Add the shrimps, sultanas, and finally the soya sauce. Turn into a dish to keep hot. Meanwhile fry the other ½ onion (chopped) with the rice in 1 oz. lard. Season with salt and when golden brown turn into a bowl putting the liver, pork, onions, shrimps on top. Place in a warm oven. Very quickly beat the eggs and make an omelette with ½ oz. lard. Slice the omelette into thin strips and scatter over the dish. Serve at once.

Grilled Pork Chops with Braised Pineapple and Forcemeat Balls

Nasi Goreng

487 Pork loaf

4 servings

1 lb. cooked minced pork
½ cooked onion
1 oz. breadcrumbs
½ oz. crumbled cornflakes
¼ teaspoon chopped fresh
  sage

½ teaspoon chopped fresh
  rosemary or thyme
salt
pepper
1 egg
¼ pint water or stock

Mix the minced pork, chopped onion, breadcrumbs and crumbled cornflakes with the herbs, salt and pepper. Bind with the beaten egg and water. Mix well, then pour into a baking tin which has been well greased and scattered thickly with breadcrumbs. Bake in centre of a moderate oven (375°F – Gas Mark 4) for 1 hour. Eat with hot apple sauce.

Pork Loaf

488 *Pork and bacon galantine*

4-5 servings

1 lb. pork belly (boned)	salt
8 oz. collar bacon	pepper
2 small onions	2 eggs
1 clove garlic (optional)	2 rashers fat bacon
1 teaspoon mixed herbs	2 long rashers lean bacon
12 crushed peppercorns	breadcrumbs

Put the pork, collar bacon, onions and garlic (if used) through the fine plate of a mincer twice. Thoroughly mix in the herbs, peppercorns, salt and pepper. Work in the beaten eggs to bind. Well grease a piece of greaseproof paper with bacon fat, lay out ⅓ of the mixture along the middle. Add 1 strip of fat and 1 strip of lean bacon. Then another ⅓ of the mixture. Repeat with the strips and add the final ⅓. Shape like a Swiss roll, roll it first in the paper and then in a cloth. Tie tightly and simmer for 2 hours. When cool re-tie the cloth tightly and place a flat tray with heavy weights on it and leave in cool place overnight. Roll the galantine in brown breadcrumbs. To serve, slice thinly.

489 *Pork and bacon croquettes*

4 servings

6 oz. minced pork belly	pepper
6 oz. minced streaky or	1 egg
collar bacon	1 egg and breadcrumbs to
4 oz. white breadcrumbs	coat
1 teaspoon thyme	small quantity milk
salt	lard for deep frying

Mix the pork, bacon, breadcrumbs, thyme, salt and pepper well together and bind with the beaten egg. Roll into croquettes and dip in egg beaten with little milk, roll in fresh white breadcrumbs and deep fry in hot lard.

Pork and Bacon Croquettes

490 *Black pudding*

4 servings

12 oz. stale bread	2 pints pig's blood
2 pints milk	1 teaspoon powdered sage or
4 oz. partly cooked rice	mint
8 oz. finely shredded suet	black pepper
4 oz. coarse oatmeal	salt

Dice the bread, put into a large dish, pour in the milk and put into the oven to warm through. Having cooked the rice, put that also in the oven and heat at the same time. Mix the soaked bread, partly cooked rice, suet, oatmeal and blood with all the seasonings very thoroughly. Put into a large, greased baking tin. Bake for about 35-40 minutes (365°F – Gas Mark 4).
Serve cut in squares with mashed potatoes and pickled cabbage or cold for breakfast.

491 *Black pudding and cabbage*

4 servings

8 oz. black pudding	1 lb. hard white cabbage
3 oz. lard	1 tablespoon soya sauce* or
	Worcestershire sauce
	salt
*soya sauce is stocked by	pepper
leading grocers	

Skin and slice black pudding and fry briskly in hot lard in a big pan. Remove and put on dish to keep hot. Shred cabbage very thinly and fry in fat. When served this should still be a little crisp, therefore, only toss for about 4-5 minutes keeping cabbage moving. Just before serving stir in soya or Worcestershire sauce and seasoning. Make a mound of cabbage with black pudding in centre.

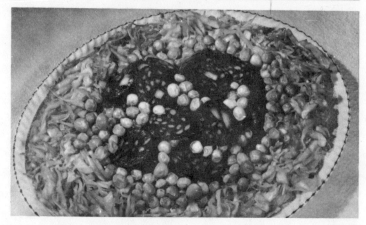

Black Pudding and Cabbage

492 *Pig's fry*

Pig's fry is the description given to a selection of offal from the pig, i.e. heart, lights, liver, sweetbreads. You either fry it in a little fat until tender or bake in the oven, covering with fat.

493 *Luxury pork liver pâté*

10-12 servings

2 lb. pig's liver	1 sprig rosemary
12 oz. butter	¼ pint sherry or port
1 onion	¼ pint tomato purée
1 clove garlic	salt
1 bay leaf	pepper
1 pinch marjoram	

Soak the pig's liver 2 hours in cold water. Heat the butter in a saucepan add the onion and garlic finely chopped and then the liver. Add all other ingredients and cook until tender. When cool remove bay leaf and pass everything through the fine plate of a mincer twice or rub through a sieve or pass through an electric liquidiser. Turn into a terrine or earthenware pot and allow to set. Serve with melba toast. The pâté will keep longer if sealed with a little melted butter over the top.

Luxury Pork Liver Pâté

494 *Trotters in parsley sauce*

4 servings

2 pig's trotters*	salt
1 large onion	pepper
bacon rind (if available)	1 knob butter or margarine
water to cover	1 tablespoon chopped parsley
½ bay leaf	cornflour to thicken

*2 large or 4 small. Very rich, so only small amount used.

Scrub the trotters and place in a saucepan with the roughly chopped onion and the bacon rind. Cover with water, bring to the boil and skim. Add bay leaf, salt and pepper and simmer until tender. Remove trotters and keep hot separately. Strain the cooking liquor into another saucepan. Stir in the butter or margarine and the parsley. Thicken with a little cornflour and water and cook for 2 minutes. Pour over the trotters and serve.

Trotters in Parsley Sauce

21. Irish stew, Southern pork casserole

22. Roast duck

495 Brawn

6-8 servings

1 pig's head or 6 pig's trotters
8 oz. stewing beef (not essential)
2 bay leaves
seasoning
pinch mixed herbs
small bunch parsley

After washing pig's head or trotters well, put into a large saucepan and cover with water. Simmer gently for 1 hour. Remove from the stock, which should be saved. Cut all meat from head or trotters, removing any gristle bones. The meat and stewing steak should be cut into neat small dice. Return the meat to the stock, adding bay leaves, seasoning, pinch herbs and the bunch of parsley and simmer gently for 1½-2 hours until the meat feels quite tender. Take out the parsley and pour into a rinsed mould or large basin. Allow to set.

496 Pork hot pot

4 servings

2 lb. potatoes
1 lb. belly of pork
1 lb. onions
seasoning
½ pint water
small quantity sage and onion stuffing (see Recipe 375)
1 large apple

Peel and slice potatoes, put into casserole a layer of potatoes, diced pork, onions and seasoning alternately. Add water, cover with lid and cook in centre of moderate oven (375°F – Gas Mark 4) for about 1 hour or until potatoes are soft. Mix the stuffing, spread on top of hot pot, arrange slices of apple in a pattern on top and return to oven for further 30-40 minutes.

Pork Hot Pot

497 Pork bake with apple rings

4 servings

4 pork chops (not too thick)

Baste:
2 rounded teaspoons dry mustard
1 heaped teaspoon soft brown sugar
2 large pinches garlic or celery salt (optional)
1 level teaspoon salt

2 tablespoons lemon or orange juice

Accompaniment:
8 apple rings (cut from 2 dessert apples)
about 1 oz. butter

To garnish:
olives (or capers or black grapes)

Trim chops of surplus fat and put into a greased baking dish. Place apple rings at the sides of the chops (or on a separate oven dish) and dot liberally with butter. Mix together mustard, sugar, garlic or celery salt and salt and form into a thin paste by gradually stirring in the lemon or orange juice. Pour over the chops. Bake towards top of moderately hot oven (400°F – Gas Mark 5) for 25-35 minutes, basting once during cooking. Transfer chops to warm platter and pour the baste from the baking dish over them. Serve with the apple rings garnished with olives (or capers or black grapes). Serve with creamed potatoes and seasonal vegetables.

Pork Bake with Apple Rings

498 To stew or braise pork

If the pork is very fat it is a good idea to cut off the surplus fat, heat this steadily and use it as a basis for frying onions or other vegetables. Put plenty of root vegetables with rather fat pork, when stewing it, to absorb the fattiness.

499 Southern pork casserole

4 servings

4 medium-sized potatoes	1 oz. cooking fat
1 medium cooking apple	1 large onion
4 pork chops	1 medium can tomatoes
1 rounded tablespoon flour	2 level teaspoons brown
1 level teaspoon salt	sugar
pepper	1 rounded tablespoon mild
	mustard

Peel potatoes, cut into thick slices, peel apple, core and slice thinly. Toss the chops in seasoned flour, then brown well in the cooking fat. Leave on one side. Slice and fry the onion. Well grease an ovenproof casserole dish, cover base with sliced potatoes then with a layer of apple. Add tomatoes with brown sugar and mustard to fried onions and heat gently. Season with salt and pour over potatoes and apple. Arrange the browned chops on the vegetables, cover casserole with a lid and bake in very moderate oven (350°F – Gas Mark 3) for 1½-2 hours. Serve with cream slaw (see below).

Southern Pork Casserole

500 Cream slaw

1 level dessertspoon mild	shake of pepper
mustard	2 teaspoons lemon juice
¼ pint soured cream	8 oz. white cabbage
½ level teaspoon paprika	1 medium green pepper
½ level teaspoon salt	(optional)

Put mustard into a small bowl and gradually stir in the soured cream. Add paprika, salt, pepper and lemon juice and toss with the finely shredded cabbage and pepper.

501 Pork rolls in cabbage

4 servings

4 outside cabbage leaves	salt
(with tough stalks	pepper
removed)	1 pinch mixed herbs
1 onion	1 bouillon cube
6 oz. belly of pork	¼ pint boiling water
1 oz. breadcrumbs	cornflour to thicken

Drop the cabbage leaves into boiling water for 2 minutes then plunge into cold water. Finely chop the onion and mix with minced pork, breadcrumbs, salt, pepper and herbs. Roll into 4 sausages and wrap each in a drained cabbage leaf. Make the bouillon with the boiling water and poach the cabbage and pork rolls in it gently for 1 hour. Remove the rolls and put to keep hot, thicken the cooking liquor with cornflour in a little water. Pour the sauce over the rolls. Serve with plain boiled rice.

Pork Rolls in Cabbage

502 Steamed pork and mushrooms

4 servings

12 oz. lean pork (from the	powdered ginger
hand and spring)	4 oz. mushrooms
salt and pepper	

Cut the pork into thin strips and season with salt and pepper and a pinch of powdered ginger. Place in a basin and steam over boiling water in covered saucepan for 15 minutes. Add ½ pint of water and the sliced mushrooms and steam for a further 25 minutes. Serve with boiled or fried rice.

Steamed Pork and Mushrooms

POULTRY AND GAME

503 *To cook poultry*

Poultry when young and tender should not be over-cooked, as over-cooked poultry is not only spoiled in flavour, but extremely difficult to carve. Poultry for casserole dishes should be cooked very slowly, unless in a pressure cooker, so that it becomes tender without being hardened in any way.

Type	How to cook	Accompaniments
Chicken	Young fowls should be roasted in moderate oven, allow 15 minutes for each lb. and 15 minutes over. For roasting see Recipes 509-511. For methods of cooking older birds, see Recipes 522, 540-546. Small broilers (i.e. frying or grilling chicken) can be used in many ways. (See Recipes 523, 537.)	Veal stuffing, bread sauce, sausages and bacon rolls, green salad
Duck	Roasted, 15 minutes per lb. and 15 minutes over. Start in a hot oven then reduce to moderate.	Sage and onion stuffing, apple sauce, thick brown gravy or orange and port wine sauce, orange salad
Goose	As duck (see Recipes 514, 551-553).	As duck
Guinea Fowl	As chicken (see Recipe 515).	As for chicken
Turkey	Roast in a moderate oven 15 minutes per lb. and 15 minutes over for a bird under 12 lb., 12 minutes per lb. and 12 minutes over for bird over 12 lb. (see Recipes 509, 512).	Veal stuffing, bread sauce, sausages, brown sauce, salads

504 *To cook game*

Much of the game available can only be obtained for part of the year and it is an offence to kill it during the closed season. Most game is best if hung for several days. An even longer period is prescribed by many people. Do keep it well basted or covered during cooking so the flesh does not dry.

Name	Important Points	Accompaniments	Cooking Time and Temperature
Capercailzie	This has a whitish breast, a little like turkey, but gamelike legs, etc., almost size of turkey, very rare but delicious	As grouse or turkey	15 minutes per lb. 15 minutes over in hot oven (450°F – Gas Mark 7) for first hour, then moderate (375°F – Gas Mark 4)
Cygnet	Young swan, very rare with fish-like flavour. (Swan and cygnet are classified as protected game in Great Britain)	Sage and onion or chestnut stuffing (see Recipes 375, 367, 368)	Best braised with brown sauce for about 3 hours in very moderate oven (350°F – Gas Mark 3)

Golden Plover As grouse but do not draw

Grouse	To roast (see Recipe 516). Older birds best casseroled in pies, etc. Must be well hung before cooking	Redcurrant jelly or bread sauce, game chips, fried crumbs, watercress	35-55 minutes or approximately 2 hours in casserole
Hare	Excellent when young (see Recipes 566, 568). If older try jugged hare (see Recipe 567)	As Recipes	As Recipes
Leveret	Young hare. As hare	As hare	As hare
Mallard	Wild duck. See duck in table overleaf	As duck	As duck
Ortolan	Imported, do not draw if cooking. Cook as quail in vine leaves (see Recipe 565)	As duck	25 minutes
Partridge	Do not hang too long: 3 days at the most. At its best when legs yellow. Can be roasted when young (see Recipe 518), halved, then fried or grilled when very young. For other methods (see Recipes 561, 563, 564)	As grouse	30 minutes
Pheasant	Roast as grouse (see Recipes 516, 517). Can be stuffed if desired, chestnut stuffing ideal, or use sliced fried mushrooms, alone or mixed with chestnut stuffing	As grouse	15 minutes per lb. and 15 minutes over
Pigeon	Very cheap and excellent value. Roast if young (see Recipes 518, 520). For other methods (see Recipes 555. 557-560, 562)	See Recipes	See Recipes
Plover	As golden plover		
Ptarmigan	This is a type of grouse and should be cooked like grouse (see Recipe 516). Hang well	As grouse	As grouse
Quail	See Recipe 565	As Recipe	As Recipe
Squab	As pigeon (see Recipes 518, 520). Very young chickens are also sometimes called squab	As Recipe	As Recipe
Snipe	Small birds can be roasted when young. Handle carefully as the skins may break. Can also be put into casseroles or puddings		25 minutes
Rabbit	Can be roasted, casseroled, put in pies, etc. (see Recipes 569-575)	As Recipes	As Recipes
Teal	Type of small wild duck. Can be cooked as duck. Excellent with orange salad (see Recipe 381) and bigarade sauce (see Recipe 348) or in casserole	As duck	25 minutes for very tiny bird – up to 35 minutes
Venison	Flesh of deer. Moderate hanging for several days improves flavour. Young venison can be identified by blue vein. Pieces to roast: best end of neck, haunch. Other cuts can be casseroled. Baste well	Cumberland sauce or espagnole sauce (Recipes 630, 355) redcurrant jelly – watercress OR as mutton	20 minutes per lb. 20 minutes over for roasting; 2 to 3 hours casserole
Widgeon	Another type of wild duck. Cook as teal or duck	As duck	25 minutes
Woodcock	Do not draw as intestines delicious. When roasting do put toast underneath (see Recipe 518). Can also be halved and fried	As grouse	25-30 minutes

505 *Pressure cooked poultry and game*

Boiling chickens should be given 7 minutes per lb. and casseroled game approximately 15-20 minutes. However, it is best in a pressure cooker to joint most poultry which means that the breast could be added a little later.

506 *How to draw poultry and game*

1 First cut off the feet, and if necessary draw the sinews from the legs.
2 Hold the bird by the legs and singe if desired.
3 Cut off the head, leaving about 3-inches of neck.
4 Insert a small pointed knife at the end of the spine and split up the skin of the neck. Pull away loose skin, then cut off the neck close to the shoulder. Keep the neck.
5 Remove the crop and windpipe.
6 Cut round the vent. Put in fingers and loosen the inside. Do this carefully so that the gall bladder (attached to the liver) is not broken.
7 Firmly draw out all the inside.
8 Cut gall bladder from the liver.
9 Put the neck, liver, gizzard, heart and kidneys into bowl of cold water. Wash thoroughly, then simmer these gently to make stock for gravy.
10 Wipe inside of bird with a clean damp cloth.

507 *To truss poultry and game*

The purpose of trussing the bird is to keep it a good shape while cooking. Stuffing should be done first.
1 Put the stuffing in the bird at the breast end. If 2 kinds of stuffing are used then 1 kind can be put the other end. Fold the skin firmly over the back at the neck end.
2 Press the legs down firmly at the sides of the bird.
3 Put a skewer right through the bird, just under the thighs. Turn the bird over and pinion the wings with the skewer. Pass string under the ends of the skewer and cross over at the back. Turn the bird over and tie the string round the tail, securing the ends of the legs.

508 *Frozen poultry*

Best results are obtained if the poultry is allowed to thaw out gradually. Do not defrost by immersing in hot water and do not cook when it is frozen.

509 *Very slow roasting poultry including turkey*

Allow 1¼ hours for first pound and then 25 minutes over up to 7 lb. and 20 minutes a pound after that. A 5 lb. bird takes 2 hours 55 minutes, but a 10 lb. bird takes 4 hours 45 minutes. Roast in a very slow oven. To brown bird raise temperature of oven for the last 25 minutes. This is an excellent way of cooking if in doubt as to tenderness of bird.

510 *Roast Chicken*

Chicken should either be covered with fat bacon or with fat of some kind as it is very important for the breast to be kept really moist. Do not overcook. If wished you can turn the bird during cooking so that the breast is downwards and is so automatically basted by fat from the legs. With a small chicken, use one kind of stuffing in both neck and body. With a large bird you can use veal stuffing at one end and a forcemeat stuffing, as with turkey, at the other. (For accompaniments see Recipe 503.)

Small spring chicken when roasted are not stuffed and because there is no fat on them they should be covered with plenty of butter or fat during cooking.

511 *Spit roasted chicken*

The modern spit is ideal for young chickens. Brush with oil or melted fat, put on to the spit and, to give a very moist bird, brush once or twice during the cooking.

Accompaniments: Bread sauce, bacon rolls (see Recipes 349, 380), tomatoes, etc.

512 *Roast turkey*

This can either be roasted in the usual way (see Recipe 503) or use the slow method of roasting (see Recipe 509). Use 2 kinds of stuffing, one the neck end and one in the body. Keep the bird very well covered in fat or cover it with fat and then wrap completely in foil. For the last 30-40 minutes you can remove the foil to crisp the skin.

Accompaniments. Choice of stuffings, veal, chestnut, cranberry and rice, etc., bacon rolls (see Recipes 377, 367-368, 369, 380), sausages. For those of you who like an unusual stuffing for turkey and chicken the following is very suitable.

Mix all the dry ingredients well together in a bowl, season well, and bind with liquids.

Clove stuffing

5 oz. white breadcrumbs	3-4 shallots finely chopped
1½ oz. butter	1 teaspoon lemon thyme
1 large tablespoon chopped parsley	grated rind of 1 lemon
juice of 1 lemon	½ teaspoon ground cloves
1 beaten egg	salt and freshly ground pepper
2 oz. fat bacon chopped	

513 *Roast duck*

For a young duckling a little melted fat can be put over the bird but with an older duck there is plenty of fat under the skin and this will keep the bird moist. After duck has been cooking for 30-45 minutes and skin is beginning to brown take a fine skewer and break the skin at intervals. Be careful not to push the skewer in too far. The purpose of this is to allow the surplus fat to run out and to give you a crisp skin. If the skewer is pushed in too far you will make the fat run into the bird and spoil the texture of the flesh.

Accompaniments. Apple sauce or orange salad, sage and onion stuffing (see Recipes 347, 381, 375). Colour plate No. 22 gives other accompaniments to roast duck. Cook with stuffing. Serve with braised or fried mushrooms and onions (or shallots) and Frankfurter or pork sausages. The sausages should be heated towards the end of cooking time in the duck fat.

514 *Roast goose*

This is roasted just like duck and since a goose is considered by many people to be too fatty, it is important that the skin should be pricked at least once, but preferably twice (see Recipe 513).
Accompaniments as duck.

515 *Roast guinea fowl*

This is cooked as grouse but since it has a very dry flesh a little butter inside the bird during cooking helps a great deal. Serve with watercress. Accompaniments as chicken or spring chicken. (Illustrated in colour on the jacket.)

516 *Roast grouse*

Cover the grouse with fat bacon or plenty of fat and roast in a hot oven for the first 15 minutes. If very young birds you can continue roasting in a hot oven for a further 15-20 minutes but if any doubt as to whether the bird is young and tender lower the heat and allow a good 45 minutes in just a moderate oven. Accompaniments as for all game.

517 *Roast pheasant*

This is cooked as grouse but since it has a very dry flesh a little butter inside the bird during cooking helps a great deal.
Accompaniments as for all game.

518 *Roast partridge, pigeon and other game*

The smaller game are roasted as grouse and pheasant and many people like to put a piece of toast under the bird during cooking to catch the rich flavour. If you have cooked the liver beforehand, this can be mashed with butter and spread on the toast.
Traditional accompaniments for game are bread sauce (see Recipe 349) or redcurrant jelly, watercress in a French dressing, fried breadcrumbs (see Recipe 371) and game chips (see below).
NOTE: It is quite correct to leave golden plover and woodstock untrussed. In other words they are cooked with liver, etc. inside.

519 *Game chips*

Peel potatoes and cut into wafer-thin slices. Dry well and cook in deep fat until crisp and golden brown. Drain well.

520 *Roast squab*

This is the name given to very young pigeons. Small game like this needs approximately 15 minutes per lb. and 15 minutes over, but wrap each bird very well in fat bacon, thinly sliced fat pork, or with buttered foil to keep it moist.

521 *Cottage gourmet chicken*

4-5 servings

1 boiling chicken (about
  4-5 lb.)
2 level teaspoons salt
about 2 pints cold water
1 large onion, skinned
2 medium carrots, peeled
2 sticks celery
6 peppercorns
2 cloves
1 bay leaf

Sauce:
8 oz. cottage cheese
1 pint chicken stock
2 oz. luxury margarine
2 oz. plain flour
seasoning

To garnish:
parsley

Cut chicken into 6-8 portions, then put jointed chicken into pan, add salt and sufficient cold water to cover. Bring to the boil. Add onion and carrots, whole, cut up celery, peppercorns, cloves and bay leaf. Simmer very gently until chicken is tender, 2½-3 hours.
Rub cheese through a sieve. Strain off 1 pint stock. Transfer chicken to a serving dish and keep hot. Melt margarine in a pan, add flour and cook for 1 minute. Remove from heat and gradually add stock. Re-heat, stirring, until sauce thickens, season, then simmer for 5 minutes. Add cottage cheese. Pour sauce over chicken. Garnish with parsley.

Cottage Gourmet Chicken

522 *Chicken with mushrooms*

Proceed as in previous recipe, but add 4 oz. sliced mushrooms to sauce.

523 *Stuffed chicken casserole*

4 servings

Stuffing:
2 oz. margarine
1 onion
2 oz. cooked rice
2 rashers bacon
2 teaspoons chopped celery
  leaves or parsley
seasoning

2 oz. margarine
small roasting chicken
1½ oz. flour
½ pint chicken stock
½ pint tomato juice
about 8 carrots
8 potatoes

First make the stuffing. Heat 2 oz. margarine in pan and fry chopped onion until transparent. Add cooked rice, diced bacon, celery leaves or parsley, and seasoning. Press into chicken and skewer firmly. Put chicken in casserole, breast down. Heat another 2 oz. margarine in pan. Stir in flour, cook for several minutes then add stock and tomato juice. Bring to the boil and cook until thick and smooth. Season. Put carrots and potatoes in with chicken, cover with sauce, put on lid and cook 1¼-1½ hours in moderate oven (375°F – Gas Mark 4).

524 *Chicken and chestnut casserole*

Proceed as previous recipe but add shelled chestnuts instead of carrots and potatoes.

525 *Chicken Kiev*

4 servings

2 small frying chickens
4 oz. butter
seasoned flour

1 egg
breadcrumbs
fat for deep frying

Halve chickens. Carefully remove the flesh from the bones of each half, trying to keep it in one piece, but leaving the drumstick unboned. Now take one of the chicken halves, flatten out the boned meat, put 1 oz. of butter on end away from drumstick and then roll the meat neatly around the drumstick. Follow the same procedure with the other 3 halves. Skewer or tie. Coat in seasoned flour, then beaten egg and crumbs. Fry STEADILY in deep fat for approximately 12-15 minutes, then drain. Pierce the flesh just as serving to allow butter to run out.

526 *Chicken and tomato bake*

4 servings

2 oz. button mushrooms
1 oz. butter or margarine
1 large onion, finely chopped
4 chicken joints
1 oz. seasoned flour

2 large tomatoes, sliced
1 can condensed kidney soup
    and ½ can water
seasoning

Gently fry mushrooms in melted butter until tender, remove from pan. Fry onion until tender and golden brown, add chicken joints coated with seasoned flour and fry until brown on all sides. Place onion, chicken, mushrooms and tomatoes in greased shallow ovenproof dish. Blend the soup with water and seasoning and pour over chicken. Cover closely and bake in a moderate oven (375°F – Gas Mark 4) for 1-1½ hours.

Chicken and Tomato Bake

527 *Golden chicken with peppers*

4 servings

1 chicken (3½ lb.)
3 oz. flour
5 oz. butter
12 small white onions
12 button mushrooms
2 stalks celery

2 red peppers
generous pinch saffron
¼ pint dry white wine
salt and pepper
¼ pint chicken stock
½ pint cream

Cut raw chicken into joints. Coat in 2 oz. flour and toss in 4 oz. melted butter, place in casserole and keep warm. Peel onions, slice mushrooms and sauté them with coarsely chopped celery and red peppers in remaining fat until golden. Dilute saffron in white wine; add to vegetable mixture and bring to the boil. Add vegetables and juices to chicken; season; pour over chicken stock and cream (or milk and cream) and simmer, covered, in a very moderate oven (350°F – Gas Mark 3) for about 40 minutes, or until tender. Drain chicken and vegetables and keep warm in casserole. Pour sauce into pan, reduce to about ½ pint, thicken with 1 oz. flour melted in 1 oz. butter, taste, add additional seasoning and pour over chicken. Serve with rice.

528 *Easy chicken marengo*

4 servings

1 chicken (2-3 lb.)
1 onion
8 oz. tomatoes
2 carrots
2 tablespoons corn oil
1½ oz. cornflour

2 small cans tomato purée
    (approx. ¼ pint)
2 chicken bouillon cubes
1¼ pints boiling water
2 tablespoons sherry
4 oz. mushrooms

Skin and joint the chicken, chop onion, tomatoes and carrots. Sauté the onion slightly in the oil then add the carrots and tomatoes and continue cooking for about 5 minutes. Add the cornflour and mix well and stir in the tomato purée. Dissolve the chicken cubes in the boiling water, pour into the saucepan and stir well. Simmer gently for 10 minutes. Rub the sauce through a sieve, return to the pan, add the sherry and the chicken joints. Cover and simmer gently for about 45 minutes or until the chicken is tender. About 15 minutes before the end of cooking, add the mushrooms peeled and sliced. For serving, put the chicken in a dish and pour the sauce over.

529 *To fry or grill chicken*

During the past years a big market has been created for very young chicken often called spring chickens or broilers. They can be fried or grilled but since the flesh is very delicate, over-cooking should be avoided and they must be kept well brushed with butter or oil. The chickens are easier to cook if halved or jointed.

530 *Crisp fried chicken in a basket*

4 servings

1 chicken (2-2½ lb.)
2 tablespoons seasoned flour
1 small egg
1 tablespoon water
dried white breadcrumbs
Parmesan, or dry Cheddar
  cheese
frying oil

To garnish:
watercress

Cut the chicken into 4 or 6 portions and coat each with seasoned flour. Beat the egg with 1 tablespoon of water. Dip the chicken joints in the egg, drain and roll in a fifty-fifty mixture of breadcrumbs and grated cheese. Press coating on firmly and if possible leave for 1 hour before frying. Heat sufficient oil to give a minimum depth of 1½-inches, and when frying temperature is reached (an inch cube of day old bread should turn golden in 30 seconds) fry the chicken over moderate heat until cooked and golden (this will take from 10-15 minutes depending on size of joint), turning once. Drain, and serve in a napkin lined basket and garnish with sprigs of watercress.
NOTE: Crisp fried chicken is excellent party fare, good served either hot or cold.

Easy Chicken Marengo

Crisp Fried Chicken in a Basket

531 *Fried chicken and mushrooms*

Fried mushrooms are an excellent accompaniment to fried chicken. Fry the chicken first, keep it hot and then fry the mushrooms in the butter remaining. For a very easy sauce a little cream can be added to the residue in the frying pan.

Fried Chicken and Mushrooms

532 Shallow fried chicken

Chicken can be fried in a small amount of fat in a frying pan, providing it is done slowly and turned frequently.

533 Chicken with orange and almond sauce

4 servings

Chicken with Orange and Almond Sauce

1 frying chicken (approx. 2½ lb.)	2 oz. margarine
	3 oranges
salt	1 level dessertspoon castor sugar
pepper	
paprika	1½ oz. almonds, shredded and browned

Cut the chicken into 4 joints and season well. Heat the margarine in a large pan and fry the joints until golden brown all over. Cover the pan, reduce the heat and cook gently for 30 minutes or until the joints are tender. Meanwhile squeeze the juice from 2 of the oranges, remove the skin and pith from the third and cut into segments. Remove the chicken joints from the pan and arrange on a hot serving dish. Drain the excess margarine from the pan and add the orange juice, segments and sugar to the pan. Bring slowly to the boil, stirring, and allow to boil rapidly for 2-3 minutes. Adjust the seasoning, pour the sauce over the joints, sprinkle with the almonds and serve.

534 Chicken Maryland

4 servings

1 frying chicken (1½-2½ lb.)	*To garnish:*
egg and breadcrumbs for coating	corn fritters (see Recipe 535)
	bacon rolls (see Recipe 380)
fat for frying	watercress
	2 bananas

Split bananas lengthways and fry. Cut chicken into 6 joints and coat each joint with egg and breadcrumbs. Heat sufficient fat in a frying pan to give a depth of ½-inch and when hot fry the joints quickly until golden brown on each side, then reduce the heat and cook gently until tender (about 25 minutes), turning once. Drain and serve on a hot dish garnished with corn fritters, fried bananas, bacon rolls and watercress.

535 Corn fritters

1 beaten egg	1 can of corn kernels or frozen corn that has been cooked and allowed to cool
2 level tablespoons self-raising flour	
salt	fat for frying
cayenne to taste	
1 teaspoon Worcestershire sauce	

Make a batter with the egg, flour and seasoning and beat well. Mix in the sauce and the drained corn. Gently fry tablespoons of the mixture in a little hot fat, for 4-5 minutes until golden brown. Turn once during cooking.

536 Grilled chicken

4 servings

1 frying chicken (1¾-2¼ lb.)	¼ teaspoon paprika
1 lemon	
salt	*To garnish:*
about 2 oz. melted butter	watercress
1 level tablespoon sugar	potato crisps

Using a strong cook's knife, split chicken in half lengthways by cutting along the breastbone and down through the backbone. Rub cut lemon, squeezing a little to release the juice, all over the chicken and sprinkle with salt. Brush both sides with melted butter. Place cut side uppermost in the bottom of the grill pan (grid removed) and cook under medium to low heat for 8-10 minutes. Turn skin-side uppermost and sprinkle evenly with mixed sugar and paprika. Continue grilling for a further 10-15 minutes, or until cooked, brushing frequently with melted butter. This rich chicken needs no other garnish than bunch of watercress and potato crisps. To serve, divide each half in half again, cutting between wing and thigh. Serve with caper sauce (see Recipe 216).

Grilled Chicken

537 Country-style chicken

4 servings

1 chicken weighing 2-2½ lb.
  or 2 halves of chicken
½ large lemon
1½ oz. butter
salt
2 rashers streaky bacon, cut
  in fine strips

2 oz. mushroom caps, sliced

To garnish:
bunch watercress
potato crisps

Cut chicken in half lengthwise unless using ready-cut chicken. Skewer each half as flat as possible and rub over with cut lemon. Melt butter in a small pan and brush generously all over chicken; sprinkle with salt. Lay halves skin side down in a grill pan (rack removed) and cook under *gentle* heat, with pan 5-6-inches below source of heat, for 12-15 minutes. Turn, brush with more butter and continue grilling for a further 12-15 minutes with 1 or 2 more applications of butter. Fry the bacon strips and sliced mushrooms in the remaining butter and when cooked add the lemon juice. Serve the chicken with the dressing poured over and garnish with watercress and potato crisps.

538 Orange rice

4-6 servings

1 stick celery, chopped with
  leaves
1 large chopped onion
3 tablespoons melted butter
¾ pint water
½ pint orange juice

2 tablespoons grated orange
  peel
1¼ teaspoons salt
pinch dried thyme
8 oz. rice

Fry celery and onion in melted butter over low heat and in covered pan, do not brown. Add water, juice, grated peel, salt and thyme and bring to the boil. Add rice slowly then reduce heat and simmer approximately 25 minutes until liquid is absorbed and rice is tender, stirring occasionally to prevent sticking and burning.

539 Devilled drumsticks

4-6 servings

1 onion
1 carrot
mixed herbs
bay leaf
marjoram
1-2 packets drumsticks
little water

2-3 oz. butter
mango chutney
salt
garlic powder
cayenne
1 teaspoon dry mustard
breadcrumbs

Dice vegetables and place with herbs and chicken drumsticks in a little water. Bring to the boil, then simmer until the meat is tender. Meanwhile, melt the butter, mix together mango chutney, pinch salt, sprinkling garlic powder, cayenne and mustard. Drain off chicken legs from stock and brush with the melted butter, then spread each leg with the mango mustard. Sprinkle with breadcrumbs and place in a baking dish. Pour the remaining butter over and bake until golden in a hot oven. Serve with orange rice (see Recipe 538).

540 Using boiling fowl

A boiling fowl is a very good 'buy' for it can form the basis of a number of meals. It can either be put in a saucepan covered with water, to which is added bay leaf, seasoning and vegetables or it can be put in a steamer and covered with buttered paper. Some people like to put a boiling fowl in the oven afterwards to crisp.

541 To tenderise boiling fowl

Method 1 – very slow treatment. Put the bird into a large container (a bread bin is admirable when large saucepan is not available) completely cover with water and add seasoning to taste. Steam, without boiling, allow 30 minutes per 1 lb. plus 2 hours over. Make certain the lid fits tightly, and see that the water has only an occasional bubble on the surface.
Method 2 – quicker treatment. Put 1 or 2 potatoes inside the bird, the steam from these helps to make it tender and keep it moist. Put into a steamer over a pan of rapidly boiling water. Sprinkle over a little seasoning. Allow 40 minutes per 1 lb.

542 Sauces with boiling fowl

Hard-boiled egg sauce (see Recipe 216) is excellent, but use ½ chicken stock and ½ milk. Add chopped whites to sauce, pour over chicken and garnish with yolks. Liver sauce is also very good. Add finely chopped chicken liver and a little parsley and cream to white or béchamel sauce (see Recipe 216) also caper sauce (see Recipe 216), parsley sauce (see Recipe 216), mushroom sauce (see Recipe 216).

543 Lemon chicken

4-6 servings

1 lemon
1 large boiling fowl
8 oz. onions, as small as
  possible
2 sticks celery
8 oz. carrots
3 bay leaves
3 white peppercorns

seasoning
4 oz. sliced mushrooms
2 oz. butter
1 egg
4 tablespoons cream
¼ pint sherry
4 oz. blanched almonds

Squeeze the lemon all over the outside of the bird, remove any pips and put the skin inside. Put the chicken with the diced vegetables (leave the onions whole if possible), bay leaves and peppercorns into a casserole, and add water to within an inch of the top. Season lightly. Put the lid on and cook for 3 or 4 hours in a very slow oven (275°F – Gas Mark 2). When tender remove chicken from liquid and keep warm. Fry mushrooms in butter. Beat the egg and cream, gradually add ½ pint of the boiling stock, stirring all the time until smooth and thick. Add mushrooms, sherry and blanched almonds. Replace chicken and surround with the sauce.

544 Chicken and mushroom casserole

4-6 servings

1 chicken
1 oz. flour
seasoning
2 oz. butter

12 tiny onions or shallots
8 oz. mushrooms
¾ pint chicken stock

Joint the chicken and roll in the well seasoned flour. Fry in the butter until golden brown, transfer to a casserole with the onions and mushrooms. Work the stock into the butter and flour in the pan, bring to the boil, cook until thickened.

Pour over chicken, cover casserole and cook in a very moderate oven (350°F – Gas Mark 3), 1¼ hours for a young chicken to 3 hours for a boiling fowl.

Chicken and Mushroom Casserole

545 Curried chicken (fresh chicken)

4 servings

2 oz. margarine or butter
2 onions
1 apple
1 tablespoon curry powder
1 tablespoon flour
¼ teaspoon powdered ginger
good pinch pepper and salt
2 teaspoons sugar
2 tablespoons sultanas or
  raisins

4 tablespoons chopped celery
½ teaspoon powdered
  turmeric
1 small boiling fowl
1 teaspoon curry paste
  (optional)
2 teaspoons jam
1 dessertspoon chutney
1 dessertspoon lemon juice
2 pints water or stock made
by simmering giblets

Heat the margarine in a large pan and fry the sliced onions and apple until just soft. Stir in the curry powder and flour and cook for about 3 minutes. Next stir in all the dry ingredients and gradually add the cold water or stock, stirring continually to keep the sauce free from lumps. Bring gradually to the boil and then put in the chicken, which should be cut into neat pieces. Add all the other ingredients, lower the heat, put on the lid of the pan and simmer gently for 2-3 hours, depending on toughness of fowl, or transfer to casserole and cook in centre of a very moderate oven (350°F – Gas Mark 3). Stir once or twice during cooking to prevent curry sauce from sticking. Serve with chutney and boiled rice or creamed potatoes.

546 Chicken pie

4 servings

small boiling fowl or ½ large
  one with giblets
seasoning
herbs
lemon rind

2 or 3 rashers of bacon or
  pieces of ham
2 hard-boiled eggs
6-8 oz. short crust or flaky
  pastry (see Recipes 207,
  338)

First simmer the fowl until just tender. Cook the giblets as well. When cooking, add seasoning, mixed herbs and little grated lemon rind. Remove meat from bone and cut into small pieces. Mix the light and dark meat together. Chop the uncooked bacon into small pieces. Slice hard-boiled eggs. The giblet meat should be mixed with the flesh as well. Season meat well. Put a layer of chicken meat, then egg and bacon into pie dish, continue until full. Cover with about ¾ pint chicken stock. Put on pastry and bake for about 45 minutes in centre of oven – start with hot oven (425°-450°F – Gas Mark 6-7), then lower to medium (375°F – Gas Mark 4). Serve hot or cold. (Illustrated in colour on the jacket.)

547 Duckling in orange sauce

4-6 servings

1 duckling (3 lb.)
salt
pepper
4 oz. margarine
3 oranges

To garnish:
watercress to garnish

Preheat the oven (375°F – Gas Mark 5). Simmer giblets to make stock for the sauce. Season the inside of the bird with salt and pepper, put 1 oz. of margarine in the body cavity and smear 2 oz. over the breast. Place in a baking tin and cook for approximately 1½ hours, basting once or twice during cooking. Remove all the skin and pith from 2 oranges and cut the pulp across into thin slices. Pare the yellow rind off the third orange and cut it into thin strips, then place it in a pan with water to cover and bring slowly to the boil; drain and set to one side. Squeeze the juice from this orange and, 10 minutes before the duckling is cooked, add it to the roasting tin and baste the bird well. When the duck is cooked, place it on a serving dish. Add ½ pint of giblet stock to the juices in the pan and boil rapidly until the sauce is reduced to a syrupy consistency. Add the shredded orange rind and pour over the duckling. Garnish with the orange slices, which have been lightly fried in the remaining 1 oz. margarine, and watercress.

Duckling in Orange Sauce

548 Casserole of duck with chestnuts

4 servings

1 lb. chestnuts	1 oz. flour
2 oz. breadcrumbs	1 pint water or stock
seasoning	¼ pint Burgundy or port wine
1 egg	2 small onions
2 oz. margarine or butter	1 bunch young carrots
1 duck	1 lb. peas

First boil the chestnuts for about 15 minutes, then remove the skins. Chop or mince half of them and mix with the breadcrumbs and seasoning, bind with 1 egg and 1 oz. of the margarine. Put this into the duck. Heat the remaining oz. of margarine in a saucepan, stir in the flour and cook over a low heat until the flour turns brown. Take from the heat and gradually add the stock or water, bringing slowly to the boil and stirring until a smooth sauce. Add the Burgundy and season well. Put the duck into a deep casserole, pour over the sauce and add the whole chestnuts, sliced onions and whole carrots. Put a lid on the casserole and cook gently for nearly 2 hours in the centre of a very moderate oven (350°F – Gas Mark 3). Add the peas and cook for a further 30 minutes. To keep the duck moist it is advisable to baste it several times with the liquid. Serve on hot dish with the vegetables round and a little sauce poured over. Serve the rest of the sauce separately.

549 Duck and cherries

Cherries, preferably fresh, are an ideal accompaniment to duck. With young roasted duck the cherries can be added to a bigarade sauce (see Recipe 348) or an Espagnole sauce (see Recipe 355).

550 Honey glazed duck

To give a really crisp outside to duck, turn after 30 minutes' roasting and brush lightly with melted honey.

551 Goose with chestnuts

Make a chestnut stuffing (see Recipe 367, 368) but add 1 lb. cooked chopped onions.
Put goose into baking dish and roast (see Recipe 514) or if using an older bird put into a casserole. Cover with 2 pints tomato sauce (see Recipe 360). Cook for 1½-2 hours in very moderate oven (350°F – Gas Mark 3), add 1 lb. shelled chestnuts and cook further 1½-3 hours, depending on size. Allow about 25 minutes per lb.

552 Goose with apple or apple and prunes

Instead of using sage and onion stuffing – stuff the goose with peeled sliced apples and a little sugar or with a mixture of sliced apples and stoned prunes. Garnish with halved lemons filled with apple jelly.

553 Braised goose

Make 2 pints brown or Espagnole sauce (see Recipes 350, 355). Put the goose in a deep casserole, pour over sauce, or add about 1 lb. mixed root vegetables. Season well. Put lid on casserole and cook in very moderate oven (350°F – Gas Mark 3), allowing 25 minutes per lb.

554 Game pies

All game is excellent in pies and you can mix various game if wished. Examples are given in this section, but other game could be used.

555 Grouse or pigeon pie

4 servings

1 grouse or 3-4 pigeons	seasoning
little flour	6 oz. flaky or short crust
1 or 2 hard-boiled eggs	pastry (see Recipes
2 rashers of bacon	338, 207)
1 small finely chopped onion	
4 oz. chopped mushrooms	*To glaze:*
½ pint stock	egg or milk

Cut the uncooked grouse into neat pieces and flour these slightly. Slice the egg or eggs and cut the bacon into neat strips. Arrange together with the onion and mushrooms in a deep pie dish, put in stock. Season well. Cover with the pastry and brush with a little egg or milk. Put into the middle of a hot oven for a good 10 minutes (for short pastry, 450°F – Gas Mark 7, for flaky pastry, 475°F – Gas Mark 8). Put a piece of paper over the pastry, lower the heat (375°F – Gas Mark 4) and cook for a further 1¼ hours. This is an economical way of serving grouse. A small quantity of steak can also be included.

556 Grouse casserole

Use the ingredients as for chicken and mushroom casserole (see Recipe 544), varying the vegetables as desired. Grouse will take approximately 2 hours to become tender.

557 Grilled pigeons mercury

Young tender pigeons can be grilled if kept well basted. Put a small knob of butter inside birds to keep them moist or cut them in half. Brush birds with melted butter and cook under moderately hot grill, putting in extra butter from time to time. For the last 5 minutes of cooking add button mushrooms. Garnish with watercress and rice moulds.

Grilled Pigeons Mercury

558 Pigeon cutlets

4 servings

2 pigeons	browned breadcrumbs
1 or 2 rashers of bacon	fat for frying
(optional)	1-1½ lb. creamed potatoes
8 oz. sausage meat	green peas
1 egg	

Cut the pigeons into halves; then, using a sharp knife, take out as many bones as possible without wasting any of the flesh. Cut the rashers of bacon into very small pieces and add to the sausage meat. Divide this mixture into 4 and press the mixture against each half of pigeon, forming into as near a cutlet shape as possible. Beat the egg, dip the pigeon cutlets into this, then coat with the bread-crumbs. Heat the fat until a faint blue haze is seen; fry the cutlets until crisp and brown on the outside. Lower the heat and cook gently for 10 minutes to make sure the pigeon is thoroughly cooked. Arrange surrounded by border of mashed potato and green peas.

559 Braised pigeons with celery

4 servings

2 large or 4 small pigeons	1½ oz. flour
1 head celery	1½ pints water plus 1 heaped
2 heads chicory	teaspoon meat or vegetable
1 large onion	extract or 1½ pints stock
2 rashers bacon	salt and pepper to taste
3 oz. table margarine	

Wash the pigeons well, dry, and if large, cut in halves lengthways. Wash celery and chicory and divide in 4 lengthways. Peel and chop onion. Cut up bacon, removing rind, and fry until beginning to brown. Remove. Add margarine to pan. heat, add pigeons, and fry until nicely browned. Remove. Add vegetables and fry until beginning to brown, turning over frequently. Add flour, and stir until bubbling. Add water or stock and stir until boiling. Cook for 3 minutes, stirring continuously. If water has been used, now stir in meat or vegetable extract. Add seasoning then return pigeons and bacon to pan, cover, and cook 2-2½ hours in centre of a very moderate oven (350°F – Gas Mark 3).

560 Pigeon ragoût

4 servings

	2 tablespoons Burgundy or
2 large, or 4 small pigeons	claret
2 large tomatoes	few olives
2 oz. dripping	
1 oz. flour	*To garnish:*
¾ pint brown stock	fried bread
seasoning	few glacé cherries

Cut the pigeons into halves. Skin and slice the tomatoes. Heat the dripping in a pan and fry the pigeons on both sides until pale brown. Put into a casserole. Toss the sliced tomatoes in the fat. Blend the flour with the stock, add to the tomato mixture and bring slowly to the boil, stirring all the time to keep the mixture from becoming lumpy. Season well. Add the Burgundy or claret and olives. Pour the sauce over the pigeons, put a lid on the casserole and place in a very moderate oven (350°F – Gas Mark 3). Cook for 1½ hours. Serve with small pieces of fried bread and, to give an unsual touch of colour and flavour, the cherries.

561 Salmis of partridge

4 servings

2 partridges, roasted	blade mace
2 oz. butter	few sprigs parsley
2 oz. small peeled	sprig thyme
mushrooms	4 oz. diced lean ham
1 sliced carrot	2 tablespoons flour
2 sliced shallots	1 pint stock
bay leaf	¼ pint dry sherry

Roast partridges (see Recipe 518). Let them get cold, skin, cut into neat joints. Heat butter, add mushrooms, carrot, shallots, bay leaf, mace, parsley, thyme and ham. Sauté until delicately browned, sprinkle in flour. Let it brown slightly, then stir in stock and sherry. Add skin from birds and simmer until liquid reduced by half. Strain, let it boil up once, add partridge pieces and, when hot but not boiling, serve with fried snippets of bread.

562 Pigeon or squabs with a sharp cream sauce

4 servings

1 onion, chopped
4 oz. lean bacon, chopped
1 bay leaf
1 tablespoon chopped parsley
1 oz. butter
4 squabs or pigeons
pepper and salt
1 pint stock or water
small piece of lemon rind

¼ pint marsala or claret
  (optional)
1 oz. butter
1 oz. flour
4 oz. mushrooms, chopped
1 or 2 cartons soured cream
  (or use single cream and
  1 tablespoon lemon juice)

Gently cook onion, bacon, bay leaf and parsley in butter without browning and place in a casserole. Place birds on top. Season with pepper and salt and add the stock or water, lemon rind and wine. Cover and simmer very gently in a moderate oven (375°F – Gas Mark 4), for about 40 minutes until tender. Remove squabs and strain the stock. Place squabs back in casserole or on hot serving dish. Make a sauce by melting other oz. of butter, stirring in flour and then strained stock. Bring to the boil, stirring. Add mushrooms and simmer 7 minutes. Remove from heat and add cream. Re-heat but do not allow to boil now. Pour sauce over squabs and serve hot. Serve with bacon rolls (see Recipe 380), and salad or green vegetables.
NOTE: A quick and delicious sauce for this is to heat condensed mushroom soup with an equal measure of the strained stock and add to it cultured cream from 1 or 2 cartons.

563 Partridge pie

4 servings

2 large or 3 small partridges
approximately 8 oz. stewing
  steak
2 or 3 rashers of bacon
2 oz. dripping
1 oz. flour
seasoning
4 oz. mushrooms

¾ pint stock or water
2 tablespoons sherry
  (optional)
6 oz. flaky pastry (see Recipe
  338)

To glaze:
egg or milk

Clean the partridges and cut each bird into 4 pieces. Cut the steak and bacon into neat strips. Heat the dripping in a pan. Mix the flour and seasoning together and roll the pieces of partridge in this. Fry in the hot fat until a very pale brown and arrange in a deep pie dish. Put the strips of steak, bacon and peeled, coarsely chopped mushrooms on top. If any flour is left, stir this into the dripping and brown for a few minutes. Add the stock gradually, bring to the boil and put in the sherry if this is being included. Season the sauce and pour over the contents of the pie dish. Allow to cool slightly, then cover with the pastry. Brush with either a little milk or well-beaten egg. Put into the centre of the oven (475°F – Gas Mark 8). After 10-15 minutes lower the heat to moderate (350°F – Gas Mark 4), and continue cooking for a further 1¼ hours. You may find it necessary to put a piece of paper over the pastry after 1 hour's cooking.

564 Partridge with cream sauce

Roast the partridge (see Recipe 518) and, when cooked lift from the tin on to a dish. Pour away all the fat but 1 tablespoon, add 1 tablespoon flour to this and cook for several minutes. Add about ½ pint cream sauce (i.e. white sauce to which a little cream is added) or ½ pint cream, thin cream can be used. Heat slowly, stirring well, then strain over the bird.

565 Quail with vine leaves

Clean and season the birds. Wrap them in a layer of young vine leaves and then in thin slices of fat pork or bacon, or in well buttered foil, and roast (see Recipe 518). Unwrap the birds, the vine leaves can be discarded or served as an accompaniment. Put the quails on toast, spread with liver paste if desired. A little sherry and a few seeded white grapes can be added to the gravy.

566 Hare and prunes

4-6 servings

2 large onions
2 oz. fat
2 oz. flour
¾ pint cheap red wine
1 jointed hare (ask for the
  blood)
2 bay leaves

1 tablespoon vinegar
8 oz. prunes, soaked
seasoning
2 tablespoons redcurrant
  jelly

To garnish:
fried bread

Fry the chopped onions in the fat, then stir in the flour and cook until golden brown. Gradually add the wine, the blood diluted with water to give another ¾ pint liquid. Bring to the boil and cook until smooth sauce. Add the hare, well washed in vinegar and water, the bay leaves, vinegar, prunes. Be sure to put in the liver of the hare. Simmer gently for about 2 hours. Season. Take out the liver, sieve, then return to the sauce with the redcurrant jelly. Simmer for a further 15 minutes to make sure the jelly has melted, then taste. If necessary add seasoning or more redcurrant jelly to sweeten. Remove bay leaves before serving and garnish with fried bread. Serve with redcurrant jelly.

567 Jugged hare

4-6 servings

1 hare, cut into joints (try
  and save as much blood as
  possible)
little vinegar
onion
carrots
2 oz. dripping or lard
2 oz. flour

little port wine
redcurrant jelly
seasoning

To garnish:
forcemeat balls (see Recipes
  377, 370)
redcurrant jelly

Put the liver of the hare on to cook in salted water and boil steadily for about 30 minutes, this will give you good flavoured liquid for the gravy. Soak the hare in cold water to which a little vinegar has been added. Fry the chopped onion and carrot in the dripping, stir in the flour, add enough stock and water to give you 1½ pints. Bring to the boil and cook until thickened. Stir in the blood of the hare, a little port wine, a good tablespoon redcurrant jelly and lots of seasoning. If you've got time, mash up the liver or rub through a sieve and stir it into the gravy. Cover the joints of hare with this and cook very slowly for about 3 hours in either a saucepan or a casserole.
Make a stuffing mixture, roll it into balls and bake for about 20 minutes in a moderately hot oven (400°F – Gas Mark 5). Serve with the hare and have plenty of redcurrant jelly.

568 Roast hare

Hare can be roasted as rabbit (see Recipe 572). It needs plenty of dripping to keep it moist. It is best stuffed with sage and onion or with a chestnut stuffing, (see Recipes 375, 367, 368). You must choose a young hare for this and allow about the same time for a rabbit or little longer for a young but meaty hare.

569 *Boiled rabbit*

4-6 servings

1 rabbit	1 pint water
little vinegar	1 oz. flour
4 oz. fat bacon	¼ pint milk
large onion	
12 oz. diced mixed root	*To garnish:*
vegetables	chopped parsley
seasoning	

Wash the rabbit in cold water to which a little vinegar has been added, to whiten the flesh. Cut into neat pieces. Dice the bacon and put into the pan with chopped onion, vegetables, rabbit, seasoning and water. Put on the lid and simmer gently for about 1½ hours until the rabbit is tender. Blend the flour with the milk and stir into the liquid. Bring to the boil, stirring well and cook until smooth and thickened. Taste and re-season if necessary. Garnish with chopped parsley.

570 *Creamed rabbit*

Follow the preceding recipe, but substitute streaky bacon for fat bacon. Omit root vegetables, using only onion and a few mushrooms. Use a little less water but increase the milk to ¼ pint and 4 tablespoons, and add 4 tablespoons thin cream.

571 *Fried rabbit with tartare sauce*

4-6 servings

1 boiled rabbit (see Recipe	1 tablespoon chilli vinegar
569)	(or use tarragon vinegar)
marinade (see below)	1 finely chopped shallot
egg	2-3 cloves
breadcrumbs	1 bay leaf
fat	1 blade of mace
tartare sauce (see Recipe 365)	salt and pepper
Marinade:	*To garnish:*
¼ pint salad oil	fried parsley

Dry the cooked rabbit well. Bone legs of rabbit and remove flesh from bone in large fillets. Place in deep dish. Combine all ingredients for marinade, mix thoroughly, pour over rabbit and leave to stand for at least 1 hour, turning frequently. Drain pieces well, coat with egg and breadcrumbs and fry in hot fat until browned. Drain thoroughly again, arrange in pyramids on hot dish, garnish with crisply fried parsley and serve with tartare sauce.

To fry parsley
Chop well dried parsley coarsely. Fry in little fat or butter until crisp. Or put in frying basket and cook for a few seconds only in hot fat.

572 *Roast rabbit*

4-6 servings

1 rabbit	fat
either sage and onion	about 4 or 5 rashers of
stuffing, veal stuffing (see	streaky bacon
Recipes 375, 377) or 8 oz.	
sausage meat	

Wash rabbit, as described in boiled rabbit (see Recipe 569), dry well and stuff. Heat knob of fat in roasting tin and spoon the hot fat over the rabbit. Cover top with the bacon and then put a lid on the tin or cover with foil. Cook for about 1½ hours in the centre of a moderately hot oven (400°F – Gas Mark 5), turning the heat down for the last 15 minutes, if necessary. Serve with roast potatoes and a green vegetable. The liver, etc. of the rabbit can be simmered to give stock for gravy. If you are not using sage and onion stuffing, an onion sauce (see Recipe 216) is excellent with roast rabbit.

573 *Rabbit pâté*

4-6 servings

1 medium sized rabbit	bunch of mixed herbs
2-3 rashers of bacon	2 tablespoons claret or
seasoning	Burgundy (if desired)
bay leaves	

Although there is quite a lot of preparation in this dish, its flavour is excellent and is certainly a very appetizing way of dealing with rabbit. First put the liver, heart, kidney, bacon and flesh from the head of the rabbit through a mincer. Add seasoning. Cut all the flesh from the bones of the rabbit. Put the bones into a saucepan, adding seasoning, bay leaves and herbs. Simmer gently for 1 hour. Take out the herbs and boil the stock fairly rapidly until it is reduced to about 1-1½ gills. Put the minced meat at the bottom of a greased basin or mould, then arrange the meat of the rabbit over this. Cut the meat into thin strips and pack tightly, adding a sprinkling of seasoning. Pour over the stock and the claret. Use the greater quantity of stock if not using claret. Cover the basin and cook in the middle of a very moderate oven (350°F – Gas Mark 3) for 2 hours. Turn out and serve cold with a salad or hot with a good brown sauce (see Recipe 350).

574 *Rabbit and bacon pie*

6 servings

Filling:	*Herb shortcrust:*
½ lb. fat bacon or ham	6 oz. plain flour
6 joints rabbit	2 oz. cornflour
1 onion, quartered	pinch of salt
seasoning	3 oz. lard
1 heaped dessertspoon	1 heaped teaspoon mixed
cornflour	herbs
	cider to mix
To glaze:	
egg or milk	

Soak bacon overnight. Cover with cold water and bring to the boil. Add rabbit and onion and simmer for about 1½ hours, until rabbit is tender. Remove rabbit and continue cooking bacon for a total of 2-2½ hours. Allow to cool in the liquid, adding rabbit to keep moist. When cold, remove meat from bones, dice roughly discarding gristle and place in a pie dish. Season well with salt and pepper. Remove fat from liquid, bring one pint to the boil and thicken with cornflour mixed with a little water. Cool. Sift flours and salt and rub in lard until the mixture resembles breadcrumbs. Mix in herbs and form into a firm dough with a little cider. Allow to rest for 15 minutes. Pour enough liquid over the meat to half-fill the dish. Cover with pastry and decorate with pastry leaves. Brush over with beaten egg or milk. Bake for about 30 minutes (375°F – Gas Mark 5-6) and serve with the remainder of the thickened liquid.

23. Grilled chicken joints with caper sauce

24. Rabbit and bacon pie

575 Rich rabbit stew

4-6 servings

1 rabbit	bouquet garni (parsley,
4 oz. streaky bacon	thyme, bay leaf)
18 button onions	2-3 cloves
2 oz. butter	6 peppercorns
1½ oz. flour	salt and pepper
1 pint stock	¼ pint claret (optional)

Joint rabbit, dice bacon and peel onions. Brown onions and bacon in butter and set aside. Then fry rabbit joints until lightly browned, add flour and continue frying until well browned. Replace onions and bacon, add the hot stock, bouquet garni, cloves, peppercorns, seasoning, cover and simmer gently for 1 hour, or until rabbit is tender. About 15 minutes before serving, add claret, and when the sauce again reaches simmering point add chopped rabbit liver and cook for 10 minutes. Serve at once.

576 Chaudfroid of chicken

¼ pint aspic jelly	*To garnish:*
½ pint mayonnaise	pieces of carrot, tomato, etc.
joints of cooked chicken	

Make aspic jelly and when it is cool, but not set, add the mayonnaise. Coat chicken with this sauce and when firm decorate with small pieces of tomato, etc.

577 Galantine of poultry or game

Recipe as galantine of beef (see Recipe 302). While cooked poultry can be used, a far better result is obtained if the poultry is minced while raw. It is coated with chaudfroid sauce (see Recipe 219) and decorated. To make the decorations 'stick' to the sauce they should be dipped in a little aspic jelly.

578 Chicken cream

4 servings

¼ oz. powdered gelatine	1 or 2 eggs
4 tablespoons white stock or	¼ pint cream from the top of
water	milk or evaporated milk
1 tablespoon water	1 tablespoon light sherry
½ pint white sauce (coating	seasoning
consistency, see Recipe	
216)	
1 lb. finely minced cooked	
chicken – as much of the	
breast as possible	

Dissolve the gelatine in the hot stock, first softening it in the tablespoon of water. Mix together the sauce and the gelatine liquid, allow to cool then add the chicken, beaten egg, cream and sherry. Taste and season well. Pour into rinsed mould or basin and allow to set. Serve with plain green salad and fingers of toast.

579 Chicken mould

4 servings

	juice of ½ lemon
1 small chicken	¼ pint white sauce (coating
2 rashers bacon	consistency, see Recipe
1 onion	216)
bunch parsley	tomatoes to garnish
2 bay leaves	
seasoning	*To garnish:*
water	tomatoes

Cut all the meat from the bones of the uncooked chicken. Chop breasts but put all rest of the meat through a mincer with the bacon, liver, etc. of chicken. Simmer the bones with onion, parsley, bay leaves and seasoning and water to cover for about 1 hour. Add ¼ pint of this stock to the minced meat, together with lemon juice and sauce. Press minced and chopped meat into a greased mould or basin and steam for 2½ hours. Cover with white sauce. Garnish with tomato rings and serve cold with peas and buttered new potatoes.

580 Chicken risotto

4 servings

	about 8 oz. chopped cooked
1 onion	chicken
2½ oz. butter	3-4 oz. grated Parmesan
8 oz. rice	cheese
2 pints chicken stock	salt and pepper

Chop the onion finely and fry it in half the butter till soft and transparent. Add the rice and stir for 1 minute or 2 till buttery all over. Pour in the boiling, well-seasoned stock. Stir, cover closely and cook over a low heat until the rice is tender and all the liquid absorbed (about 25 minutes). Stir in the chopped chicken, the rest of the butter and 1 oz. of the cheese, add seasoning and heat through gently. Hand the rest of the cheese round separately and serve the risotto with a green salad. Chopped cooked mushrooms and ham or bacon can be added as well as the chicken and a few peas for colour, if you like.

581 Turkey risotto

As in preceding recipe but add the chopped cooked turkey liver to the rice as well as the turkey meat.

582 Curried poultry and game

Any left-over poultry or game can be heated in a good curry sauce of which there are a number in this book (for example see Recipe 584). Adjust the accompaniments according to whether poultry or game. Game needs a rather sweet chutney, etc.

583 Devilled poultry

A very good way of using pieces of cold turkey, chicken, etc. is to devil it. Make up the devilled paste (see Recipe 539), spread it over the pieces of turkey and heat in the oven or under a moderate grill.

584 Chicken curry

4 servings

1 oz. dripping
12 oz. chopped onions
1 clove garlic
1 small apple
1 dessertspoon curry powder
1 dessertspoon flour
½ pint water
1 chicken bouillon cube
a few drops of liquid
    seasoning
1 dessertspoon lemon juice
1 teaspoon tomato purée or
    1 tomato
1 tablespoon condensed milk
1 tablespoon coconut
1 tablespoon sultanas

cold roast or boiled chicken
    pieces
1 oz. rice per person, cooked
    and drained well

To garnish:
lemon
parsley
paprika

Accompaniments:
crisp bacon
cucumber slices
lemon
banana
grated coconut
margo chutney
salted peanuts
gherkins
chillies

Melt the fat and fry the onions and garlic. Add the chopped apple. Stir in the curry powder and flour and add the ½ pint water and the chicken bouillon cube, gradually bringing to the boil while stirring. Add a few drops of liquid seasoning. Cover and simmer gently for 30 minutes. Add lemon juice, tomato purée, condensed milk, coconut, sultanas and chicken. Heat gently until meat is thoroughly hot. Dish with a border of rice and garnish with lemon fans, chopped parsley and paprika. Hand small dishes containing small squares of crisp bacon, slices of cucumber and lemon, banana and lemon, fresh grated coconut, mango chutney, chopped salted peanuts, fan-shaped gherkins decorated with chillies.

585 Fricassée of chicken

4 servings

1½ oz. butter
1½ oz. flour
½ pint chicken stock

¼ pint and 4 tablespoons milk
1 lb. cooked chicken
little cream
seasoning

Heat butter in pan, stir in flour and cook gently. Add stock and milk and stir until smooth. Put in diced chicken and heat gently for about 20 minutes. Stir in cream and seasoning. Serve with creamed potatoes or cooked rice.

586 Chicken and cucumber salad

4 servings

1 large cucumber
12 oz. cooked chicken meat

Dressing:
2 tablespoons thin cream
2 tablespoons mayonnaise
2 teaspoons lemon juice
1 teaspoon finely chopped
    fresh mint
shake of salt

To garnish:
2 firm tomatoes, sliced
1 hard-boiled egg, sliced

Cut the cucumber in half; thinly slice one half, cut the other into ¼-inch cubes. Cut the chicken into small pieces. Prepare the dressing by mixing cream, mayonnaise, lemon juice, mint and salt together. Stir in cucumber cubes and chicken Set aside in a cool place for 1 hour for the flavours to blend. When ready to serve pile the chicken in the centre of a flat dish, circle with cucumber slices and garnish with sliced tomato and hard-boiled egg.

Chicken and Cucumber Salad

587 Duckling with apricot and almond stuffing

4-6 servings

duckling (3-4 lb.)

Stuffing:
1 oz. margarine
1 chopped onion
1 oz. almonds, blanched and
    shredded
2 oz. white, fresh
    breadcrumbs

1 teaspoon chopped parsley
1 8 oz. can apricots
    drained and sliced
rind and juice of ½ lemon
salt and pepper to taste

To garnish:
orange slices
lettuce leaves

Make stuffing: Fry onion in margarine until soft but not coloured, add almonds, fry for 2-3 minutes. Add other ingredients, mix well. Stuff duckling and put in roasting tin. Cook 1¼-1½ hours (see Recipe 513). Remove from tin and cool. Carve and put on serving dish, garnish with stuffing, orange slices and lettuce.

Duckling with Apricot and Almond Stuffing

588 *Salmis of duck*

4 servings

1 oz. fat, preferably dripping
   from cooking the duck
2 medium-sized onions
1 oz. flour
¼ pint stock (made by
   simmering giblets)

2 tablespoons orange juice or
   1 tablespoon lemon juice
2 tablespoons chopped
   gherkins or sliced olives
seasoning
about 12 oz. cooked duck
slices bread
fat for frying

This is a particularly good way of re-heating left-over duck. Heat the fat in a pan, slice and fry the onions until just soft, turning well but trying not to break them. Blend the flour with the stock, pour gradually into the pan and stir all the time until the sauce has come to the boil and thickened. Add the orange juice, gherkins and seasoning and the pieces of duck. Turn the heat very low and simmer gently for just on 30 minutes. When nearly ready to serve fry 1 piece of bread for each person, pile the salmis on these and serve at once.

589 *Kromeskies*

4 servings

2 oz. margarine
1 oz. flour
¼ pint milk
3 oz. cooked chicken, turkey
   or duck
2 oz. ham or boiled bacon
2 oz. mushrooms
3-4 oz. quick cooking rolled
   oats

1 finely chopped onion
¼ teaspoon mixed herbs
seasoning
1 egg
quick cooking rolled oats for
   coating
2 oz. fat to fry

Melt half margarine in a saucepan, add the flour and cook for a few seconds over a gentle heat. Slowly add the milk. Return to the heat and cook until the mixture leaves the sides of the pan. Chop up the chicken and ham. Melt remaining margarine in a saucepan. Fry the prepared chopped mushrooms, quick cooking rolled oats and finely chopped onion. Add this together with the chicken, ham, mixed herbs and seasoning to the thick sauce. Turn on to a plate and allow to cool. Divide the mixture into pieces and shape into croquettes. Coat with beaten egg and rolled oats and fry in hot fat until golden brown. Serve hot.

590 *Giblet, bacon and egg pie*

4 servings

chicken, turkey or goose
   giblets
very little flour
seasoning
6-8 oz. short crust or flaky
   pastry (see Recipes 207,
   338)

2 hard-boiled eggs
4-6 oz. lean bacon

To glaze:
egg or milk

Simmer giblets until tender, strain off nearly all the stock, keep about 2 tablespoons for pie. Cut all meat from the neck of the bird, chop liver, heart and kidney finely, then dust lightly with well-seasoned flour. Roll out pastry and line a glass pie-plate or sandwich tin with half of this. Cover pastry with half the giblet meat, the sliced hard-boiled eggs and bacon. Pour the reserved stock over it, then cover with the last of the giblet meat. Put pastry over top and decorate with tiny leaves. Brush with milk or a little beaten egg. If you are using short crust pastry, bake in the centre of a hot oven (450°F – Gas Mark 7) for about 20 minutes, then lower heat to moderate for a further 20 minutes. For flaky pastry use a slightly hotter oven for the first 15 minutes, then reduce the heat to moderate for the final 25 minutes.

591 *Turkey with sweet sour sauce*

4 servings

8 oz. chestnuts
½ pint white wine or cider
4 large tomatoes
2 or 3 pieces celery
seasoning

1 good tablespoon sugar
1 teaspoon capers
approximately 12 oz. to 1 lb.
   cooked turkey – cut into
   neat pieces

Split the skins and boil the chestnuts for about 10 minutes, then skin, while hot. Put the wine, sliced tomatoes, chopped celery, seasoning, sugar, capers and whole chestnuts into a saucepan; simmer for about 30 minutes, add the turkey and continue simmering for 20 minutes. Serve with creamed potatoes and Brussels sprouts.

BACON, HAM, SAUSAGES

592 *Bacon, ham and sausages*

Should look moist and not too dry. Bacon may be blanched to remove excess of salt before adding to other dishes. Do not confuse ham and bacon – they have been cured in entirely different ways, giving quite distinct flavours. The hams of the pig are simply the legs which are cut off and are dry cured individually. While the various hams have their own methods of curing they are, unlike bacon, generally unsmoked. It takes from 3-5 months to cure a ham. At the end of that time a perfect ham has a faint green mould, known as the 'bloom'. Never take this off until you are ready to cook it. Gammon, on the other hand, is also the leg of the pig, but this is cured with the whole bacon side before being cut away. It is, on the whole, cheaper than ham and can be used in any recipe where ham is indicated. Naturally where cooked ham is suggested it must be cooked gammon used in its place. When soaking, hams should have 24 hours' soaking before cooking, whereas bacon varies quite a bit. Green bacon, for example, is very lightly salted and needs little soaking at all. The other bacon can be soaked for several hours, up to 24 hours.

Purpose	Cuts to Choose	Cooking Time	Accompaniments
Roasting or Baking	Gammon slipper Middle gammon Back and ribs Joint top streaky Top streaky Prime streaky Thin streaky	20 minutes per lb. and 20 minutes over. If well done bacon is preferred cook like pork for 25 minutes per lb.	Mustard Salads Unusual garnishes such as baked apples, oranges, pineapple, etc.
Grilling or Frying	Gammon slipper Middle gammon Corner gammon Long back Short back Back and ribs Top back Prime collar	Few minutes only for thin rashers, but with thick slices of gammon cook outside fairly quickly then reduce heat to cook through to the middle. Keep gammon well brushed with fat when grilling.	Eggs, tomatoes, mushrooms, etc. for breakfast. Vegetables or salads for main meals
Boiling or Braising	Forehock Prime streaky Flank Gammon slipper Gammon hock Middle gammon Corner gammon Long back Back and ribs Top back Prime collar End of collar Oyster cut	Soak well if you want very mild flavour, then simmer gently for 20-25 minutes per lb. and 20-25 minutes over. Do not boil too quickly. A pressure cooker can be used (see Recipe 604). Ham or bacon stock is excellent for soups.	Any vegetables – beans and peas are particularly good with boiled bacon. Salads, etc.

593 When roasting bacon

Always soak bacon in cold water overnight, before roasting. Choose gammon, slipper, forehock, middle gammon, back bacon or ribs, or a joint of top streaky bacon. To give an attractive glaze the skin can be removed after most of the cooking time, then the fat scored with a sharp knife, a little brown sugar sprinkled over the top, together with a small quantity of mixed spice or a few cloves.

594 Jutland bacon whirl

8 servings

piece of long back (2½ lb.)

Stuffing:
8 oz. sausage meat
8 oz. cooked sieved chestnuts
2 teaspoons chopped parsley
1 small chopped onion
seasoning

To glaze:
2 tablespoons brown sugar
1 teaspoon made mustard
3 tablespoons orange juice

Mix all the ingredients for the stuffing together. Spread over the inner edge of the bacon and roll firmly. Secure with string or skewers and cover with foil or greased paper. Cook in a moderately hot oven (375°-400°F – Gas Mark 4-5) for approximately 1½ hours. If bacon is wrapped well in the paper or foil it will not need basting. Otherwise baste with a little hot bacon fat. Remove the paper or foil and cut the rind off the bacon. Blend the ingredients for the glaze together and spread over the fat of the bacon, scoring this in a neat design first. Return to the oven for a further 25-30 minutes until crisp and a rich, golden brown. Jutland bacon whirl makes a hot meal for 4, with enough over for 4 when cold. Serve hot with Brussels sprouts and roast potatoes, or cold with a salad and jacket potatoes.

595 Bacon baked with sweet-sour sauce

4 servings

4 slices of collar bacon (each weighing 3 to 4 oz.) about ¼-inch thick
3 tablespoons brown sugar
1½ tablespoons made mustard
4 tablespoons wine vinegar

4 tablespoons water
2 tablespoons redcurrant or crab apple jelly

To garnish:
parsley

Soak slices of bacon 2-3 hours in water to cover. Cook uncovered, in a very moderate oven (325°-350°F – Gas Mark 3) for about 1 hour. Mix the sugar, mustard, vinegar and water together. Remove bacon slices to a warmed serving dish, add 2 tablespoons of redcurrant or crab apple jelly to the sugar mixture in pan, cook over a low flame, stirring until the jelly is melted and the sauce slightly thickened and syrupy. Pour a little over the bacon slices and serve rest separately. Garnish with parsley. The dish is excellent served with lightly cooked cabbage or sauerkraut.

596 To bake ham

When ham is baked it is either wrapped in foil or in a flour and water paste as the southern casserole (see Recipe 597). You retain all the flavour of the ham and good soaking is essential.

597 Baked British ham southern style

10-12 servings

5 lb. piece of ham, or you can use boned gammon
1½ lb. plain flour
cold water to mix

small can pineapple chunks
2 dozen cloves
8 oz. demerara sugar

If using ham, soak for 24 hours. If using smoked bacon, soak it overnight to remove surplus salt. Make a plain dough of the flour and water and roll out ⅓-inch thick. Place drained pineapple chunks into the hole left by removing the bone, wrap the ham in the paste and bake in very moderate oven (350°F – Gas Mark 3) for 1¼ hours. Take out and allow to cool sufficiently to handle. Break off crust. Skin the gammon and score across the fat diagonally. Stud with cloves and cover with the sugar. Bake in moderately hot oven for 30 minutes (400°F – Gas Mark 5). Baste frequently with pineapple juice. Delicious hot or cold.

Baked British Ham Southern Style

598 *To fry bacon and gammon*

Thin rashers Put into a frying pan, arranging the rashers so the lean of the second rasher is on the top of the fat of the first. Fill the pan in this way. This makes sure the fat moistens the lean part of the bacon.
Bacon chops i.e. back rashers of bacon. Fry steadily to cook through to the centre.
Gammon Score the edges with scissors at ½-1-inch intervals to encourage the fat to become crisp. Heat a little fat in the pan and cook steadily, turning when the underside is well cooked.
Gammon Veronique Heat cider and halved de-seeded grapes in fat in pan. Pour over gammon, garnish with watercress.

599 To grill bacon and gammon

Thin rashers of bacon should just be put under a hot grill and cooked quickly, preferably on the rack of the grill pan so that the surplus fat drains away.
Bacon chops i.e. back rashers of bacon cut rather thickly are excellent grilled and served as a main meal. They need no extra fat but should be grilled steadily until crisp and brown on the outside and cooked through the middle.
Gammon is a very lean part of the bacon so brush well with melted butter. Cut the fat at ½-1-inch intervals to encourage this to crisp and brown. Put under a COOL grill, i.e. do not pre-heat the grill, this prevents the bacon from curling up. Cook steadily to make sure it is tender through to the middle.
If wished glaze by sprinkling a little brown sugar on top and returning to the grill for 1 minute.
Serve with grilled tomatoes, mushrooms and vegetables or with glazed pineapple rings or halved peaches or apricots and a crisp green salad.

600 Bacon fraize

4 servings

8 oz. streaky bacon
sage
thyme
pepper

Pancake batter:
3 oz. flour
1 egg
¼ pint and 4 tablespoons water or milk and water
1 tablespoon melted butter
fat for frying pancakes

Cut the streaky bacon into strips, and cook gently in a frying pan, sprinkle the bacon while cooking with sage, thyme and a little pepper. Put aside to keep hot, make the pancake, with flour, egg, liquid and butter, and cook separately. Roll the bacon pieces into the pancakes and serve piping hot.

Bacon Fraize

601 To fry ham

Put a good knob of butter in the frying pan and heat the ham in this, taking care not to over-cook.

602 To grill ham

Cooked ham can be heated under a grill; it should be brushed with melted butter. If the slices are thin it needs only a minute or so to heat thoroughly.

603 Fried ham with mustard sauce

4 servings

sprinkling of flour
4 thick slices cooked ham
2 oz. butter

1 teaspoon made mustard
2 tablespoons water
little brown sugar

Flour the ham lightly, heat the butter and toss it in this until piping hot. Lift on to a hot dish, add mustard, water and sugar to fat remaining in pan. Pour over ham. Serve with fried potatoes and eggs.

604 To boil bacon and ham

Put into cold water. Bring up steadily to boiling point. Skim if necessary and take care that the liquid does not boil too quickly. Vegetables can be added if desired but generally speaking the ham stock is sufficient flavour without them. IN PRESSURE COOKING allow approximately 7 minutes per lb.

605 Bacon with garnet sauce

8-10 servings

collar of bacon (3½-4 lb.)
1 sliced carrot
1-2 sticks celery
1 sliced onion

pepper
water or water and cider to cover
crisp breadcrumbs

Put the bacon into a saucepan, add the vegetables and freshly milled pepper to taste, and water to cover, or use half water and half cider. Bring to the boil and simmer allowing 25 minutes to the pound. Remove rind and sprinkle with breadcrumbs. Serve with jacket potatoes and Brussels sprouts. Serve the garnet sauce (see Recipe 606) separately.

606 Garnet sauce

8 oz. redcurrant jelly
4-5 tablespoons port wine
1 teaspoon shallots, chopped
   and scalded
thin rind of 1 orange
thin rind of 1 lemon

juice of 1 orange
juice of ½ lemon
1 teaspoon dry mustard
dash cayenne pepper
1 shallow teaspoon
   arrowroot

Melt redcurrant jelly in port wine. Add chopped scalded shallots. Cut the orange and lemon rind into thin strips. Cover with boiling water. Leave for 6 minutes. Rinse in cold water and add them to the sauce. Add the orange and lemon juice, dry mustard and cayenne pepper. Stir the arrowroot blended with water into the boiling sauce. It clears at once. Serve sauce with the hot or cold bacon.

607 To casserole bacon or ham

Soak the bacon or ham well and then put into the casserole. Bacon blends very well with almost any vegetable and quite a number of fruits so your casserole can have onion, carrots, peas, beans, mushrooms or be more unusual with apples, raisins, pineapple, etc.

608 Welsh gammon and leeks in tomato sauce

4 servings

4 small leeks (white part
   only)
4 thin gammon rashers
1 tablespoon tomato purée

1 teaspoon Worcestershire
   sauce
1 pinch cayenne pepper
salt

Parboil the leeks in salted water for 5-6 minutes. Drain thoroughly but save cooking liquor. Roll each leek in a rasher of gammon. Use some of the leek water to make a thinnish sauce with the tomato purée. Season with Worcestershire sauce, cayenne and salt. Put the rolls in a small casserole, cover with the sauce, place on the lid and bake 25 minutes in a moderate oven (375°F – Gas Mark 4). Serve with creamed or jacket potatoes.

609 To heat ham in sauces

Slices of ham can be heated in either an Espagnole, Madeira or good brown sauce (see Recipes 355, 356, 350). Do not over-cook.

610 Bacon olives

4 servings

8 thin slices forehock

Stuffing:
1½ oz. butter
1 large chopped onion
4 oz. breadcrumbs
1 tablespoon chopped parsley
pinch mixed herbs
1 egg
seasoning

Sauce:
water or stock
bottle tomato juice
1 oz. butter
1 oz. flour
seasoning

First prepare stuffing. Heat butter and fry onion in this, add crumbs, parsley, herbs, egg and season well. Spread on the slices of bacon. Roll firmly and secure with cocktail sticks or cotton. Put into a casserole.

Sauce:
Add enough water or stock to the tomato juice to make ¾ pint. Heat butter in pan, stir in flour and cook for several minutes, then add liquid and seasoning. Stir until smooth. Pour sauce over bacon olives.
Cover casserole and cook for about 1¼ hours in centre of very moderate oven (350°F – Gas Mark 3). Serve with creamed potatoes and diced mixed vegetables.

611 Jambalaya

4 servings

4 oz. ham, including fat
4 oz. salt pork or bacon
2 onions, chopped fine
1 clove garlic
1 medium can tomatoes

1 red pepper
salt and pepper to taste
few oysters (optional)
1 lb. raw shrimps shelled
6-8 oz. rice

Dice the ham and pork and fry slowly in a large, heavy pan until all fat has been fried out, add onions and garlic and cook in fat until clear; add tomatoes and chopped pepper, season, and simmer slowly for an hour, adding water as needed. Add oysters and liquor and shrimps, 1½ pints of water and raw rice. Bring to the boil, cover tightly and simmer for 20 minutes. Serve immediately.

612 Sausage roly poly

4-6 servings

1 lb. uncooked sausage meat
½ teaspoon herbs
breadcrumbs

Suet crust:
1 lb. flour
1½ teaspoons baking powder
4 oz. suet
seasoning to taste
1 egg

Bind the flour, baking powder, suet and seasoning together with a well-beaten egg, add sufficient water, if required, to produce a firm suet crust, roll out on a well-floured board into an oblong shape, spread with the uncooked sausage meat mixed with herbs. Wrap up in kitchen foil and boil for 3 hours. Remove the foil and roll in breadcrumbs. Place in a moderate oven to brown (375°F – Gas Mark 4).

Sausage Roly Poly

613 *Chipolata gratin*

Make up a packet of tomato soup according to directions with ¾ pint water and when quite smooth and thickened add 1 lb. chipolata sausages. Simmer a further 10 minutes. Surround with a border of spaghetti. Sprinkle with grated cheese and brown under grill.

614 *Sausage shepherd's pie*

4 servings

4 rashers bacon	salt and pepper
1 lb. pork sausages	1 can condensed vegetable
1½ lb. hot mashed potatoes	soup

Cut bacon into small pieces and fry gently until crisp. Remove and fry sausages for approximately 15-20 minutes. Put a layer of potatoes into a deep dish. Cover with sausages and bacon and pour over gently heated, seasoned, condensed vegetable soup.

Sausage Shepherd's Pie

615 *Hungarian pork sausages in lace*

4-5 servings

1 lb. 12 oz. pork (belly or hock)	1 clove garlic if desired
1 teaspoon salt	pork flair (a thin skin like tissue covered in a lace like pattern of fat. Available from pork butchers on request giving 24 hours notice)
½ teaspoon paprika	
pinch ground black pepper	
pinch ground white pepper	
1 bread roll or thick slice bread	1 teaspoon lard
¼ pint milk	

Mince pork through coarse cutter, then put the meat into a dish, salt and pepper it, adding to it the roll steeped in some of the milk, together with the rest of the milk and crushed garlic. Mix this sausage stuffing thoroughly and put in a cool place or refrigerator for 1 hour. Wash the pork-lace in several waters, spread it out and cut into 10 pieces of equal size. Divide the stuffing into equal parts, lay them over the pieces of pork-lace, then roll them up tightly in the shape of a sausage. Grease the inside of a pan of suitable size with lard, place the sausages in it in a neat row, and bake them brown in a hot oven (425°-450°F – Gas Mark 6-7). Garnish with mashed potatoes and cooked cabbage.

USING LEFT-OVER MEAT

616 *California sunshine savoury*

4 servings

8 oz. diced cooked lamb	1 oz. cornflour
1 medium-sized onion	¼ teaspoon salt
1 small green pepper	⅛ teaspoon pepper
4 oz. seedless raisins	1 teaspoon Worcestershire sauce
small can pineapple chunks	
pineapple juice and water to make ½ pint	1 tablespoon soya sauce or 1 beef extract cube dissolved in 1 tablespoon hot water
5 tablespoons vinegar	
2 teaspoons dry mustard	
2 oz. brown sugar	

Place lamb in baking dish. Slice onion and green pepper into rings and place in layers on top of lamb. Top with raisins and pineapple. Combine pineapple juice and vinegar, blend together dry ingredients with small amount of liquid. Bring rest of liquid to boil and pour on blended cornflour mixture, return to heat and stir until mixture thickens. Stir in Worcestershire sauce and soya sauce. Pour over lamb and raisins. Bake in centre of moderate oven (375°F – Gas Mark 4) for 45 minutes. Serve with rice.

Hungarian Pork Sausages in Lace

California Sunshine Savoury

617 *Durham cutlets*

4 servings

8 oz. cooked meat
1 oz. margarine
1 onion (optional)
1 oz. flour
¼ pint gravy, stock, or water
   flavoured with a little beef
   or yeast extract
salt, pepper, mustard
1 tablespoon chopped parsley
pinch mixed herbs
2 oz. breadcrumbs

To coat the cutlets:
1 egg
crisp breadcrumbs

To fry:
dripping or lard

To garnish:
parsley
fried tomatoes

Mince or chop meat. Heat the margarine in a saucepan, you can if you wish fry about 1 tablespoon chopped onion in this to give additional flavour. Stir in the flour, away from the heat, and cook the *roux* for about 5 minutes, until it begins to turn slightly brown. Don't let it burn. Remove pan from the heat, then gradually stir in the gravy or stock. Bring to the boil and cook, stirring well until it is a thick sauce. Add seasoning, meat, parsley, herbs and breadcrumbs. Let the mixture cool, turn out of saucepan, and form into 4 cutlet shapes. Beat the egg on a flat plate, then, using a pastry brush, coat the outside of the cutlets with the egg. Put about 2 tablespoons crisp breadcrumbs (or raspings) in a piece of grease-proof paper and turn the cutlets round in this gently until they are completely covered with the crumbs. Pat the crumbs well into the cutlets then shake each cutlet well to get rid of surplus crumbs. Heat about 2 oz. dripping or lard in a frying pan, put in the cutlets, fry steadily for about 4 minutes to crisp and brown the underside, then turn with a knife and cook for the same time on second side. Lower the heat and allow a further 4 minutes to make sure they are heated right through to the middle. To drain, lift on to crumpled tissue paper on a hot dish for about 2 minutes, then transfer to hot plates or another dish, garnished with parsley and fried tomatoes.

618 *Shepherd's pie*

4 servings

12 oz. cooked meat
1 oz. dripping or lard
1 large onion
2-3 tomatoes
¼-½ pint gravy or stock

seasoning
good pinch mixed herbs
1-1½ lb. mashed potatoes
1 oz. margarine

Cut the cooked meat into small pieces. Heat the dripping in a pan and fry the sliced onion and tomatoes until tender. Add the meat, stock, seasoning, and mixed herbs. Vary the amount of stock according to personal taste. Pour this into the bottom of a pie dish. Mash the potatoes and when they are very soft and smooth pile on top of the meat mixture. Fork into an attractive shape or use a large potato pipe and a cloth piping bag. Put the margarine in tiny pieces over the potato and bake in the centre of a moderately hot oven (400°F – Gas Mark 5) for 30 minutes until the top is crisp and brown. If both meat filling and potatoes are very hot this dish will only need browning under a hot grill or near the top of a hot oven.

619 *Shepherd's pie in scallop shells*

4 servings

8 oz. minced cooked meat
1 chopped and lightly fried
   onion
2 teaspoons chopped parsley
pepper, salt and nutmeg

about ¼ pint Spanish sauce
  (see Recipe 354)
1 lb. mashed potatoes
4 slices tomato

Grease 4 scallop shells. Mix the minced meat, onion, parsley and seasoning with enough sauce to make a dropping consistency. Divide the mixture between the 4 shells. Surround with a border of mashed potato and cover the meat with a tomato slice. Place in a moderately hot oven (400°F – Gas Mark 5) to re-heat and lightly brown the potatoes. Serve hot, with parsley.

620 *Other ways of using left-over meat*

There are a number of ways of using left-over meat given in this book but care must be taken when storing the meat that it is absolutely fresh, also that if any members of the family suffer from gastric or duodenal ulcers they must not be given re-heated meat in any form. If you re-heat in gravy make sure the gravy, or sauce, is really hot before you put in the meat, heat for a few minutes only to prevent it toughening.

Curried cutlets Follow the recipe for Durham cutlets (see Recipe 617). Add curry powder to sauce and serve with chutney.

Meat fritters Cut slices of cooked meat, dip in fritter batter (see Recipe 7) and fry steadily.

Stuffed tomatoes Use minced meat or finely chopped left-over meat, mix with sauce or mayonnaise as a filling for tomatoes. Mix pulp with meat, season well and serve hot or cold.

621 Corned beef hash

4 servings

12 oz. can corned beef	1 oz. dripping for frying
approx. 8 oz. mashed potatoes	
	To garnish:
1 egg	sliced beetroot
seasoning	parsley

Flake the corned beef and mix with the potatoes and beaten egg. Season well. Heat the dripping in a pan and put in the mixture. Spread this evenly and allow to cook slowly until the underside is golden-brown and the mixture really hot. Fold like an omelette and turn on to a hot dish. Garnish with beetroot and parsley.

622 Corn beef and cabbage hash

Ingredients as previous recipe but add cooked cabbage mixed very well and fry.

623 Spiced corn beef hash

Ingredients as Recipe 621 but add a good pinch of curry powder, 1 tablespoon of chutney and a little mixed spice to the ingredients.

624 Fruit hash

Add 1 tablespoon of dried fruit and a little chutney to ingredients in Recipe 621.

625 Quickie hot pot

4 servings

8 oz. tomatoes	1 beef cube
12 oz. corned beef	½ pint boiling water
paprika pepper	½ oz. cornflour
1 onion, finely chopped	8 oz. cooked potatoes
3 sticks celery, sliced	1-2 oz. butter

Peel and slice tomatoes. Break up the corned beef, put in the bottom of a casserole and sprinkle lightly with paprika. Add the chopped onion and the tomato and celery slices. Dissolve the beef cube in the boiling water, mix the cornflour smoothly with 1 tablespoon cold water, add to the stock and bring to the boil. Pour the thickened stock over the ingredients in the casserole and arrange the potatoes in slices on top. Cover and bake about 15 minutes in a hot oven (425°F – Gas Mark 6). Remove the lid, dot the potatoes with butter and return to the oven for 10-15 minutes to brown.

626 Chopped pork and ham

Canned chopped pork mixed with ham can provide the basis for a number of dishes hot and cold. To serve hot, slice the meat and re-heat in a little hot margarine or butter. It can be fried with an egg, used as omelette filling, served with garnished rice. Or you may like to try one of the recipes given below.

627 Fritters

Either chop the meat and mix with the fritter batter (see Recipe 7), or slice it thinly and coat with the fritter batter. Fry until hot. Serve with rings of apple, pineapple or vegetables.

628 In salads

Dice the meat and mix with diced apple, celery, cucumber. Toss in mayonnaise and serve on a bed of salad.

629 Using canned stewed steak

Most people will just heat this as a quick meal but it can be used as a filling for pies, puddings, for savoury dishes like stuffed marrow, etc.

UNUSUAL SAUCES

630 Cumberland sauce

1 orange and lemon	3 tablespoons port wine
8 oz. redcurrant jelly	seasoning
1 teaspoon made mustard or 1-2 teaspoons ready prepared mild or French mustard	½ teaspoon cornflour
	2 teaspoons water

This is an old traditional English sauce for game and ham and there are many versions of it. All of them contain redcurrant jelly and mustard. Here is one method. Thinly peel orange and lemon, cut into fine shreds and simmer this peel with the fruit juice and jelly for 5 minutes. Blend in the mustard. Cool and add wine. Season further to taste. Blend cornflour with water, stir into sauce, bring to the boil and stir until thickened. If preferred, peel can be simmered in ¼ pint water and at the end of 10 minutes removed. Add rest of ingredients, blending in cornflour.

631 Golden basting sauce

Melt 4 oz. butter or margarine. Fry gently in it, 1 tablespoon chopped onion and 1 tablespoon chopped parsley without browning. Blend in 1 tablespoon brown sugar, 2 tablespoons mild mustard, dash of cayenne, ½ level teaspoon salt, ¼ pint bouillon (water with bouillon cube or savoury essence). Simmer 5 minutes and spoon over hot hamburgers or meat.

632 Golden glaze

A delicious result is obtained when baked ham is brushed with brown sugar, stuffed with cloves and glazed in the oven for about 30 minutes. This glaze can be varied by blending the sugar with orange or lemon juice or pineapple or apricot syrup.

633 *Marinade for venison*

¼ pint vinegar
½ pint red wine
½ teaspoon each of coarsely crushed peppercorns and cloves
1 dessertspoon soft brown sugar
1 tablespoon made mustard
3 crushed bay leaves

1 crushed clove of garlic
¼ pint olive oil
2-3 leeks or an onion

This makes enough marinade for about 4 lb. of venison, preferably haunch

Bring this mixture to the boil and then cool. Spoon over the venison and leave in a cool larder. From time to time turn the meat and spoon the mixture over it. This makes the venison very tender.

634 *Piquant sauce*

½ pint milk
bay leaf
1 onion
2 oz. margarine or butter
3 or 4 large mushrooms

1 oz. flour
seasoning
1 dessertspoon lemon juice
1 teaspoon Worcestershire sauce

Heat the milk gently together with the bay leaf and onion and let it stand in a warm place for as long as possible before making the sauce – this will allow it to absorb the flavour of the onion, then strain. Melt the margarine in a saucepan and fry the chopped mushrooms until just soft. Blend the flour with the milk, add to the margarine and bring slowly to the boil, stirring all the time until a smooth sauce, and add seasoning. Take pan off the heat and whisk in lemon juice and Worcestershire sauce. Re-heat without boiling. Excellent with ham, tongue or boiled chicken.

635 *Sweet-and-hot mustard sauce*

Mix 4 level tablespoons brown sugar, 3 level tablespoons dry mustard, pinch salt. Stir in 3 tablespoons hot vinegar. If liked a tablespoon of olive oil can be added and a piece of cut clove garlic. Cover and stand for a day or two. Excellent with hot boiled beef, tongue or ham.

636 *Sweet-sour sauce*

Mix equal quantities of redcurrant jelly and French or mild mustard. Delicious with roast pork, veal or lamb and with grilled meat.

637 *Tangy cream*

Warm ¼ pint soured (cultured) or fresh cream or yoghourt with 1 or 2 egg yolks and 2 tablespoons mild mustard. Serve immediately with fried or roast veal, roast chicken or fish.

638 *A bouquet garni*

This is the name given to a collection of fresh herbs added to water or stock in all savoury dishes to give flavour. The herbs are tied together with a piece of cotton, or tied into a piece of muslin, and removed before serving.

CARVING AND BONING

639 *To carve meat*

To carve beef
Carve large thin slices ACROSS joint. If sirloin is cooked on bone, first remove backbone or chine, then cut first slices along bone. Turn and carve at right angles.

To carve lamb or mutton
Cut thickish slices DOWNWARDS but carve some joints as follows:
SADDLE: Cut very long slices first across the centre of the joint, cutting downwards. Next cut slanting slices from the remainder of the joint.
SHOULDER: Follow the contour of the bone, cutting slices round it.

To carve pork
Cut shoulder or leg as lamb.

To carve veal
Carving depends on joint. Leg or shoulder is carved downwards or round bone as lamb, loin is cut downwards into chops, fillets are carved across as beef.

To carve chicken
This depends on size of bird. For tiny chickens, serve one per person, or if slightly larger cut in half. Cut firmly down, slightly to one side of centre of breast bone. Medium-sized chickens can be jointed, rather than carved. Make one or two joints of each and two joints of breast and wings.

To carve a turkey or goose
Cut off leg on one side or pull it away from body. Cut large slices from the breast.

To carve a duck
Halve small duckling as tiny chickens, there is not much meat on breast. Larger birds will cut into 4 joints – 2 from breast and 2 from legs. For a very large duck, thick slices can be cut from breast instead of leaving whole.

To carve game
Serve small birds whole or halved. Carve or joint large chickens.

Index

ACKNOWLEDGMENTS

Illustrations by courtesy of the following:

Angel Studios: Colour plate no. 14.

Batchelors Foods Ltd.: Black and white photographs accompanying Recipes 15, 283, 299.

Blue Band Luxury Margarine: Black and white photographs accompanying Recipes 21, 112, 194, 218.

British Travel Association: Black and white photographs accompanying Recipes 123, 504.

Brown and Polson: Colour plate no. 15.

California Raisin Bureau: Black and white photographs accompanying Recipes 44, 440, 616.

Campbell's Soups Ltd.: Black and white photographs accompanying Recipes 18, 234, 263, 282, 298, 335, 439, 473, 526, 614.

The Cheese Bureau: Black and white photographs accompanying Recipes 177, 200, 202, 287, 295.

Chicken Information Council: Black and white photographs accompanying Recipes 530, 536, 586.

Colman's Mustard: Colour plates nos. 14, 16, 18. Black and white photographs accompanying Recipes 27, 70, 497, 499.

Cookeen: Black and white photographs accompanying Recipes 92, 275, 484, 486, 487, 493, 502.

John Cowderoy: Black and white photographs accompanying Recipes 539, 550.

Express Dairy Products: Black and white photograph accompanying Recipe 521.

Fleetway Publications: Colour plates nos. 6, 9, 10, 11, 12, 13, 17, 21.

Flour Advisory Bureau: Black and white photographs accompanying Recipes 94, 341, 343, 344.

Fruit Producers Council: Colour plate no. 19.

George Newnes Ltd.: Colour plate no. 4.

Herring Industry Bureau: Black and white photographs accompanying Recipes 88, 96.

H. J. Heinz Ltd.: Black and white photograph accompanying Recipe 108.

Housewife: Black and white photographs accompanying Recipes 417, 418.

Japanese Canned Foods: Black and white photograph accompanying Recipe 145.

Judge International: Black and white photograph accompanying Recipe 415.

Kraft Foods Ltd.: Black and white photographs accompanying Recipes 17, 23, 290, 464.

Lard Information Bureau: Colour plate no. 24.

MacFisheries Ltd.: Black and white photographs accompanying Recipes 14, 142, 533, 547, 587.

Mushroom Growers Association: Black and white photographs accompanying Recipes 242, 444, 531, 544.

National Milk Publicity Council: Black and white photographs accompanying Recipes 36, 76, 175, 300.

New Zealand Lamb Information Bureau: Black and white photographs, accompanying Recipes 435, 457, 458.

Odhams Syndication: Colour plates nos. 8, 22, 23. Black and white photograph accompanying Recipe 392.

The Pig Industry Development Authority Home Service: Black and white photographs accompanying Recipes 481, 485, 489, 491, 494, 496, 501, 502, 597, 600, 612.

Potato Desk: Black and white photograph accompanying Recipe 53.

Public Relations Associates: Colour plates nos. 5, 20. Black and white photographs accompanying Recipes 165, 279, 528.

Rice Council of U.S.A.: Black and white photographs accompanying Recipes 323, 474.

Spry Cookery Centre: Black and white photographs accompanying Recipes 31, 136, 303, 334, 462, 465.

Sunkist Growers: Black and white photographs accompanying Recipes 232, 475.

Uncle Ben Rice: Black and white photograph accompanying Recipe 133.

United Fresh Fruit and Vegetable Association: Black and white photograph accompanying Recipe 266.

John West Middle-Cut Brand Tuna: Black and white photographs accompanying Recipes 205, 206, 207.

White Fish Authority: Colour plates nos. 1, 2, 3, 7. Black and white photographs accompanying Recipes 34, 42, 73, 178, 447.

Woman's Realm: Black and white photograph accompanying Recipe 447.